CISCAUCASIA

CAUCASUS

TRANSCAUCASIA

CAUCASUS MOUNTAINS

Kura River

Lake Sevan

▲ Mount Ararat

Araxes River

Lake Van

ARTU

Greater Zab River

Hasanlu

Dinkha Tepe

Lake Urmia

TURKMENISTAN

Amu Darya River (Oxus)

Caspian Sea

Kara Kum Desert

Atrek River Anau

KOPET DAG

Yaz-depe

Kuchuk Tepe

Namazga-Depe

Altyn-depe

MARGIANA

BACTRIA

PARTHIA ○ Tepe Hissar

Mursab River

Tedzhen River

ELBURZ MOUNTAINS

MEDIA

Dasht-i-Kavir Desert

Nineveh

Kalkhu

...hur

Nuzi

Tigris River

...OTAMIA

ZAGROS

Diyala River

○ Godin Tepe

LURISTAN

Eshnunna

AKKAD

Sippar ○

Babylon ○

Kish ○

Tigris River

SUSIANA

MOUNTAINS

Nippur ○

Isin ○

Umma ○

ELAM

Susa ○

Euphrates

BABYLONIA

○ Lagash

Uruk ○

Larsa ○

SUMER

Eridu ○ Ur ○

Karun River

...River

Tepe Sialk ○

IRAN

SIMASHKI

Dasht-i-Lut Desert

Helmand River

Anshan ○ ○ Pasargadae

○ Persepolis

Failaka Island ▸

Persian Gulf

Tepe Yahya ○

○ Bampur

Bahrain

DILMUN

QATAR

Shimal ○

Gulf of Oman

Hili ○

MAGAN

ARABIAN PENINSULA

OMAN PENINSULA ○ Maysar

Arabian Sea

The Ancient Near East

An Encyclopedia for Students

Ronald Wallenfels, *Editor in Chief*

Jack M. Sasson, *Consulting Editor*

Volume 4

CHARLES SCRIBNER'S SONS
An Imprint of The Gale Group

NEW YORK   DETROIT   SAN FRANCISCO   LONDON   BOSTON   WOODBRIDGE, CT

Developed for Charles Scribner's Sons by Visual Education Corporation, Princeton, N.J.

For Scribners
PUBLISHER: Karen Day
SENIOR EDITOR: Timothy J. DeWerff
COVER DESIGN: Lisa Chovnick, Tracey Rowens

For Visual Education Corporation
EDITORIAL DIRECTOR: Darryl Kestler
PROJECT DIRECTOR: Meera Vaidyanathan
WRITERS: Jean Brainard, John Haley, Mac Austin, Charles Roebuck, Rebecca Stefoff
EDITORS: Dale Anderson, Carol Ciaston, Linda Perrin, Caryn Radick
ASSOCIATE EDITOR: Lauren Weber
COPYEDITING MANAGER: Helen Castro
COPY EDITOR: Marie Enders
PHOTO RESEARCH: Sara Matthews
PRODUCTION SUPERVISOR: Marcel Chouteau
PRODUCTION ASSISTANT: Brian Suskin
INTERIOR DESIGN: Maxson Crandall, Rob Ehlers
ELECTRONIC PREPARATION: Cynthia C. Feldner, Christine Osborne, Fiona Torphy
ELECTRONIC PRODUCTION: Rob Ehlers, Lisa Evans-Skopas, Laura Millan, Isabelle Ulsh

Library of Congress Cataloging-in-Publication Data

The Ancient Near East : an encyclopedia for students / Ronald Wallenfels, editor in chief; Jack M. Sasson, consulting editor.
    p. cm.
   Includes bibliographical references and index.
   ISBN 0-684-80597-9 (set : alk. paper) — ISBN 0-684-80589-8 (vol. 1)
— ISBN 0-684-80594-4 (vol. 2) — ISBN 0-684-80595-2 (vol. 3) — ISBN
0-684-80596-0 (vol. 4)
    1. Middle East—Civilization—To 622—Dictionaries, Juvenile.
[1. Middle East—Civilization—To 622—Encyclopedias.] I. Wallenfels, Ronald. II. Sasson, Jack M.

DS57 .A677 2000
939'.4—dc21
                                     00-056335

TABLE OF CONTENTS

VOLUME 1   Abraham–Cities and City-States

VOLUME 2   Clay Tablets–Inheritance

VOLUME 3   Inscriptions–Phoenicia and the Phoenicians

VOLUME 4   Phrygia and the Phrygians–Zoroaster and Zoroastrianism

MAPS & CHARTS

COLOR PLATES

A Time Line of the Ancient Near East

	Neolithic Period ca. 9000–4000 B.C.	Chalcolithic Period ca. 4000–3000 B.C.

Mesopotamia	Neolithic culture in northern Mesopotamia
	   Earliest permanent farming settlements, ca. 7000 B.C.
	   Earliest evidence of pottery, ca. 6500 B.C.
	Ubaid settlements in southern Mesopotamia
		Late Ubaid period
		Uruk and Jamdat-Nasr periods
		   Development of city-states
		   Invention of writing

Anatolia	Earliest permanent farming settlements, ca. 7000 B.C. Çatal Hüyük inhabited Earliest evidence of pottery, ca. 6300 B.C.	Development of agricultural and trading communities
Syria and the Levant	Agriculture first practiced, ca. 8500 B.C. Settlement of Jericho Domestication of animals, ca. 7300 B.C. Earliest evidence of pottery, ca. 6600 B.C.	Development of agricultural and trading communities
Egypt	Earliest permanent farming settlements in northern Egypt, ca. 5200 B.C. Earliest evidence of pottery in northern Egypt, ca. 5000 B.C. Evidence of predynastic graves in southern Egypt, suggesting the existence of permanent settlements, ca. 4000 B.C.	Predynastic period Invention of hieroglyphics
Arabia	Earliest evidence of pastoralism and pottery in western Arabia, ca. 6000 B.C. Contact between eastern Arabia and southern Mesopotamia	Permanent settlements established Contact between western Arabia and Syria and the Levant Continued contact between eastern Arabia and southern Mesopotamia
Iran	Earliest permanent farming settlements in southwestern Iran, ca. 7000 B.C. Earliest evidence of pottery in southwestern Iran, ca. 6500 B.C. Susa founded	Proto-Elamite culture
Aegean and the Eastern Mediterranean	Earliest permanent farming settlements on Crete, ca. 7000 B.C. Earliest permanent farming settlements on the mainland, ca. 6700 B.C. Earliest evidence of pottery on the mainland, ca. 6300 B.C. Earliest evidence of pottery on Crete, ca. 5900 B.C.	Development of agricultural and trading communities

Early Bronze Age ca. 3000–2200 B.C.	Middle Bronze Age ca. 2200–1600 B.C.

Sumerian Early Dynastic period
Akkadian empire
   Sargon I (ruled ca. 2334–2278 B.C.)
   Unification of Sumer and Akkad
	Gutian and Amorite invasions
	Second Dynasty of Lagash
	   Gudea of Lagash (ruled ca. 2144–2124 B.C.)
	Third Dynasty of Ur
	   Ziggurat of Ur
	Dynasties of Isin and Larsa
	Old Assyrian period
	Old Babylonian period
	   Hammurabi (ruled ca. 1792–1750 B.C.)
	Hurrian immigrations

Development of city-states
   Troy
   Alaca Hüyük
	Old Assyrian trading colonies
	Old Hittite period
	   Khattushili I (ruled ca. 1650–1620 B.C.)
	Hittites invade Babylon

Development of city-states
Sumerian-style urban culture
   Kingdom of Ebla
      Akkadians conquer Ebla
	Rise of Amorite city-states

Early Dynastic period
Old Kingdom period
   Djoser (ruled ca. 2630–2611 B.C.)
      First pyramids
   Great Pyramid of Giza
	First Intermediate period
	   Civil war between dynasties at Thebes
	   and Heracleopolis
	Middle Kingdom period
	Second Intermediate period
	   Hyksos conquest

Levantine, Mesopotamian, and Iranian influence in the northwest Magan and Dilmun trade with Mesopotamia	Mesopotamian and Iranian influences along coast of Arabian Gulf
Old Elamite period Wars with Mesopotamia Susiana under Akkadian and Sumerian domination	Sukkalmakh dynasty Susiana allies with Elam Babylonians control Elam
Early Cycladic culture	Minoan culture on Crete Mycenaeans invade Peloponnese Volcanic eruption at Thera

A Time Line of the Ancient Near East

	Late Bronze Age ca. 1600–1200 B.C.	Iron Age ca. 1200–500 B.C.
Mesopotamia	Hittites invade Babylon Dark Age Middle Babylonian (Kassite) period Hurrian kingdom of Mitanni Middle Assyrian period	Second Dynasty of Isin Neo-Babylonian period Neo-Assyrian empire 　Sargon II (ruled 721–705 B.C.) Late Babylonian period (Chaldean dynasty) 　Nebuchadnezzar II (ruled 605–562 B.C.) Persians conquer Babylonia
Anatolia	Hittite empire 　Shuppiluliuma I (ruled ca. 1370–1330 B.C.) 　Hittite wars with Egypt Destruction of Khattusha	Dark Age Rise of Neo-Hittite states Kingdoms of Urartu and Phrygia Cimmerian invasion Kingdoms of Lydia and Lycia Median expansion Greek city-states in western Anatolia Persians conquer Lydia
Syria and the Levant	Canaanites develop aleph-beth Egyptian domination Hittite invasions Hurrian domination Sea Peoples	Aramaean migrations Israelites settle in Canaan Philistine and Phoenician city-states Kingdoms of Israel and Judah Assyrian conquests Babylonian conquests
Egypt	Expulsion of Hyksos New Kingdom period Expansion into Syria, the Levant, and Nubia Invasion of the Sea Peoples	Third Intermediate period 　Libyan dynasty 　Nubian dynasties 　　Taharqa (ruled 690–664 B.C.) Assyrian conquest Late period 　Saite dynasty
Arabia	Decline of Dilmun Qurayya flourishes Arabia dominates aromatics trade	Qedar tribe dominates northern Arabia Syria dominates in the east Neo-Babylonians control trade routes Sabaean rulers
Iran	Middle Elamite period Aryans (Medes and Persians) enter Iran	Neo-Elamite period Median kingdom Zoroaster (lived ca. 600s B.C.) Persians overthrow Medes Cyrus the Great (ruled 559–529 B.C.) 　Conquest of Babylonia Persian empire established 　Darius I (ruled 521–486 B.C.)
Aegean and the Eastern Mediterranean	Decline of Minoan civilization Rise of Mycenaeans Mycenaeans colonize Aegean	Trojan War Dorian invasions Fall of Mycenae Dark Age Greek colonization Competition with Phoenician trade

Persian domination Alexander the Great (lived 356–323 B.C.) enters Babylon	Seleucid empire Parthian empire
Persian domination Macedonian conquest	Roman rule

Persian domination
   Jews return from Babylon
   Second temple of Jerusalem
Macedonian conquest
	Ptolemaic kingdom and Seleucid empire
	Maccabean Revolt
	Hasmonean dynasty
	Roman rule

Persian domination
Local dynasties of native Egypt
Macedonian conquest
	Ptolemaic dynasty
	   Ptolemy I (ruled 305–282 B.C.)
	   Cleopatra (ruled 69–30 B.C.)
	Roman rule

Nabatean kingdom in Jordan Persian domination	Trade with Hellenistic world Roman conquest
Persian empire dominates the ancient Near East Greek invasions Macedonian conquest Alexander the Great	Seleucid empire Parthian empire
Persian wars Classical period Peloponnesian War Macedonian conquest	Hellenistic dynasties Roman conquest

Phrygia and the Phrygians

Phrygia (FRI•jee•uh) was a land in west-central ANATOLIA (present-day Turkey). The Phrygians were an important power in the region after the fall of the HITTITES in the 1100s B.C. At first, the Phrygians were part of an alliance of Anatolian peoples. Eventually, however, Phrygia emerged as a kingdom, and its most famous ruler was a semilegendary king named Midas. After the kingdom of Phrygia collapsed shortly after 700 B.C., aspects of Phrygian culture survived for many centuries.

Origins and Early History. Phrygia took its name from the Phryges, a people who migrated into central Anatolia in the 1100s B.C., sometime after the fall of the Hittite empire. The ancient Greeks believed that the Phrygians came from MACEDONIA and Thrace, north of Greece. This belief is supported by the fact that the Phrygian language is an INDO-EUROPEAN LANGUAGE related to Greek or Thracian. After leaving their homeland, the Phrygians moved from Anatolia's Black Sea coast south along the Sangarios River into the center of Anatolia.

Between 1100 and 900 B.C., various Anatolian peoples competed for territory and power in the absence of a strong central government such as that of the Hittites. Although the Phrygians had not formed an organized state during this period, by the 700s B.C., their kingdom had been established. It was centered on a city named Gordium, located 60 miles southwest of Ankara, the capital of present-day Turkey.

The Kingdom of Midas. The Phrygian kingdom achieved its peak of greatness under King Midas, who took the throne around 738 B.C. Not many details are known about Midas. Some ancient historians claimed that he married a Greek princess and dedicated his throne to the Greek sun god Apollo. He may have founded Ankara and another settlement called Midaeion (Midas City). Under Midas's rule, the Phrygians controlled most of west-central Anatolia, and they had considerable influence over Syrian and Anatolian states to the east and southeast.

Midas tried several times to stir other rulers into rebellion against the Assyrians, but around 709 B.C., he sought an alliance with King SARGON II of Assyria. By that time, perhaps, Midas had begun to fear a greater threat than Assyria—the Cimmerians, warlike horsemen from southern Russia who had migrated south through the CAUCASUS and were rampaging across Anatolia. Around 696 B.C., the Cimmerians conquered Phrygia, burned Gordium, and—according to one ancient source—drove Midas to commit suicide by drinking the blood of a bull.

The Cimmerians eventually withdrew, and the Phrygians rebuilt Gordium around 600 B.C. By that time, power in Anatolia shifted to the Lydians, whose homeland was west of Phrygia. After the mid-500s B.C., Anatolia came under the domination of the PERSIAN EMPIRE. The Phrygians, however, remained a distinctive ethnic group within the Anatolian population.

Phrygian Culture. The Phrygians were known for their skills in weaving, wood carving, and metalwork. In addition to bronze (an alloy of copper and tin), the Phrygians knew how to make brass (an alloy of copper

See map in Anatolia (vol.1).

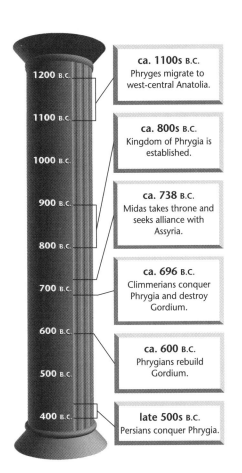

ca. 1100s B.C.
Phryges migrate to west-central Anatolia.

ca. 800s B.C.
Kingdom of Phrygia is established.

ca. 738 B.C.
Midas takes throne and seeks alliance with Assyria.

ca. 696 B.C.
Climmerians conquer Phrygia and destroy Gordium.

ca. 600 B.C.
Phrygians rebuild Gordium.

late 500s B.C.
Persians conquer Phrygia.

1200 B.C.
1100 B.C.
1000 B.C.
900 B.C.
800 B.C.
700 B.C.
600 B.C.
500 B.C.
400 B.C.

Phrygia and the Phrygians

Dating from around the 700s B.C., this painted jug, decorated with images of animals between panels of geometric patterns, was excavated from a Phrygian burial mound at Gordium in Anatolia. During the Iron Age (ca. 1200–500 B.C.), the Phrygians buried the dead with many grave gifts, including pottery, painted tiles, furniture, and sculpture.

* **archaeologist** scientist who studies past human cultures, usually by excavating material remains of human activity

and zinc). In fact, the bright yellow color of brass may have given rise to the legend of Midas's golden touch.

Phrygia's economy, like that of other Near Eastern societies, was based on agriculture. As late as the 400s B.C., the Phrygians were said to have more flocks and herds and larger harvests than any other people in the region. Long before that time, they had earned a reputation for horsemanship. A few of their artworks—including a small square of ivory carved with the image of a rider and a miniature bronze chariot and horses from a child's tomb—reveal how they used horses.

Archaeologists* working at Gordium in the late A.D. 1900s uncovered a large citadel—a fortified cluster of buildings—that dates from the time of Midas. It contained rooms for food and textile production, storage, and eating. Some archaeologists believe that the citadel may represent a centralized palace economy in which all raw foods came to the palace to be prepared and distributed to the people.

The citadel also provides information about Phrygian art. For example, the floor of one room is tiled with designs of colored pebbles and is probably one of the earliest mosaic floors of the ancient world. Other types of Phrygian art reflect a fondness for unusual shapes and tiny geometric patterns. The Phrygians also produced POTTERY with exaggerated spouts and handles and in the shape of animals. Some pieces were painted with lively pictures of animals, mythological scenes, or soldiers, in addition to the geometric patterns.

Little is known about the Phrygians' religion other than that they worshiped a mother goddess called Matar or Cybele. Many statues of her, most dating from several centuries after Midas's time, have been found at Gordium.

The Phrygians used a version of the Greek alphabet that had been developed in the 700s B.C. This fact, together with Greek influences in art and the stories of Midas's Greek wife and his devotion to a Greek god, suggests that Phrygia had close contact with Greek culture during the 700s B.C. (*See also* **Lydia and the Lydians.**)

Midas's Resting Place

Burial tumuli are mounds of earth covering separate graves. Burial tumuli found at Gordium served to mark the location of and to protect the one-room wooden tombs beneath them. The largest of the 85 tumuli found there is called the Midas Mound, which stands 174 feet high and measures 984 feet in diameter. Although the occupant of the tomb is a short man who died in his early 60s, archaelogists are unsure whether he is King Midas or another member of Phrygian royalty.

Physicians

See *Medicine.*

PIGS

* **domesticate** to adapt or tame for human use
* **Levant** lands bordering the eastern shores of the Mediterranean Sea (present-day Syria, Lebanon, and Israel), the West Bank, and Jordan

Wild pigs were found throughout well-watered regions in the ancient Near East. First domesticated* in southeastern ANATOLIA (present-day Turkey) between 8500 and 8000 B.C., pigs were being raised in MESOPOTAMIA and SYRIA by at least 6000 B.C. and in the Levant* within another thousand years. Interestingly, the domestication of pigs was widespread during the early development of Near Eastern societies but declined steadily with the growth of cities.

As early societies were established, people raised pigs in abundance, probably because they reproduce more quickly than such animals as GOATS and SHEEP. However, pigs thrive only in specific environments, preferably wetlands, areas with abundant rainfall, and forests. Yet AGRICULTURE required the clearing of forests and draining of marshes to create fields. Thus, as agricultural settlements grew larger to support cities, the environment was changed in ways that made it much more difficult to raise pigs. By about 1500 B.C., the number of pigs in the ancient Near East had declined substantially.

Although pigs can be an important source of meat, the consumption of pork was not very widespread in the Near East. A number of cultures developed taboos against eating pigs or even using them for sacrifices. The Hebrew BIBLE, for example, declared pigs to be unclean and unfit to eat, and such taboos generally were practiced throughout the Levant, except among the PHILISTINES. Even in societies where the consumption of pigs was not prohibited, few people ate them after about 1200 B.C. One reason may be that pigs, like humans, feed on grain. Because of competition with humans for grain resources, the domestication of pigs may have been discouraged in favor of animals that ate grasses, such as sheep and

Planets

CATTLE. An exception to this trend occurred in the Egyptian city of AMARNA, where pigs became a basic foodstuff of the working class after about 1500 B.C. (*See also* **Animals, Domestication of; Food and Drink.**)

PLANETS

In ancient times, astronomers were primarily concerned with the SUN, moon, and STARS, in part because these bodies exhibited regular movements that could be used to tell time. However, these early observers also noted the existence of other heavenly bodies—the planets—whose seemingly irregular movements distinguished them from other objects in the sky.

Because the stars do not revolve around the sun, their position in the night sky is fixed in relation to the earth. Thus, each star seems to rise and set at the same place on the horizon on the same date each year. However, since planets revolve around the sun, their observed position changes from one night to the next. This motion led the ancient Greeks to call them *planetes,* or "wanderers."

Ancient astronomers were familiar with the five planets that can be seen with the naked eye: Venus, Jupiter, Mercury, Mars, and Saturn. The earliest recorded astronomical observations were compiled in Babylonia during the 1600s B.C. and tracked the movement of Venus, the brightest and most important planet to early astronomers. *Venus* is a Roman name, but the planet was first associated with the Mesopotamian goddess ISHTAR and later with the Greek goddess Aphrodite. Over time, astronomers were able to note and predict the movements of these five planets and their relation to the fixed stars. This eventually led to the development of the ZODIAC, which divided the sky into 12 equal parts, or houses. The positions of the planets among the stars were believed to influence events on earth. (*See also* **Astrology and Astrologers; Astronomy and Astronomers.**)

POETRY

Like other forms of LITERATURE in the ancient Near East, poetry developed from the traditions of presenting literature orally before an audience. The influence of these traditions is reflected in the literary devices used in poems, such as repetition of lines, standard descriptions or phrases, and simple plots and characters. These techniques helped make it easier for oral storytellers and those listening to a poem to remember the basic story. At the same time, most poetry also contained rich and unusual imagery and words that made poetic language distinct and separate from the common spoken language.

Poems were usually recited before an audience, and the storyteller added new details at each performance. Rather than simply being spoken, poems were generally sung or chanted in a rhythmic manner, often accompanied by musical instruments and sometimes by the clapping of hands. When poems were written down, they were recorded by scribes*, who probably recalled them from memory and thus introduced new variations into the works. These texts became standardized versions of the poems, which were passed down relatively unchanged through the centuries.

* **scribe** person of a learned class who served as a writer, editor, or teacher

* **epic** long poem about a legendary or historical hero, written in a grand style

* **deity** god or goddess

Brains Over Brawn

One of the main themes in Sumerian epic poetry is that a weaker or less important person can win over a stronger or more important one because of luck or intelligence. For example, in the epic *Gilgamesh and Khuwawa,* Gilgamesh defeats Khuwawa, a fearsome guardian of the forest, by tricking him into giving away his seven coats of protective splendor. The moral of such stories is that wisdom and cunning are better and more effective than force. This lesson also appears in the *Iliad,* by the Greek poet Homer. The Greeks capture the city of Troy by hiding men inside a giant wooden horse given to the Trojans as a gift.

* **consort** companion or partner of a monarch, sometimes but not always a spouse

* **Levant** lands bordering the eastern shores of the Mediterranean Sea (present-day Syria, Lebanon, and Israel), the West Bank, and Jordan

* **prophetic** relating to or containing a prediction

The earliest known examples of ancient Near Eastern poetry are Sumerian works dating from around 2500 B.C. Most of these barely understood early works are mythological epics* that focus on the deeds of deities* and rulers. They point out their bravery, intelligence, leadership, and dealings with foreign rulers and deities.

The best-known versions of these epics, dating from around 2000 B.C., are about Enmerkar, Lugalbanda, and GILGAMESH, semilegendary rulers of ancient URUK. Another great early work, attributed to a priestess, Enkheduanna, was written in praise of the goddess Inanna (Ishtar). Most of the Sumerian epics available to modern scholars are copies written during later periods (ca. 1700–1600 B.C.). The earliest material is very brief and often difficult to understand. However, it contains the seed of what scholars later recognized as mythological epic poetry.

Another typical form of early Mesopotamian poetry consisted of royal HYMNS that celebrated existing rulers and hymns dedicated to particular gods. Hymns to the gods generally played an important role in temple rituals and ceremonies. Love poetry was also quite widespread in ancient MESOPOTAMIA. There were three basic types of love poems. The first told of the love between two deities. A second type dealt with the love between a ruler and his consort*. The least common type of love poetry involved love between ordinary people.

Many of these same types of poetry were popular outside Mesopotamia, and other types flourished as well. In the Levant*, poems intended to teach a moral lesson were common. They addressed subjects such as aging, death, female virtue, and the creative process. The poetry of ancient Israel included prophetic* poems, love poems, and PROVERBS. The best-known Israelite poems are the PSALMS of the Hebrew BIBLE. Interestingly, the ancient Israelites had almost no tradition of epic poetry similar to that of Mesopotamia. In ancient Egypt, the main forms of poetic expression were hymns to the gods and love poetry. (*See also* **Creation Myths; Entertainment; Epic Literature.**)

POLYGAMY

* **concubine** mistress to a married man

Polygamy (puh•LI•guh•mee) is the practice of having more than one spouse at the same time. When a woman has more than one husband it is called polyandry. The marriage of a man to more than one woman is called polygyny, and this is the only type of polygamy known to have existed in the ancient Near East. Most ancient Near Eastern societies allowed men to enter into polygamous marriages, but even where such unions were possible, they were not common. Although rich and powerful men could afford to maintain many wives, most humble folk could not.

Persian, Hittite, and Egyptian kings often had several wives. Their lofty status entitled them to many wives as well as concubines*, along with other privileges and pleasures. Other instances of polygamy were concerned chiefly with the production of CHILDREN and heirs. The Greek historian HERODOTUS reported that polygamy existed in the PERSIAN EMPIRE and that the Persians encouraged it to promote population growth. Some Persian men with more than one wife had as many as a dozen children.

In MESOPOTAMIA, men whose wives had not borne sons could take second wives, although the first wife's status in the household and community remained higher. Sometimes a childless wife adopted a second woman as a sister and let that woman also marry her husband. A man could also take a second wife if his first wife was ill and unable to perform her marital duties. The man still had to support the first wife and could not divorce her, although she could voluntarily leave his house.

In ancient Egypt, a man was free to take a second wife as long as he maintained and supported his first wife and her children properly. However, the first wife did not have to tolerate another wife and could divorce her husband. According to Egyptian records, some second wives had much lower social status than first wives did, perhaps because few men could afford two wives of equal status. Among the Israelites, the ideal marriage was monogamous (having only one spouse at a time). However, a number of figures in the Hebrew BIBLE, including several of the patriarchs and some early kings, had numerous wives. (*See also* **Divorce; Family and Social Life; Marriage.**)

Population Movements

See Migration and Deportation.

POTTERY

Pottery—objects made of hardened clay—provides the primary evidence of ancient Near Eastern cultures and is also one of the most useful records of past civilizations. Unlike wood or TEXTILES, pottery does not deteriorate or change form over long periods of time. Even if broken into pieces, called shards or potsherds, pottery lasts for a long time. Pottery can tell archaeologists* and historians a great deal about the people who created it and the culture in which it appeared.

* **archaeologist** scientist who studies past human cultures, usually by excavating material remains of human activity

CERAMIC TECHNOLOGY

The art and technology of making hardened objects of clay by means of heat or fire is known as ceramics. Clay, the basic ingredient in ceramics, was abundant in the river valleys of the ancient Near East. In such regions as MESOPOTAMIA, which lacked adequate sources of timber and STONE, clay became an important building material. Ancient builders made clay BRICKS by mixing clay with straw or animal manure, shaping it in molds, and placing the molds in the sun so that the bricks would dry and harden.

Pottery was invented when humans learned how to fire clay in a kiln to make it hard and durable. Potters could then make cups, plates, containers, and other items from clay. Evidence suggests that the first pottery was made in the Near East by at least 8000 B.C. By the fourth millennium B.C.*, pottery was being produced in large quantities to supply the needs of people in towns and cities throughout the region. The demand for pottery led to the appearance of craft specialists—full-time potters skilled at making various types and sizes of objects.

* **fourth millennium B.C.** years from 4000 to 3001 B.C.

* **artisan** skilled craftsperson

Gender Roles

Archaeologists are unsure whether most potters were men or women in the ancient Near East. Based on studies of modern-day potters in the region, it is likely that most of those who worked with potter's wheels were men. Women and children, on the other hand, probably made most handmade pottery. This division of labor may reflect the responsibilities of men and women in the ancient world. Because the production of handmade pottery did not require full-time attention, it could be completed when other household chores—which were performed by women and children—were not pressing.

See color plate 9, vol. 4.

Making Pottery. Clay is found in various textures and consistencies. In making pottery, ancient artisans* first had to choose the proper type of clay for the object they planned to make. Delicate, thin-walled objects, such as cups and plates, were made from fine-textured clay. To make sturdier items, such as storage jars and cooking pots, artisans used coarser clay. Potters could make clay stiffer by adding sand, crushed shells, ash, or vegetable matter, such as the dry husks, or outer coverings, of grains and grasses. These materials also helped prevent the clay from shrinking and cracking during the baking process.

Ancient potters shaped clay into objects using various techniques, all of which are still used today. In a technique known as coil building, a potter used ropelike pieces of clay, generally placed in spiral-shaped patterns, to form the base and sides of an object. The surface of the clay was then smoothed or flattened, either by hand or with a simple tool. Another technique, known as molding, involved placing wet clay in a preformed mold made of wood, stone, hardened clay, or metal. The clay thus took on the shape of the mold. A third technique, called throwing, required the use of a device known as a potter's wheel. As the wheel rotated, a potter shaped the moist clay by hand or used simple tools to form the desired shape.

Once the clay was formed into the desired shape, the object was set aside to dry. Then it was placed in a kiln and baked slowly at high temperatures. The earliest kilns were simply open fires on which dried pots were placed. The pots were covered with a layer of brush, straw, or manure, which both protected the pottery and served as a source of fuel for the fire. Later kilns were walled, circular chambers made of fire-hardened brick. Beneath the kiln was a pit into which the potter fed fuel for the fire. Holes in the floor of the kiln allowed the heat and gases from the fire below to rise into the chamber containing the pottery. A layer of potsherds resting on top of the pottery formed the roof of the kiln. Kilns such as this were used throughout the ancient Near East, and they are still found in many parts of the region.

Decorating Pottery. Ancient potters decorated pottery in many ways. Before the object began to dry, patterns could be pressed or carved into the clay with tools. Wet clay could also be trimmed with bits of clay added to the surface. In the Near East, such additions often took the shape of animal heads or other natural objects.

When a pot was partially dry, a potter could use tools to incise, or cut, lines or figures into its surface. Partially dried pots could also be rubbed with a smooth, hard object such as a pebble to create a glossy finish with markings. This technique, known as burnishing, also helped compact the clay, making it less likely that liquids would be able to seep through the walls of the finished pot.

Before an object was fired in a kiln, potters could coat the surface with slip—a watery solution of fine clay, water, and natural coloring agents. After firing, the slip produced a red or black finish, with the final color depending on how the pottery was fired. Other forms of decoration—including paint and glaze, a transparent coating—could also be added to pottery, generally after firing in a kiln.

Pottery

CERAMIC ANALYSIS

Pottery techniques, forms, materials, and decoration can indicate how an object was used by the society that produced it. The relative abundance of certain types of pottery in various regions can also provide information about the lifestyles of the people. The analysis of pottery by experts, known as ceramic analysis, can thus supply important evidence of the cultural, economic, political, social, and technological dimensions of ancient societies, as well as the changes and developments that took place from one time period to another.

Archaeologists call the various types and forms of ceramics used at a particular time and place an assemblage. Assemblages provide a snapshot of certain aspects of a culture. For example, a large concentration of similar undecorated pots at an archaeological site probably indicates an urban center with a steady demand for plain and inexpensive pottery. When archaeologists have identified different assemblages in a particular area, they analyze them on the basis of various classifications, or typologies.

The Trojan tradition of depicting human features in relief is illustrated in the vase shown here. It was excavated at Troy and dates from the late third millennium B.C. This vessel is known as a trick vase because the liquid poured out from an unexpected place. In this case, liquid was poured into the pot on the woman's head, but it filled the pot on her chest.

Pottery

These typologies group the objects according to similarities in size, shape, style, decoration, type of clay, method of manufacture, and other features. Grouping and comparing pottery in this way helps scholars establish relative dates for objects found at different sites and allows them to determine various factors about the objects and the societies that produced them.

Using ceramic analysis, archaeologists can learn a great deal about different topics. For example, plotting discoveries of pottery on maps helps archaeologists determine the location of ancient settlements. Collections of potsherds at sites can help archaeologists trace the rise and development of urban centers, and the appearance of foreign pottery types at a site may suggest trade relationships with other cultures. Studying the composition of the clays in pottery can tell archaeologists whether an object was made from local clay or was an import, made of clay from a more distant source. Examining how a piece of pottery was fired may provide information about the types of fuel used in ancient kilns; this, in turn, can reveal something about the vegetation available for fuel in the area.

CERAMIC TRADITIONS IN THE NEAR EAST

Humans may have discovered the process of firing clay from the early practice of heating limestone to produce plaster. Fired clay pottery first appeared in SYRIA around 8000 B.C., and evidence of it in western IRAN dates from at least 7500 B.C. However, pottery did not become widespread in the ancient Near East until after 7000 B.C.

Mesopotamian Pottery. Shortly after 7000 B.C., people in northern Mesopotamia began producing hand-formed clay pots in kilns. Because the clay they used was mixed with large amounts of vegetable matter, it produced a very coarse type of pottery. Over time, the Mesopotamians developed advanced technology, using finer clays and applying slips and other, more elaborate decorations.

The early use of kilns in Mesopotamia suggests that pottery making had already become a specialized skill. Just before 6000 B.C., potters began to decorate their work with geometric designs and naturalistic figures, such as horned animals. The early sixth millennium* B.C. marked a high point of Mesopotamian pottery, with detailed and beautifully painted pottery of all types. Much of the pottery produced at this time constituted luxury items created by skilled artisans for export and trade.

Early pottery in southern Mesopotamia varied greatly in quality. The best-preserved pieces are often warped and show other evidence that they were fired at excessive temperatures. Archaeologists have also unearthed many soft and easily broken pieces, which indicate too little heat during firing. Some scholars believe that these variations indicate that potters were experimenting with firing techniques and ways to achieve the best temperatures in kilns.

The introduction of a fast potter's wheel in southern Mesopotamia during the fourth millennium B.C. allowed artisans to mass produce pottery to meet the demands of a society experiencing increased urbanization*.

Form Follows Function

Archaeologists can learn much about an ancient society by studying its pottery, but they can also learn about pottery from various cultural sources. For example, texts from ancient Mesopotamia have provided important clues to the uses of the variously shaped vessels found at many archaeological sites. The symbols used in early Mesopotamian writing to indicate different liquids correspond to the types of vessels used to store those liquids. For example, the symbol for beer looks like an upright jug with a straight spout. Beer was a popular drink in Mesopotamia, and remains of this type of pot are commonly found in the region.

* **sixth millennium B.C.** years from 6000 to 5001 B.C.

* **urbanization** formation and growth of cities

Pottery

* **faience** decorated object made of quartz and other materials that includes a glaze

* **Levant** lands bordering the eastern shores of the Mediterranean Sea (present-day Syria, Lebanon, and Israel), the West Bank, and Jordan

See color plate 13, vol. 2.

Painted decoration largely disappeared at this time so that pottery could be produced faster and more cheaply.

Although the fast potter's wheel was used in northern Mesopotamia after 4000 B.C., pottery in the region differed greatly from that of the south. While undecorated and mass-produced objects dominated southern Mesopotamian pottery, potters in the north still exhibited a great deal of innovation. When a glassmaking industry developed in the north in the 1300s B.C., potters quickly mastered glazing techniques, which provided decoration and produced a watertight seal over the clay. Glazed pottery largely replaced more expensive stone and glass containers for storing valuable liquids such as PERFUMES.

Egyptian Pottery. In Egypt, most pottery was plain and practical, generally lacking in decoration or interesting forms. Yet the Egyptians knew the basic pottery techniques used by other ancient cultures, and some Egyptian works feature burnished, incised, and painted decorations. During certain periods, Egyptian potters typically produced works of a single color—such as yellow, red, black, or blue—that had geometric patterns, animal figures, and scenes from the Nile River. Among the animal figures decorating this pottery were hippopotamuses, crocodiles, sheep, and goats.

The potter's wheel was first used in Egypt in about 2400 B.C. Before this time, potters used rotating platforms that they turned with one hand while shaping clay with the other. Mold-made pottery flourished between about 1500 and 1200 B.C., and these works show a great deal of creativity and playfulness. They include animal shapes, bottles shaped like nursing mothers, and women holding pets or playing musical instruments. By this time, faience* and a blue-painted pottery had become popular in major cities such as MEMPHIS.

After about 500 B.C., pottery in Egypt showed increasing signs of Greek influence. The conquest of Egypt by ALEXANDER THE GREAT in the late 300s B.C. led to the dominance of Greek pottery styles. This pattern of increased Greek influence was repeated throughout the Near East as Alexander's armies conquered the entire region from ANATOLIA (present-day Turkey) to the frontiers of India.

Pottery in the Levant and Syria. The earliest pottery in the Levant*, which appeared around 6000 B.C., was quite crude. Made from coarse clay and fired at low temperatures, it was decorated with simple geometric designs made from slip applied to the surface before firing.

After 4000 B.C., new pottery forms were introduced in the region, and the craftsmanship improved. New types of decoration included geometric designs and hand-cut patterns. Some pieces were made on a rotating platform that was turned by hand, much like a potter's wheel. By the late fouth millennium B.C., distinct ceramic traditions had emerged in Syria and the Levant, including red and gray burnished pottery and red-painted pottery. By this time, the wheel had also come into use.

The period between 2000 and 1500 B.C. marked a high point of urban culture in the Levant, and the pottery of this time reflected the wealth and sophistication of the people in CANAAN. There is also evidence of much influence from other cultures, and pottery from Cyprus and other Mediterranean civilizations was introduced around this time. After about 1500 B.C., pottery in the region reflected a significant decline in creativity, with few new forms. However, imports increased dramatically, especially those from Cyprus, Crete, Greece, and Egypt.

Around 1200 B.C., new cultural traditions began to appear in Syria and the Levant, perhaps because of the movement of the Sea Peoples into the region. The Philistines (believed to be one of the Sea Peoples) produced pottery with beautiful geometric and bird designs similar to Late Bronze Age Greek works from Rhodes and Cyprus. In Phoenicia, potters created delicate pottery featuring a red finish and burnished surface. Archaeologists have established rough dates for Phoenician expansion and colonization by tracing the appearance of their distinctive pottery in various places throughout the Mediterranean region.

After about 500 B.C., much of the local pottery in the Levant imitated imported designs from areas to the east and west. Imported pottery from Greece began to increase greatly at that time as well, and Greek designs eventually replaced the local styles in most places. (*See also* **Archaeology and Archaeologists; Art, Artisans, and Artists; Clay Tablets; Economy and Trade; Glass and Glassmaking; Wheel.**)

See color plate 5, vol. 3.

PRAYER

* **pantheon** all the gods of a particular culture

* **deity** god or goddess

* **archeologist** scientist who studies past human cultures, usually by excavating material remains of human activity

* **incantation** written or recited formula of words designed to produce a given effect

* **lamentation** expression of grief; act of grieving

* **third millennium B.C.** years from 3000 to 2001 B.C.

* **funerary** having to do with funerals or with the handling of the dead

* **plague** contagious disease that quickly kills large numbers of people

Defined as a verbal act of worship to one god or to a pantheon*, prayer played an important role in the Religions of the ancient Near East. Because ancient Near Eastern peoples considered their deities* powerful, mysterious, and unpredictable beings, their prayers praised the gods and showered attention on them. People also prayed to the gods to ask for protection against misfortune and evil, to apologize, to request help, to complain about injustices, and to give thanks for good deeds.

Modern scholars know very little about the everyday prayers spoken by ordinary individuals in ancient times. The Book of Psalms in the Hebrew Bible is an example of a religious text that records prayers intended to be spoken by priests and individuals. These prayers were probably meant to be recited with the help of an expert in ritual. They follow a basic form and contain general terms, suggesting that they could be used in a wide range of circumstances.

Most of the ancient prayers discovered by archeologists* have been either those recited by priests or diviners on specific occasions or group prayers intended to be spoken by an entire community. An example of a communal prayer was found in ancient Ugarit. It was meant to be recited by the people to the storm god Baal during times of danger from attack. It begins, "O Baal, drive away the mighty one from our gates, the warrior from our walls." An Egyptian prayer, meant to be recited by a temple priest during the morning ritual, begins: "I worship your majesty with the chosen words, with the prayers that enhance your prestige."

Ancient prayer took many forms, including Hymns, incantations*, letters, and magic spells. In Mesopotamia, the prayers recited in ancient Sumer and Akkad included many lamentations*, which were poetic responses to real or imaginary disasters, such as the destruction of temples

Pregnancy

and cities or the death of a king. By the end of the third millennium B.C.*, a type of prayer called the letter-prayer had emerged in Sumer. These prayers, written on CLAY TABLETS and placed before a god in a temple, were a form of private communication between worshipers and the gods. Letter-prayers opened with an elaborate greeting that emphasized the divine qualities that would best serve the needs of the worshiper, such as healing qualities, wisdom, or forgiveness.

Among the most important types of Egyptian prayers were funerary* prayers, which were expressions of mourning as well as magical formulas that would help the dead reach the AFTERLIFE. The Egyptian BOOK OF THE DEAD contains collections of such prayers. The prayers of the HITTITES of Anatolia (present-day Turkey) were similar in form and content to Mesopotamian prayers. Occasionally, the Hittites added elements typical of their own culture or in reaction to specific events. Some prayers became masterpieces of Hittite LITERATURE, such as the prayer crafted by King Murshili II when plagues* were devastating the empire.

Ritual was a crucial part of worship. To gain the attention of the gods, prayers had to be recited while the person praying performed specific ritual movements. The typical gesture of prayer in Mesopotamia was lifting the hand to the mouth. In Egypt, priests recited prayers while standing with their arms at their sides. Like the Mesopotamians, it seems that the Hittites raised their hands when praying, although they sometimes kneeled, as did the Israelites. (*See also* **Death and Burial; Gods and Goddesses; Priests and Priestesses; Religion; Rituals and Sacrifice.**)

PREGNANCY

* **fertility** ability to become pregnant and bear children or to father children

* **incantation** written or recited formula of words designed to produce a given effect

In the ancient Near East, people considered pregnancy a natural part of the cycle of life, one that humans shared with animals. They also regarded pregnancy as a special condition of females that might be treated with MEDICINE, MAGIC, religious ritual, or all three.

The main purpose of MARRIAGE in the Near East was to produce and raise CHILDREN who could help their parents with work, enter into advantageous marriages, support parents in their old age, perform funeral rituals for deceased parents, and inherit property. Childless people became objects of pity and sometimes of scorn. To avoid such a fate, women sometimes sought medical or magical aids to improve their fertility*. The HITTITES of ANATOLIA (present-day Turkey) performed fertility rituals for men and women, and texts from ancient Egypt and MESOPOTAMIA describe treatments thought to remedy female infertility.

Pregnancy was a time of potential—and of mystery. Magical incantations* from ancient Mesopotamia describe the unborn child as a ship with an unknown cargo, sailing across a dark sea to the world of the living. The Egyptians and Babylonians devised tests to determine whether a woman was pregnant and, if so, whether the child would be a boy or a girl. Certain tests for pregnancy that involved the use of various herbs might have had some basis in scientific fact. However, many tests were based purely on superstition, such as the Babylonian belief that a pregnant woman was carrying a boy if she always stepped to the right, a girl if she stepped to the left.

Women facing the difficulties of pregnancy and CHILDBIRTH often sought magical and supernatural aid. Mesopotamian women, for example, wore amulets* during pregnancy to protect them from the demon Lamashtu, who preyed on mothers and infants. They might also ask for aid from goddesses such as Nintu, the Lady of Birth, who was occasionally portrayed holding a baby.

Even in social and economic environments that encouraged large families, women sometimes wanted to avoid pregnancy. The same Egyptian and Mesopotamian texts that describe infertility remedies also list contraceptive treatments—such as herbal potions to be drunk or applied to the body—that were meant to prevent pregnancy or cause an abortion. Breast-feeding gave women at least partial control over the spacing of children, as women are somewhat less likely to become pregnant when nursing a child. For instance, because they generally breast-fed children for about three years, Egyptian women reduced their chances of conceiving another child during that time. (*See also* **Amulets and Charms; Family and Social Life; Gender and Sex; Women, Role of.**)

PRIESTS AND PRIESTESSES

Religion was a very important aspect of life in the ancient Near East, and priests and priestesses played a crucial role in society. The duty of all humans was to serve the gods, and kings served as the primary link between the world of the gods and the world of humans. Although rulers were the chief priests of their societies, they could not be present at every religious function or ceremony. Consequently, religious duties were often delegated to priests and priestesses.

Qualifications for Priesthood. Throughout the ancient Near East, priests and priestesses came primarily from the elite, often including individuals of royal descent, particularly for the chief positions at large temples. At its higher levels, the priesthood was often a hereditary position passed down from generation to generation. In MESOPOTAMIA, priestly positions were inherited, and this practice was even more widespread in Egypt. Among the HITTITES of ANATOLIA (present-day Turkey), the chief priests of major temples came from royal families, while village priests were not of the nobility and had a lower social status. Most priests in ancient Israel also inherited their positions.

The main qualification to become a priest or priestess was that individuals be "pure." This generally meant that they had no visible imperfections, such as marks on the skin or skin diseases, or any physical deformities. An individual not only had to be pure to enter the priesthood, but that purity had to be maintained afterward as well. Each society had its own rules about maintaining both physical and symbolic or ritual purity.

To remain pure, priests had to wash themselves several times each day. This process was often carried out in a sacred lake or in special washbasins at the entrances to temples. The maintenance of purity also usually required wearing special clothing and eating specific foods while

Priests and Priestesses

serving the gods. In Egypt, temple priests shaved their heads and dressed in white linen. Mesopotamian priests also wore special clothing and often had shaved heads. They sometimes performed their duties in the nude, as did the Elamite priests of IRAN. For the Hittites, impurity on the part of a priest was punishable by death. Their great concern for ritual purity is evident in *Instructions for Temple Personnel,* an ancient Hittite text about religious administration.

In general, priests and priestesses did not have to remain chaste*. In Egypt, however, they had to refrain from sexual relations while serving in the temple, but otherwise they could marry and, often, have children. Sometimes priests and priestesses married each other. Priests had to obey various moral rules to maintain their ritual purity and serve in temples. An ancient Egyptian INSCRIPTION lists some of these rules: "Do not come in sin, do not enter in impurity, do not utter falsehood in his house, do not covet things, do not slander, do not accept bribes, do not be partial as between a poor man and a great . . . do not reveal what you have seen in the mysteries of the temple."

Role and Organization of the Priesthood. The primary role of priests was to attend to the needs of the gods by properly conducting religious rituals and ceremonies. The basic daily ritual in temples was the "care and feeding" of the gods, who were represented by statues. The temple was considered the home of the gods, and priests cleaned, dressed, fed, and entertained these statues as if they were living beings. Providing for such needs kept the gods healthy and happy and helped ensure that they would favor their subjects. In addition to their role in temple rituals, priests and priestesses also took part in various public religious ceremonies.

Priests performed a variety of roles beyond attending to the needs of the gods and performing religious rituals. They served as teachers, scientists, doctors, psychologists, and judges. Some priests were considered magicians, and others practiced divination* by interpreting DREAMS and OMENS from the gods. Sometimes the individuals who served as musicians, cooks, and administrators in temples were members of the priestly class as well. Temple scribes* responsible for learning, performing, and passing down sacred texts and rituals were among the most important members of the priesthood.

In most Near Eastern societies, priestesses held positions that were similar to those held by priests. They were also organized in the same ways as the men. Often, but not always, priestesses served goddesses while priests served gods. Those priestesses who served a male deity*— often called a "bride of the god"—sometimes had more power than the highest male priest serving the same god. In ancient BABYLON, for example, priestesses of the god MARDUK had great power. Some women who were attached to the family of the Sumerian sun god Shamash could marry, but they were not allowed to have children. Elamite priests and priestesses were equals. In some regions of the Near East, some priestesses served as prostitutes, and the money they made went to the gods or goddesses they served. Israel was unique in that women were not permitted to serve in priestly functions, but they could be prophets* for Yahweh.

* **chaste** not participating in sexual relations; virtuous or pure

* **divination** art or practice of foretelling the future

* **scribe** person of a learned class who served as a writer, editor, or teacher

* **deity** god or goddess

* **prophet** one who claims to have received divine messages or insights

Dating from the 400s B.C., this Phoenician sculpture from Carthage depicts a priestess with open arms. Priestesses and priests in the ancient Near East held similar roles in society. They generally had to meet the same requirements and performed the same religious duties.

Every ancient Near Eastern society had various classes of priests, from village priests to the high priests of great city temples. Some priests served major deities, while others served lesser ones. The priesthood was also organized according to priestly duties and responsibilities, such as performing daily rituals, keeping track of temple records, performing music, singing HYMNS, and serving in other specialized roles. Various priestly titles signified rank, responsibilities, and the god or goddess served.

Ancient Egypt had a highly organized priesthood. There were two main classes of priests and priestesses: the "servants of god," or prophets; and the "pure ones," or *waab* priests. The "servants of god" included the highest priestly ranks, while the "pure ones" were individuals of lesser rank. Most Egyptian temples had between 10 and 25 priests; larger temples had many more, however. Egyptian priests were divided into four groups, called *phyle,* made up mostly of *waab* priests. Each *phyle* was usually led by a "servant of god," or prophet. The *phyles* served at the temple on a rotating basis: One *phyle* served for one month while the other three *phyles* were off duty.

Until about the 1500s B.C., Egypt had no full-time, professional priesthood. Scribes from the upper classes of society performed priestly service as a part-time job. Among this elite, priesthood was a normal part of people's

15

Property and Property Rights

lives and not a separate profession. Moreover, individuals often served several temples at different ranks all at the same time. For example, a man who served as a prophet in one temple might also be a *waab* priest in another.

The Egyptian priesthood included many priestly titles, such as "father of the god," "provost of the mysteries," and "lector priest." Lector priests, who read sacred texts, were sometimes called magicians. Some priests were called "scribes of the sacred book" in the "House of Life," which was essentially a library and school connected to the temple. This is where most of the science, history, and literature of Egyptian society was kept.

The structure of the priesthood was less complex in other areas of the Near East. In ancient Sumer, many temples were organized around the *en*, a priest or priestess considered the spouse of a god or goddess. Apart from the *en*, the highest figure in most temples was the *sanga* (bookkeeper), who performed both administrative and religious duties for the temple. At some small temples, the bookkeeper was the only temple worker.

Among the Hittites, the highest religious official was the *sanga*, followed by a priest known as the "anointed." One of the most important priestesses was known as the "mother of the god." These priests and priestesses performed most of the actual OFFERINGS to the gods and were the ones who approached the gods most directly. Other temple personnel included musicians, singers, cooks, and administrators.

Among the Israelites, the biblical Priestly Code gave priests more power than in many other areas of the Near East. According to the Priestly Code, all law was regarded as religious law and could be enforced by priests. This meant that, in addition to all their other duties, Israelite priests served as judges, physicians, and even state administrators for the society. (*See also* **Death and Burial; Gods and Goddesses; Occupations; Palaces and Temples; Prayer; Rituals and Sacrifice; Scribes; Women, Role of.**)

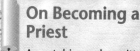

On Becoming a Priest

An autobiography written around 850 B.C. describes how the author entered the priesthood of Horus:

I was introduced into the [temple] to sanctify the mysterious image of the god who is in Thebes, to satisfy him with his offerings.

I . . . had rid myself from all that was evil in me, had exchanged evil with purity, and had loosened clothes and ointments according to the purification of Horus and Seth. I entered the presence of the god . . . while I was afraid and in awe of him. The king praised me; he made my position. He appointed me in the steps of my father.

PROPERTY AND PROPERTY RIGHTS

In ancient times, both private individuals and public institutions, such as the palace or the temple, could own property in the Near East. Within each Near Eastern culture, however, a web of laws and customs determined the kinds of property different individuals could hold and what they could do with it. Women, for example, could not own property in their own names in some cultures. Slaves, who were themselves considered a form of property, could sometimes own property.

Property consisted of real estate (land and buildings), movable property (money and possessions), and human property, or slaves. Another category included nonphysical things, such as offices and occupations that could be passed from a father to his oldest son, water rights that gave landowners a share in the water from nearby streams or canals, and businesses. A slave's labor was also a form of property. For instance, a document excavated in Egypt states that a specific number of people owned a slave together and that each owner was entitled to the slave's labor for a certain number of days each year. This labor was property that the slave owner had the right to resell.

In MESOPOTAMIA and Egypt, where agricultural societies developed early, ownership of farmland was an important element of the social order.

* **nomadic** referring to people who travel from place to place to find food and pasture

* **dowry** money or property that a woman brings to the man she marries

* **will** document in which one dictates the division of one's property after death

* **disinherit** to exclude someone from a share in an estate

A Woman's Place

In Mesopotamia, during the period of the Old Babylonian empire (ca. 1900–1600 B.C.), there appeared a social and economic practice by which families with daughters and no sons could keep wealth within the family. Rich young women became *naditus*. These women were sent to live in special communities maintained by donations from their families. There they led lives of devotion to the gods but were forbidden to marry, preventing the wealth from being given away as a dowry. The *naditus* maintained control of their property, engaged fully in business activities, made profits, and could dispose of property as they wished.

Although much land belonged to powerful individuals (kings and high priests) or to state institutions (palaces and temples), some land was privately owned in every society. Such privately owned property was passed from one generation to the next by means of one of several methods. Nomadic* peoples generally divided a father's property equally among his sons. However, equal division of farmland spelled disaster, for within a few generations, a farm would be reduced to many plots, each too small to support a family. For ancient Mesopotamians, the solution was shared ownership of property by extended families rather than by individuals. After about 2000 B.C., as Mesopotamian society grew more centralized, land laws placed increasing emphasis on individual ownership. The state found it easier to deal with one owner than with a group of brothers, uncles, and cousins.

Primogeniture, in which the oldest son inherited the land, was another solution to the problem of land division. This type of inheritance was customary in Egypt, although sometimes both sons and daughters could own and inherit land. The Israelites divided their land among sons but gave the oldest son a double share.

Every society was concerned with keeping family property within the family, which was defined by the father's bloodline. For this reason, sons usually inherited land and most other property. A daughter's share of the estate was her dowry*, which she took to her marriage. The dowry then became part of her husband's family's property. In the case of DIVORCE, however, a portion of that property might be returned to the wife or her family. The family that lost property in the form of a daughter's dowry might expect to regain the loss when sons married and brought their wives' dowries into the family's estate.

Customs and laws were not the only factors that shaped the handing down of property from one generation to the next. A will* from ancient Egypt reveals a woman disinheriting* some of her children for not taking proper care of her. In another will, a man disinherits a female relative because she failed to nurse him when he was ill. Although the general pattern of property transfer reflected the needs and values of the larger society, individuals could still express their personal preferences and family feelings through the disposal of their property. (*See also* **Egypt and the Egyptians; Family and Social Life; Land Use and Ownership; Law; Women, Role of.**)

Prophecy

See *Oracles and Prophecy.*

PROVERBS

Proverbs are short, sometimes witty, often educational sayings meant to express some common truth or useful thought. Proverbs created primarily to educate were among the earliest forms of LITERATURE in the ancient Near East. A type of instructional text classified as wisdom literature, proverbs record observations about the nature of reality and provide simple instructions and rules of behavior based on experience and thought

Psalms

about the meanings of life. Proverbs provided valuable advice to everyone from kings to ordinary people.

Among the earliest proverbs were so-called "wisdom of events," sayings about simple factual situations based on observations of occurrences in nature and society. Later proverbs taught lessons by describing an action and its result. For example, the lesson of the Egyptian proverb "You beat my back; your teachings entered my ear" was probably that one should appreciate a strict instructor. Some proverbs used ridiculous situations to make their point, as in the Sumerian proverb "Would you pay cash for a pig's squeal?"

Many ancient Near Eastern proverbs were written in the form of a father (or teacher) speaking to his son (or student). It is not surprising, then, that the lessons taught often involved such subjects as respect for one's elders and the gods, the value of modesty and caution, the importance of financial responsibility, and the avoidance of the "wrong" types of people. The earliest known proverbs of this type were Egyptian sayings in which a pharaoh* gave advice to his son. The subject matter of these proverbs was essentially directed toward preparing Egyptian princes and their high officials for later responsibilities in government.

* **pharaoh** king of ancient Egypt

The most famous proverbs are found in the Book of Proverbs in the Hebrew BIBLE. These biblical proverbs—intended to help individuals make sensible choices in their lives—deal with a range of sacred and secular* themes that have universal appeal. Some portions of the Book of Proverbs share similarities with earlier works of wisdom literature, including an ancient Egyptian text called *The Instruction of Amenemope.*

* **secular** nonreligious; connected with everyday life

Ancient Sumer, Babylonia, Egypt, and Assyria also had collections of proverbs. The oldest Mesopotamian proverbs are contained in a work called *Instructions of Shuruppak.* Another collection—*Sayings of Ahiqar*—probably put together in Assyria in the 600s B.C., deals with themes similar to earlier proverbs, such as devotion and submission to the gods, the value of discipline, and respect for superiors. This collection is remarkable for its fablelike comparisons involving animals. (*See also* **Books and Manuscripts; Education; Religion.**)

PSALMS

* **first millennium** B.C. years from 1000 to 1 B.C.

* **canonical** included in the canon, the officially recognized books of the Bible

Psalms are ancient Hebrew songs that address or call on the god YAHWEH. The word *psalm* originally came from a Greek translation of the Hebrew word *mizmor,* which literally means "song accompanied by a stringed instrument." This indicates that psalms were used as HYMNS, or religious songs, in ancient Israel. Many psalms are pleas or songs of praise, thanksgiving, and mourning. It is also clear that some psalms were chanted or used as prayers. Some psalms were written for specific religious occasions, such as the Sabbath, the day of worship and rest. The majority of psalms were written in terms that made them suitable for various occasions. Most psalms were written during the first millennium B.C.* and were later adopted for use in the Jewish and Christian religions, in which they continue to play an important role.

The best-known psalms are the 150 canonical* psalms that appear in the Book of Psalms in the Hebrew BIBLE. The canonical psalms were said to have been written by King DAVID, who took the throne of Israel just after 1000 B.C. However, scholars no longer think that David wrote many, if any, of these psalms. Instead, they believe that the psalms were written by a number of people. In fact, some scholars believe that Psalm 104 borrowed phrases and ideas from an Egyptian hymn written in the 1340s B.C. called the *Hymn to Aten.*

Besides the canonical psalms, the *Psalms of Solomon* is also well known. These 18 psalms were said to have been written by King SOLOMON of Israel, David's son and successor. Although Solomon's psalms are similar to many of the canonical psalms in their subjects and forms, they are not included in the Bible.

Other psalms are recorded in the Dead Sea Scrolls, which were composed by members of a Jewish sect* between 200 B.C. and A.D. 100. These scrolls were recovered in the A.D. 1940s and 1950s from caves bordering the Dead Sea, between present-day Israel and Jordan. Hymns found in the Dead Sea Scrolls borrow phrases from the canonical psalms, indicating that the writers of later Jewish hymns based their work on ancient Hebrew psalms. Psalms continued to be produced in medieval times by European and Middle Eastern Jews. (*See also* **Hebrews and Israelites; Judaism and Jews; Religion.**)

* **sect** group of people with a common leadership who share a distinctive set of religious views and opinion

PTOLEMY I

ruled 305–282 B.C.
King of Egypt

* **coronation** act or ceremony of crowing a leader

* **Hellenistic** referring to the Greek-influenced culture of the Mediterranean world and western Asia during the three centuries after the death of Alexander the Great in 323 B.C.

* **diplomacy** practice of conducting negotiations between kingdoms, states, or nations

Ptolemy I (TAH•luh•mee) was a highly decorated general under ALEXANDER THE GREAT of MACEDONIA. He went on to become one of the most famous kings of Egypt. He also founded the Ptolemaic dynasty, a long line of rulers from the Ptolemy family that governed Egypt for almost 300 years and led it through its last great period of empire and grandeur.

Born into a Macedonian noble family around 366 B.C., Ptolemy probably started his career at an early age as a page in the royal court. When Alexander took the throne in 336 B.C., Ptolemy became his bodyguard. He was later promoted to the position of general in command of the navy and proved to be one of Alexander's most capable officers. When Alexander died in 323 B.C., Ptolemy convinced Alexander's other generals to divide up the empire with him. Each former general became a governor of a different province. Ptolemy governed Egypt until 305 B.C., when he named himself king of Egypt. His coronation* marked the beginning of the Ptolemaic dynasty.

Ptolemy worked hard to make Egypt a great Hellenistic* power. Using diplomacy* as well as military might, he first stabilized and then expanded his kingdom. Under his rule, Egypt became the supreme NAVAL POWER in the Mediterranean. Although he brought Hellenistic culture to Egypt, especially to its royal court, he won the loyalty of the Egyptian people by adopting their religion, building temples to the Egyptian gods, and restoring the temples of their earlier kings. In addition, Ptolemy introduced coins to Egypt, founded a famous library at the city of Alexandria, and wrote a history of Alexander the Great, which is now lost. After he died in 282 B.C., Ptolemy was designated a god by the Egyptian people.

Pyramids

Ptolemy's first few successors were strong and able kings who maintained the overseas holdings and wealth of the empire. However, later Ptolemaic rulers were both weak and corrupt. By 200 B.C., they had lost many of the empire's overseas lands and faced revolts by the Egyptian people. The last rulers of the dynasty were Ptolemy XV and his mother, the famous Egyptian queen CLEOPATRA. Their rule and the Ptolemaic dynasty both came to an end in 30 B.C., when the Romans conquered Egypt. (*See also* **Dynasties; Egypt and the Egyptians; Pharaohs; Seleucid Empire.**)

PYRAMIDS

The pyramids are tombs that were built for Egyptian kings between about 2650 and 1650 B.C. Most of the pyramids were built during the Old Kingdom period (ca. 2675–2130 B.C.), which is why that period is sometimes referred to as the pyramid age.

In addition to many smaller pyramids, 35 major pyramids still stand in Egypt today. The most famous are three giant pyramids at GIZA, on the west bank of the NILE RIVER, not far from Cairo. These three pyramids are among the best-known monuments of ancient Egypt. The biggest of the three, called the Great Pyramid, is the largest all-stone structure ever built. Because of their preservation and significance, the pyramids are one of the most important sources of information about ancient Egypt.

How the Pyramids Originated. Because the ancient Egyptians believed in an AFTERLIFE (life after death), they tried to protect the bodies of the dead by burying them in tombs. These tombs could hold provisions and guides to help the soul in the afterlife. Before the pyramids, tombs of kings and other important people took the form of mastabas. These were long, low rectangular structures with a gently curving roof and slightly sloping sides or with a flat roof and sides that had numerous false doors. These moundlike structures, often made of sand and rubble, covered a pit in the ground in which the dead body was placed. Over time, mastabas became bigger and more solidly built. The sides were covered in bricks and arranged in steps to make the tomb stronger and more durable.

The shape of the mastabas and pyramids had religious significance for the ancient Egyptians. The mastabas symbolized the creation of the world, which the ancient Egyptians believed occurred when a hill emerged from the waters of chaos. Scholars also believe that the sloped sides of the mastabas and pyramids represented the rays of the sun, reflecting the Egyptians' relationship with the sun god AMUN. Egyptians believed that the sun god was the king of the gods and that he had created the universe.

Builders of the Pyramids. The first pyramid in ancient Egypt was built for King DJOSER (ruled ca. 2630–2611 B.C.) by his chief architect, Imhotep. The pyramid started out as a mastaba, but Imhotep enlarged it and then added five layers of rocks and bricks above the first, each layer somewhat smaller than the one below. The result was a six-stepped pyramid rising more than 200 feet and covering almost 150,000 square feet at the base.

Pyramid Robbery

From the very beginning of the pyramid age, many pyramids were broken into and robbed of their valuable contents. This often occurred soon after a king's body was entombed. As a result, builders of later pyramids introduced architectural features to prevent robbers from gaining easy access to the tombs' interiors. These features included passages with dead ends, large granite rock plugs for entranceways, and hidden trapdoors. Despite these attempts to block robbers' efforts, the pyramids continued to be robbed of their treasures, leading later Egyptian kings to abandon pyramids altogether and to adopt less obvious rock-cut tombs for burial.

Pyramids

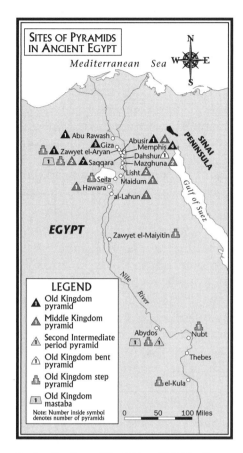

SITES OF PYRAMIDS IN ANCIENT EGYPT

Mediterranean Sea

SINAI PENINSULA

Abu Rawash
Giza
Zawyet el-Aryan
Saqqara
Abusir
Memphis
Dahshur
Mazghuna
Lisht
Seila
Maidum
Hawara
al-Lahun

Gulf of Suez

EGYPT

Zawyet el-Maiyitin

Nile River

Abydos
Nubt
Thebes
el-Kula

LEGEND

▲ Old Kingdom pyramid
△ Middle Kingdom pyramid
⬡ Second Intermediate period pyramid
⬠ Old Kingdom bent pyramid
🏛 Old Kingdom step pyramid
1️⃣ Old Kingdom mastaba

Note: Number inside symbol denotes number of pyramids

0   50   100 Miles

During the time of the Old and Middle Kingdoms, many kings of ancient Egypt built mastabas and pyramids to hold their mummies and the items necessary for the afterlife. Generally, the pyramids were built in the region surrounding the city of Memphis, which was the capital of Egypt in ancient times. Middle Kingdom pyramids were concentrated near Lisht, the site of Egypt's capital during that period. During the Second Intermediate Period, two pyramids were built at Abydos.

* **mud brick** brick made from mud, straw, and water mixed together and baked in the sun

* **relief** sculpture in which material is cut away to show figures raised from the background

* **funerary** having to do with funerals or with the handling of the dead

Most of Djoser's successors followed his lead and built pyramids for themselves. Some of the earliest pyramids were never completed, perhaps because the kings died prematurely. In those cases, the workers apparently abandoned the building site and began work on a new pyramid for the dead king's successor.

The first true pyramid—with straight sides instead of steps—was built by King Sneferu (ruled ca. 2625–2585 B.C.). Sneferu also built two other large pyramids as well as two smaller pyramids, making him the most productive builder in ancient times. One of Sneferu's pyramids is called the Bent Pyramid because its sides are steeper at the bottom than at the top. Some scholars believe that following the collapse of one of Sneferu's earlier steep-sided pyramids, the architects corrected the angle of the slope.

Sneferu's son and successor, King KHUFU (ruled 2585–2560 B.C.), was probably the most famous pyramid builder of ancient times. He built the Great Pyramid at Giza, which towered more than 480 feet in the air. Not far from the Great Pyramid, Khufu built three smaller pyramids as tombs for his mother and two principal queens. Khufu's son and successor, King Khafre, also built a huge pyramid at Giza. He intended it to match his father's pyramid in height, but it turned out to be slightly smaller. Khafre was succeeded by his son Menkaure, who built the third largest pyramid at Giza. Although considerably smaller than the other two, it is still very impressive.

After about 2500 B.C., kings continued to build pyramids but on a smaller scale. Larger pyramids were built once again starting around 1900 B.C., but they were less solidly constructed than earlier pyramids had been. Instead of being built of solid stone, they were built of mud bricks* and had stone outer walls. The last pyramids built for Egyptian kings were constructed during the Second Intermediate period (ca. 1630–1539 B.C.), but none of these has survived intact. After this time, most Egyptian kings were buried in tombs cut into rock cliffs.

Structure of the Pyramids. Most pyramids were built with a square base and four triangular sides that sloped inward to form a peak at the top. Inside they usually contained several rooms—burial chambers for members of the royal family and areas for storing provisions needed for the afterlife. The most important room was the central chamber, where the king's body was placed. In the earliest pyramids, this chamber was located deep underground at the bottom of a shaft. By the time of King Khufu, however, the king's burial chamber was placed high up in the pyramid. The later position reflected the belief that the king became one with the sun god after his death. The inside walls of the pyramids were decorated with paintings and reliefs*.

Most pyramids were surrounded by a large complex of other structures. Most often, these included a chapel and a funerary* temple, which were joined by a passageway, and a small pyramid, which may have been intended for the dead king's soul. The interiors of all these structures were elaborately decorated as well. In addition, a covered trench was located on one or more sides of the pyramid. This trench contained the funerary boats that the king would use to meet the sun god. Usually, the whole complex was surrounded by a large brick wall.

Pyramids

How the Pyramids Were Built. Building the pyramids required vision, planning, organization, and skills. Their construction reflects strong central governments and powerful kings who had control over both people and resources.

The exact position of a pyramid may have been determined by astronomical observations, and the site was leveled with precision. For example, the 13-acre base of the Great Pyramid is only about half an inch higher on one side than on the opposite side. All other types of MEASUREMENT also were made with incredible accuracy.

Quarrying* the limestone blocks used for building the pyramids was a major undertaking. Stones were not just broken off and dragged away randomly. Instead, each stone block was marked in the quarry, cut to the exact shape desired, and then removed. As a result, the massive stone blocks fit tightly together without any gaps. For the Great Pyramid, more than 2 million stone blocks, weighing an average of 2.5 tons, were quarried in this way. Although most of the limestone quarries were relatively close to the building sites, moving the huge stone blocks still required great planning and effort. Paths were leveled, and rollers and heavy sleds were used to make dragging the stone blocks easier. Some stones, such as the granite that was used for columns and chambers inside the pyramids, came from as far away as 500 miles. These stones had to be carried down the Nile River by ship or barge.

After the stone blocks were transported to the building site, they were carefully fitted into place. The stones were lifted into place by means of giant ramps, which were built against the sides of the growing pyramid, and levers, which made it easier to move the blocks up the ramps and

* **quarry** to excavate pieces of stone by cutting, splitting, or (in modern times) blasting

The Egyptian Fourth Dynasty king Khufu and his successors constructed several pyramids at Giza. Khufu referred to his complex, shown here, as the "Horizon of Khufu." The three larger pyramids at Giza are the most famous pyramids in the world. The complex also includes several smaller pyramids and the Great Sphinx.

into their settings. One of the most impressive achievements in the construction of the pyramids was the positioning of 40-ton granite blocks almost 200 feet high in the roof of the king's burial chamber inside the Great Pyramid.

In the 400s B.C., the Greek historian HERODOTUS wrote that more than 100,000 workers labored for up to 20 years to build each pyramid. However, modern historians believe that as few as 20,000 laborers may have been involved and that construction may have been completed in as few as 6 years. However, this is still a very large workforce, especially considering that the laborers were provided with housing, food, and medical care while they worked on the pyramids. (*See also* **Egypt and the Egyptians; Pharaohs.**)

Qanat

See *Irrigation.*

QUEENS

* **diplomacy** practice of conducting negotiations between kingdoms, states, or nations

The highest-ranking women of the ancient Near East were queens. These women were either the principal wives or the mothers of KINGS. Although these royal women were necessary for the continuation of kingships and they sometimes had considerable responsibility and influence, queens rarely played a direct role in the GOVERNMENT of their land. Very few of them ruled in their own right. Many queens did, however, fulfill important duties in diplomacy* and religion, and some have emerged from the pages of history as forceful and distinctive women.

Sumer. Little is really known about many of the earliest rulers of Sumer beyond their names—and even less is known about their wives. The tomb of Pu-abi, the wife of a king of UR, dating to around 2600 B.C., provides an exception. Buried in a tomb next to that of the king, she lay on a bed wearing jewelry made of gold, silver, lapis lazuli*, and carnelian. Also buried nearby were a wooden wardrobe, two ox-drawn wagons, and the bodies of 59 attendants and soldiers, all sacrificed to accompany the king and his wife in their AFTERLIFE.

* **lapis lazuli** dark blue semiprecious stone

Assyria. In the Assyrian empire of northern MESOPOTAMIA, the king's wives and concubines*, along with their young children, lived in a harem* ruled by the queen mother (mother of the king). This arrangement gave the queen mother tremendous power in the royal household. It also led to much plotting and competition, as various women tried to get their sons named heir to the throne.

* **concubine** mistress to a married man
* **harem** section of a household designated for women

An Assyrian king's wife possessed estates occupied by large households. A female official called a *shakintu* administered her household, which also included a scribe*, a cook, and makers of sweets. The identities of the Assyrian queens are, for the most part, unknown. Few of them appear in sculptures or texts. Even when their names remain, their origins

* **scribe** person of a learned class who served as a writer, editor, or teacher

Queens

are not always clear, although it seems that some Assyrian kings married women from Assyrian and foreign noble families.

Egypt. The status of royal women in Egypt depended on their relationship to the king, as revealed in such titles as "king's daughter," "king's wife," "king's mother," and "king's sister." Kings in Egypt were believed to be descended from the gods and to have divine aspects themselves. Egyptian tradition also associated queenship with the divine. Consequently, queens were frequently portrayed wearing or carrying symbols associated with such goddesses as HATHOR, the universal mother goddess of ancient Egypt.

By the 1500s B.C., if not earlier, Egyptian kings had begun taking two or more wives. One wife was identified as the principal wife, although it is not clear how the king chose her. A principal wife could be of royal or nonroyal birth. Some kings married their sisters, half sisters, or daughters and had children with them, a tradition that may have developed to mirror the relationships among Egyptian deities*, who also intermarried. After Egypt became a leading power in the ancient Near East, its kings sometimes married foreign princesses. In some cases, defeated rulers may have sent their daughters to the Egyptian kings as signs of submission. Other marriages to foreign women may have been diplomatic alliances.

Egyptian queens and queen mothers owned independent estates run by officials who only served the royal women. As partners of the divine kings, the royal women occupied an important place in rituals, but they did not have any officially recognized political positions. Still, some of them managed to attain considerable power. Ahmose Nefertari, mother of Amenhotep I, was so highly honored that a cult* worshiped her for centuries after her death. Tiy, the nonroyal principal wife of Amenhotep III, appears in sculpture on an equal scale with her husband rather than on the usual, smaller scale. A few Egyptian queens, including NITOKRIS, HATSHEPSUT, and CLEOPATRA, even ruled Egypt in their own names.

Anatolia. Among the HITTITES of ancient ANATOLIA (present-day Turkey), royal women had significant status and responsibilities. In the Hittite kingdom of KHATTI, the king maintained a harem of numerous women, but only one woman held the title of queen. In addition to bearing the king's highest-ranking children, including the son who would inherit the throne, the queen was responsible for supervising much of the king's household. Groups of officials helped her oversee the complex administration of the royal establishment.

Some Hittite queens were also involved in diplomatic communication with other states and in governing the empire. Queen Pudukhepa, wife of KHATTUSHILI III, wrote letters to the Egyptian court and appeared on royal SEALS with her husband and her son. Many of the queens of Khatti were foreigners whose marriages to Hittite kings were arranged by diplomats to seal alliances or reflect relationships between states. In the same way, Hittite princesses were given in marriage to foreign kings or princes.

The Buried Queens of Kalkhu

Modern archaeologists have found the tombs of several Assyrian queens in the palace at Kalkhu (present-day Nimrud). It was the Assyrians' custom to send their dead into the afterlife with the finest items their family could afford. The royal family was especially expected to spend lavishly on grave goods. The queens' graves at Kalkhu contained some of the finest known examples of Mesopotamian metalwork and jewelry, including heavy gold cuffs inlaid with semiprecious stones and decorated with images of stars and figures—finery that told of a queen's high status, living or dead.

* **deity** god or goddess
* **cult** system of religious beliefs and rituals; group following these beliefs

This relief-decorated limestone block from Hermopolis depicts Kiya, a secondary wife of the Egyptian king Akhenaten (ruled ca. 1353–1336 B.C.). It was common for Egyptian kings to have several wives. In addition to Kiya, Akhenaten married many other women, including princesses from Mitanni and Babylonia, as well as Nefertiti, who became his principal wife.

The most powerful royal woman in Khatti held the title and position of Tawananna, after the name of the first Hittite queen. The queen became Tawananna after the death of the previous Tawananna, who was usually the queen mother. The Tawananna had much influence in the empire, even if her husband died and a new king came to the throne. Hittite history records several power struggles between widowed queens and their sons or stepsons. King Murshili II, for example, removed his Babylonian stepmother from her position as Tawananna.

Israel. The queen mother was the most powerful woman in the Israelite kingdom. Her title was *gebirah,* meaning "mighty lady." She wore a crown, and her throne could be set alongside that of the king, her son. Among the Israelites and Judeans, who sometimes worshiped a goddess named Asherah, the wife of the god YAHWEH, the queen mother played an important role in Asherah's cult.

The queen mother's duties were not simply religious. Passages from the Hebrew BIBLE show that her position was that of adviser to the king, and her political role may have been even greater than those passages suggest. She was most likely also involved in the administration of the harem and the female workers within the palace. The king's wife, in contrast, had less of a public role. Although she may have had some influence on the king or the court, she had no official position or responsibilities—until

25

her son became king and she became queen mother in her turn. (*See also* **Athaliah; Nefertiti; Semiramis; Valley of the Queens; Women, Role of.**)

Ra

See *Amun*.

RAMSES II

ruled ca. 1279–1213 B.C.
King of Egypt

* **pharaoh** king of ancient Egypt

* **delta** fan-shaped, lowland plain formed of soil deposited by a river

Ramses II (RAM•seez) was one of the most celebrated Egyptian kings. His unusually long reign of nearly 70 years was a time of prosperity and stability in Egypt, marked by an extraordinary number of monumental building projects that included some of the most famous structures of the ancient world.

Ramses was the son of the dynamic pharaoh* SETY I. Although Sety reigned for less than 15 years, he not only led several military campaigns to secure Egyptian control over CANAAN, but he also built lavish temples to the main Egyptian gods. Ramses actively participated in many of these ventures, and Sety eventually named him heir to the throne. Ramses was in his 20s when Sety died, leaving the young pharaoh a large kingdom to run and many temples and buildings to complete.

After burying his father in a huge underground tomb in the elaborate cemetery known as the VALLEY OF THE KINGS near THEBES, Ramses turned his attention to matters of state. He speeded completion of Sety's temple at the Egyptian city of ABYDOS and drew up plans for his new capital, Pi-Ramese, on the delta* of the NILE RIVER. To finance these works, he increased production of gold from mines in the kingdom of Nubia.

Ramses next set out to strengthen Egypt's military position in Canaan. In the fourth year of his reign, he conquered the Syrian kingdom of Amurru, which had been controlled by the HITTITES of ANATOLIA (present-day Turkey). He then attempted to retake the nearby city of Qadesh, which had been seized by the Hittites during the reign of the Egyptian king AKHEN-ATEN, around 100 years earlier. However, the Hittites laid a trap for Ramses that nearly destroyed the Egyptian army. Only his bold action and the well-timed arrival of reinforcements allowed him to fight the Hittites to a draw. For several years, the two powers clashed in Canaan before finally signing a peace treaty. Ramses also acknowledged KHATTUSHILI III as the rightful Hittite ruler and later married two of his daughters.

At home, Ramses' construction projects spread along the length of the Nile. His capital featured a magnificent palace and temples and was linked with the Nile to create a port for ships from the Mediterranean Sea. At KARNAK, he completed the great columned hall that was begun by Seti. He also finished the huge temple of Abydos and his own colossal temple, called the Ramesseum, in the city of Thebes. At ABU SIMBEL in Nubia, he built two spectacular temples, one for himself and the sun god, the other for his queen, Nefertari, and the goddess HATHOR.

Ramses outlived several of his sons, and his successor, Merneptah, was at least 60 years old when he came to the throne. Merneptah ruled for ten years and was followed by a series of undistinguished kings until RAMSES III inherited the throne in the 1180s B.C. (*See also* **Egypt and the Egyptians; Nubia and the Nubians; Palaces and Temples.**)

RAMSES III

ruled ca. 1187–1156 B.C.
King of Egypt

* **Levant** lands bordering the eastern shores of the Mediterranean Sea (present-day Syria, Lebanon, and Israel), the West Bank, and Jordan

* **delta** fan-shaped, lowland plain formed of soil deposited by a river

The reign of Ramses III (RAM•seez), second ruler of the Twentieth Dynasty of Egypt, was marked by a series of invasions that he successfully fought off and by internal difficulties. At the time he assumed power, Egypt had just recovered from a series of civil wars.

Within five years of becoming king, Ramses faced an invasion by tribes from Libya, which lies just west of Egypt. He defeated the LIBYANS and their allies, whom he brought back to Egypt as slaves. Two years later, however, a dangerous coalition of invaders known as the SEA PEOPLES began to threaten Ramses' kingdom. Perhaps originating in ANATOLIA (present-day Turkey) and islands in the Mediterranean Sea, the Sea Peoples advanced against Egypt by both land and sea. However, Egypt crushed their land army in the Levant* and destroyed their fleet by drawing it into the narrow channels of the NILE RIVER delta*. Some of the defeated Sea Peoples settled on the Levantine coast and eventually forced Egypt to abandon the territory it controlled in that region.

Despite these military successes, Ramses' later years were plagued with internal problems. Difficulty in the delivery of food rations led to the first recorded strike by workers at the royal tombs in the ancient city of THEBES. Then one of Ramses' wives plotted to kill him and put her son on the throne. This plan was foiled, but Ramses died soon afterward and was succeeded as king by his son Ramses IV. (*See also* **Egypt and the Egyptians; Kings; Pharaohs.**)

RECORD KEEPING

* **city-state** independent state consisting of a city and its surrounding territory

* **archaeologist** scientist who studies past human cultures, usually by excavating material remains of human activity

* **Levant** lands bordering the eastern shores of the Mediterranean Sea (present-day Syria, Lebanon, and Israel), the West Bank, and Jordan

The oldest known communication code before the invention of WRITING emerged in the ancient Near East around 8000 B.C. It was a form of record keeping that used small clay objects called tokens to represent the items being recorded. This simple method of accounting remained in use for more than 5,000 years and was directly related to two of the major milestones in Near Eastern civilization: the beginning of AGRICULTURE and the growth of city-states*. The token system of record keeping also opened the way to new forms of communication. It gave rise to the earliest known system of writing and led to the invention of abstract numerals, which became the basis of all MATHEMATICS.

Tokens and Their Use. Archaeologists* have found record-keeping tokens in ANATOLIA (present-day Turkey) and the Levant*, but the greatest numbers of them were found in MESOPOTAMIA and IRAN. Ranging in color from brownish-pink to green and black, the tokens are small, handmade objects of baked clay that measure up to one inch across.

The first tokens consisted of simple geometric shapes, such as cones, spheres, disks, and cylinders. A few were shaped like objects, such as oil

Record Keeping

jars and animals. Each token shape represented a particular item. For instance, a cone and a sphere each represented different measures of grain. Tokens added an element of abstraction to the simple act of counting. By using tokens, people could not only count things without actually handling or even looking at them, but they could add and subtract numbers of things as well. Tokens also provided a permanent, mobile record of counting calculations and transactions.

The token system represented a great leap forward in record keeping, but it had some drawbacks. The counters conveyed only simple economic quantities, and they provided no information about the quality of goods or the kinds of transactions involved. Moreover, large numbers of tokens were difficult to store and keep together.

To keep the tokens together, people developed the idea of placing groups of them inside hollow clay balls, which served as a type of envelope. Once a ball was sealed, however, the tokens were no longer visible and could not be counted. To solve this problem, record keepers devised a system of marking the clay envelopes. They pressed the tokens, like SEALS, on the outer surface of the envelopes while the clay was still soft. The resulting impressions represented the tokens inside the balls, just as the tokens themselves stood for real items.

Why Keep Records? Human communication evolved to keep pace with other cultural developments. The token system appeared at about

Clay tokens were used in record keeping as early as 8000 B.C., coinciding with the rise of agriculture. These tokens were excavated at Susa. Dating from around 3300 B.C., they represent different goods. The tokens at the top represent (from left to right) a unit of oil, a measure of honey, an unknown item, and a sheep. The tokens at the bottom represent a unit of metal, a wool fleece, and an unknown item.

the same time that people began farming. Once their survival started to depend on harvesting and storing grains and other crops, people needed a way to count and keep records of their goods. Although a single family did not need to keep such records, larger units of society did. Record keeping may therefore be related to the development of new and more complex political and social structures, such as an urban economy and an elite class that oversaw the distribution of goods.

Between about 4000 and 3500 B.C., complex tokens appeared, although the simple ones remained in use. The complex tokens featured more realistic forms, such as miniature tools, fruit, and people. Markings also began to appear on tokens at around this time. The new variety and complexity of tokens was probably related to the growth of city-states. This resulted in an increase in workshops and products, a varied urban economy, and centralized institutions, such as palace and temple bureaucracies*, all of which needed accurate and detailed accounting.

Record keeping became the glue that held the increasingly complex states of the Near East together. It allowed those in power to know how much grain a farmer produced or how many animals he owned—and therefore how much he should be taxed. Scribes* used the token system to record gifts given to temples, the number of people who lived in a district or city, and the amount of grain sent from one district to another. This method of accounting became the key to controlling the goods themselves. Archaeologists have found tokens in tombs of wealthy individuals, which suggests that counting and record keeping were the privilege of an elite segment of society and a sign of authority.

From Record Keeping to Writing. During the next 400 years, accountants went from placing the tokens inside hollow clay balls to drawing diagrams of the tokens on CLAY TABLETS. The illustrations were scratched into the tablets and ranged from realistic to abstract drawings of the objects they represented.

Soon scribes began to use a stylus—a reed with a triangular-shaped tip—to press the shape of the symbol into the surface of the clay. Once the principle of communicating by these symbols and pictures was established, people applied it to things other than tokens, such as personal names, words, and phrases. This marked the beginning of CUNEIFORM writing, which developed in Sumer before 3000 B.C.

The invention of writing allowed for more extensive record keeping in the ancient Near East. Scribes in the city-state of URUK, where writing may have been invented, kept records of transactions and inventories for the temple there, which had vast economic interests. This type of record keeping, for both the government and the temple, was one of the main duties of many scribes in the ancient Near East. Additionally, they gathered and recorded information for tax collection purposes.

Writing as a method of record keeping was also important to private individuals who engaged in trade. Writing allowed them to maintain cuneiform records of their business transactions in the form of contracts, bills of sale, letters of credit, and debt statements. These records were crucial because they could be referred to if a dispute arose between the two parties concerning their agreement after it had taken place.

* **bureaucracy** system consisting of officials and clerks who perform government functions

* **scribe** person of a learned class who served as a writer, editor, or teacher

Red Sea

From Record Keeping to Mathematics. In addition to paving the way for writing, the token system also led to the invention of abstract numerals and thus to the development of mathematics. The record keeping of prehistoric cultures suggests that people did not possess knowledge of abstract numbers. In other words, they had no concept of "sixness" aside from six actual things possessed or being counted. To represent six oil jars, for example, the token system used six tokens, not one token for oil jar and another representing the number 6.

Around the time that the practice of impressing or scratching symbols into clay envelopes or tablets was developing into the earliest form of writing, a new kind of symbol came into use: abstract numbers. A numeral stood for a number as an idea apart from any particular object. For example, a tablet from ancient Iran records 33 jars of oil—but not as 33 repetitions of the token symbol for jar of oil. Instead, the symbols are a single jar of oil sign accompanied by three circles, each representing ten, and three wedges, each representing one, for a total of 33. Over time, the symbols for numerals became even more abstract, and people began combining and manipulating them in new ways. In this manner, the ancient counting technology that the farmers had used for simple record keeping gave rise to mathematics.

The Near Eastern practice of the use of clay as a medium for recording transactions has allowed modern scholars and archaeologists to see records made thousands of years ago. Because baked clay is durable, records have survived—often in archives—allowing historians to track the evolution of record keeping from a token-based system to the invention and continued use of writing and mathematics. (*See also* **Communication; Libraries and Archives; Numbers and Numerals.**)

RED SEA

See map in Arabia and the Arabs (vol. 1).

The Red Sea is a narrow body of water that separates the western shore of Arabia from the eastern shore of North Africa. Its northernmost point lies some 100 miles south of the Mediterranean Sea, and at its southern end, it connects to the Arabian Sea by way of the Gulf of Aden. The Red Sea stretches about 1,200 miles from north to south, but its widest point is no more than about 190 miles across. Parts of the sea are quite deep, dropping to nearly 10,000 feet below sea level. Although the water of the sea is generally colored a brilliant bluish green, the sea sometimes turns red when a particular type of algae dies. This phenomenon is believed to be the source of its name.

The sea has been an important waterway for thousands of years. It is the subject of some of the earliest recorded references to large bodies of water. By around 2000 B.C., Egyptian ships had begun to use the Red Sea as a major trade route, despite the fact that it is difficult to navigate. Egyptian navigators had probably compiled accurate charts of the sea by about 1500 B.C. Queen HATSHEPSUT sailed on the sea at that time, and it is unlikely she would have risked the journey if its currents and other dangers were not well known.

Around 600 B.C., Phoenician ships traveled through the Red Sea as part of a journey in which they circumnavigated (sailed entirely around)

Africa. In 497 B.C., the Persian king DARIUS I recut a canal begun by the pharaoh* NECHO II that joined the Red Sea and the NILE RIVER, anticipating the present-day Suez Canal by nearly 2,400 years.

Because of a misinterpretation of the Hebrew BIBLE, the Red Sea is frequently thought to be the sea that YAHWEH parted during the Israelites' flight from slavery in Egypt to Canaan. The Bible, as it was written in ancient Hebrew, stated that the Israelites crossed the "Sea of Reeds," which could refer to three separate bodies of water. The misinterpretation occurred in the 200s B.C., when Greek writers translated all three bodies of water as simply the Red Sea. This mistake was carried into later Latin and English translations, each culture adding its own nuances. Modern scholars have restored the translation to its original wording and do not believe that the sea mentioned in the Bible refers to the Red Sea. (*See also* **Economy and Trade; Shipping Routes; Ships and Boats; Trade Routes; Transportation and Travel.**)

* **pharaoh** ruler of ancient Egypt

RELIGION

* **deity** god or goddess

* **archaeological** referring to the study of past human cultures, usually by excavating material remains of human activity

* **artifact** ornament, tool, weapon, or other object made by humans

* **amulet** small object thought to have supernatural or magical powers

* **cult** system of religious beliefs and rituals; group following these beliefs

* **pantheon** all the gods of a particular culture

Religion is the belief in and worship of one or more deities*. Historians know about the religions of the ancient Near East from archaeological* remains of temples and tombs, from religious artifacts* such as statues and amulets*, and from ancient religious writings such as myths and HYMNS. Although these sources reveal a great deal about the state cults* of ancient Near Eastern religions, far less is known about the religious practices of the common people.

Religions of the ancient Near East shared certain basic features. Most were polytheistic, meaning that they were based on the worship of many deities. Each pantheon* usually included a chief god and a number of other gods and goddesses, each responsible for different aspects of the universe or human existence. As regions became large states as a result of unification or conquest, local pantheons, which often had similar gods, merged to form larger national pantheons.

Religion was not a separate facet of life in the ancient Near East but an essential part of both governments and economies. Priests were often beneficiaries of kings and governors, and many temples were involved in commerce and trade. Religious practice also included MAGIC and MEDICINE—all three were seen as ways to influence the supernatural world for the benefit of humankind.

Mesopotamia. Some of the most important deities in ancient Sumer and Akkad were ANU, ENLIL, Enki (EA), Inanna (ISHTAR), Utu (Shamash), and ADAD. Anu, the god of heaven, presided over the other gods. Enlil was the god of the atmosphere and winds, whom Sumerians believed separated heaven and earth. Enki (Ea) was the god of water and the protector of humanity. Inanna (Ishtar), the goddess of love, was the most important goddess in ancient MESOPOTAMIA. Utu (Shamash) was the sun god and the god of justice. Adad was the storm god, responsible for rain and thunder.

Each city and city-state* in ancient Mesopotamia had a main temple for its patron* deity and smaller temples for lesser deities. The gods were

* **city-state** independent state consisting of a city and its surrounding territory

* **patron** special guardian, protector, or supporter

31

קרשתאבגדהוזחטיכדלמסנזקרשתאבג

Religion

* **sanctuary** most sacred part of a religious building

* **incense** fragrant spice or resin burned as an offering

Feeding the Gods

A common feature of ancient Near Eastern religions was the offering of food to statues of the gods. Obviously, the statues did not actually eat the food. Instead, the food was eaten by the temple's staff and their families. For temples with very large staffs, this could be an enormous amount of food. An ancient text from Mesopotamia lists the following daily food offering at one major temple: 40 sheep, 3 bulls, 8 lambs, 70 birds and ducks, 4 wild boars, 3 ostrich eggs, dates, figs, raisins, 54 containers of beer and wine, and more than 1,000 pounds of bread.

* **incantation** written or recited formula of words designed to produce a given effect

* **stela** stone slab or pillar that has been carved or engraved and serves as a monument; *pl.* stelae

represented by statues, which were kept in the sanctuaries* of the temples. The temples were equipped like palaces, with a kitchen for preparing the deity's meals, a reception suite for receiving visitors, and bedrooms for the deity's divine family and servants. PRIESTS AND PRIESTESSES carried out the many tasks involved in worshiping the deity at the temple. The chief priest managed the temple and its practical affairs, while a priestess served as the spouse of the deity. Several priests performed the daily rituals, which included offering the deity two daily meals, music, and burning incense*. On certain occasions, the statue was taken out of the temple so that the deity could meet with the gods of other cities or attend public festivals, during which the common people could make offerings. The practices of the Mesopotamian priests and people reflected their belief that their survival depended on their ability to honor the gods and fulfill their needs.

Egypt. Major deities of the Egyptian pantheon included Ra, AMUN, HATHOR, HORUS, ISIS, and OSIRIS. Amun was the creator god of THEBES, who later became the chief god of Egypt. Hathor was goddess of women and dance. Horus was god of the sky and of kingship. He was identified with the Egyptian king, who was considered a living manifestation of the god. Isis was the mother of Horus and the goddess of magic. Osiris was the father of Horus and the god of the netherworld, or the world of the dead.

Although temples were built for worshiping one god, the god was not the only divine being there. Usually, temples housed divine families of father, mother, and son. Statues representing these family members were kept in the temple's sanctuary. In principle, only the king was allowed to approach directly and worship the deities, because he was considered a god or a son of a god. In practice, however, most of the temple responsibilities fell to priests and priestesses acting on the king's behalf. Each day, the temple priests bathed the statues, and dressed and perfumed them. They offered the gods food and drink and entertained them with songs and dance. On special occasions, they performed additional rituals, which might include the recitation of prayers and incantations* to gain the deities' attention and favor. The Egyptians feared that the gods would become angry if not worshiped properly, and then Egypt would be destroyed.

During the frequent religious festivals, statues of the deities were carried outside the temples and through the streets of the city in a procession. On these occasions, the common people could ask questions of the deities, and priests would convey the deities' responses. Although the common people were barred from entering the temples, during and after the Middle Kingdom period (ca. 1980–1630 B.C.), they were allowed to set up a statue or stela* outside a temple to establish a link between themselves and the deity within. Some families also had altars in their homes, where they prayed and made offerings.

The religion of ancient Egypt had a number of unique features. The Egyptian king was believed to be Horus, hence divine. After his death, he was Osiris and was worshiped as a god. The ancient Egyptians also had a strong belief in the AFTERLIFE, which greatly influenced their religious practices. Bodies of the dead were preserved as MUMMIES and buried in tombs,

Making sacrifices and offerings to the gods was an important element of worship in many ancient Near Eastern religions. At the center of this Neo-Hittite relief from the Lion Gate at Malatya in Anatolia, a ruler pours an offering during a sacrifice to the storm god. At left, the storm god approaches in his chariot, and to the right, a servant holds a bull for offering.

See color plate 13, vol. 1.

* **dynasty** succession of rulers from the same family or group

* **prophet** one who claims to have received divine messages or insights

* **monotheistic** referring to the belief in only one god

and their descendants regularly brought them offerings of food to meet their needs in the afterlife. Toward the end of ancient Egypt's civilization, certain animals, including bulls, cats, and snakes, were increasingly worshiped as gods. Many of these sacred animals were also mummified and buried in tombs.

Iran. The Elamites, early inhabitants of ancient IRAN, worshiped many different deities. Kirisha was goddess of the sky and mother of the other Elamite deities. Khumban was god of storms and ruled over the heavens. Napirisha was god of wisdom and ruled over the earth. Ishushinak—originally the city god of Susa—became the most important god of the Elamites and was responsible for their peace and security.

In Elam, the king was the chief priest. Next in rank was the high priest, who always accompanied the king, even in times of war. Other priests served the deities in their city temples and in groves that were believed to be sacred. Music was always part of worship, as was the use of fire and alcoholic beverages. However, the most important part of worship was the sacrifice of animals, most often rams. During some religious festivals, great feasts were held for the public, during which large numbers of rams were sacrificed and then roasted and shared among the people in attendance.

After the Elamite kingdom ended in the 600s B.C., Iranians began to worship other deities, including Mithra, god of the sun and of war; AHURA MAZDA, god of goodness; and AHRIMAN, god of evil. After the Achaemenid dynasty* took over Iran in 522 B.C., the state religion of Iran was based on the teachings of the prophet* Zoroaster, who taught that Ahura Mazda was the only true god. In this monotheistic* religion,

33

Religion

called Zoroastrianism, animal sacrifice was condemned, and an offering of flour and wine to Ahura Mazda became the most important aspect of worship. Later Ahura Mazda was seen as the chief god among others.

Anatolia. The HITTITES of ancient Anatolia (present-day Turkey) had a very complex pantheon because they adopted many gods and goddesses from other Near Eastern peoples. Most of these deities came from the HUR-RIANS who heavily influenced the Hittites around the 1400s B.C. The Hurrian pantheon was headed by the storm god TESHUB, who ruled the heavens, and his wife, the sun goddess KHEPAT. Among the other gods worshiped by the Hurrians were KUMARBI, god of fertility and grain, and Shimegi, god of the moon.

Many deities had their own temples, where they were represented by statues. Worship at outdoor sites, such as groves, was common. The highest-ranking priest was the king, whose most important duty as head of state was performing religious rituals. The state paid a hierarchy* of other religious personnel, including many types of priests, who were involved in worshiping the deities or managing the temples. The people of Anatolia also celebrated numerous religious festivals throughout the year, some lasting more than a month. The festivals involved processions of the king and statues of the deities, feasts, and entertainment, such as gymnastics and mock battles. The common people could attend the festivals, as well as pray to deities on their own.

Syria and the Levant. Some of the most important deities of Syria and the Levant* included EL, BAAL, and ANAT. In the religion of the Syrian city UGARIT, El was considered the creator of earth and the father of humanity. He presided over the other gods. In the Canaanite and Phoenician religions, Baal was the storm god and god of war. Anat was Baal's sister and guardian of the king.

In the countryside, deities were worshiped at thousands of outdoor sites that were believed to be sacred. In the cities, temples were built as places of worship and homes for the deities. The deities were represented in the temples by statues kept in the sanctuaries. Although kings were not usually priests, they played an important religious role because they had the power to appoint priests. The chief priest managed the temple, and additional priests were responsible for the daily sacrifices, hymns, and other aspects of worship. The main role of women in the temples was as wives or mistresses of temple gods. Common people could come to the temple to pray to the deities or seek an oracle*. They could also pray in the privacy of their own homes.

Another important god in ancient times was YAHWEH, the Hebrew deity associated with storms and thunder, who became the national deity of Israel and Judah. Yahweh came to be worshiped as the one and only god of the Israelites, and their religion, which eventually led to Judaism, was one of the first major religions to be based on monotheism. (*See also* **Ashur (deity); Aten; Cults; Gods and Goddesses; Israel and the Israelites; Marduk; Monotheism; Mythology; Oracles and Prophecy; Palaces and Temples; Priests and Priestesses; Psalms; Rituals and Sacrifice; Seth; Theology; Witchcraft.**)

Gods Galore

In the ancient Near East, each community had its own local pantheon containing many deities. As a result, as kingdoms, regions, and nations developed, they had an astonishing number of deities. At one time, scribes in ancient Sumer attempted to list Sumerian and other deities. The list they produced contained a total of 3,600 gods and goddesses. Of course, only a small fraction of these deities were actually worshiped in any one place at a given time.

* **hierarchy** division of society or an institution into groups with higher and lower ranks

* **Levant** lands bordering the eastern shores of the Mediterranean Sea (present-day Syria, Lebanon, and Israel), the West Bank, and Jordan

* **oracle** priest or priestess through whom a god is believed to speak; also, the location (such as a shrine) where such utterances are made

Rhodes

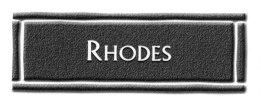

RHODES

* **maritime** related to the sea or shipping

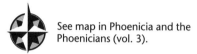

See map in Phoenicia and the Phoenicians (vol. 3).

* **city-state** independent state consisting of a city and its surrounding territory

* **confederacy** group of cities or states joined together for a purpose; an alliance

* **Hellenistic** referring to the Greek-influenced culture of the Mediterranean world and western Asia during the three centuries after the death of Alexander the Great in 323 B.C.

* **siege** long and persistent effort to force a surrender by surrounding a fortress or city with armed troops, cutting it off from supplies and aid

* **sack** to loot a captured city

The largest island of the Dodecanese (Greek for "twelve islands"), Rhodes is located in the AEGEAN SEA near the southwestern coast of present-day Turkey (ancient ANATOLIA). According to Greek mythology, the island was named for Rhodos, the daughter of the goddess Aphrodite and wife of the sun god Helios. Some believe that Rhodes got its name from the Phoenician word for snake, *erod,* because the island was known to have many snakes.

Rhodes prospered in ancient times as one of the major maritime* and trading powers of the eastern Mediterranean. Throughout its history, the island earned its living from the sea and from trade, and it developed a powerful navy to defend its TRADE ROUTES in the Mediterranean and Aegean Seas. By the late 200s B.C., the island had become one of the most important NAVAL POWERS in the region. Its navy played a significant role in keeping the region free of pirates.

Among the early inhabitants of Rhodes were Minoans from CRETE, who may have established a colony there before 1500 B.C. Between about 1200 and 1000 B.C., a people from mainland Greece known as the Dorians settled on the island and established three city-states*: Lindus, Ialysus, and Camirus. These city-states became very prosperous from trade, and by the 500s B.C., they had established colonies in Anatolia, Sicily, and northeastern Spain.

After the PERSIAN WARS in the early 400s B.C., Rhodes became a member of the Delian League, a group of Greek city states allied against the PERSIAN EMPIRE. It remained in the league until the late 400s B.C., when the Peloponnesian Wars broke out between the Greek city-states of Athens and Sparta. Around 408 B.C., the three major city-states of Rhodes united in a confederacy*, whose capital was a newly founded city also called Rhodes.

Dominated by Caria on the Anatolian mainland in the mid-300s B.C., island of Rhodes was occupied by ALEXANDER THE GREAT in about 332 B.C. It regained its independence after Alexander's death in 323 B.C. and entered the period of its greatest power, prosperity, and cultural achievements. During the Hellenistic* period, Rhodes was home to a famous school of Greek philosophy. More famous, however, was a gigantic statue of the god Helios that stood at the entrance to the harbor of the capital city. Known as the Colossus of Rhodes, this immense statue was built in the early 300s B.C. to celebrate a victory over Demetrius I, ruler of the Macedonians, who had laid siege* to the city. The statue, destroyed by an earthquake in 227 B.C., is considered one of the Seven Wonders of the Ancient World.

Between 215 and 148 B.C., Rhodes became involved in a series of conflicts between Macedonia and the Roman Empire. At first, Rhodes cooperated with the Romans against the Macedonian king Philip V and the Seleucid king Antiochus III, but it later withdrew much of its support for the Romans. In turn, the Romans shifted their support of Rhodes to the Aegean island of Delos, which became a tax-free port. This caused Rhodes to lose much of its trade, wealth, and power in the Mediterranean. The Romans conquered the island and sacked* its capital in the middle of the first century B.C. (*See also* **Greece and the Greeks; Mediterranean Sea, Trade on; Minoan Civilization.**)

Rituals and Sacrifice

RITUALS
AND SACRIFICE

* **secular** nonreligious; connected with everyday life

A ritual is a series of formal actions and words that have special meaning when performed and spoken. Usually found within the context of religious worship, rituals also accompany important secular* events, such as birth, passage into adulthood, MARRIAGE, and death. Sacrifices are ritual OFFERINGS of food, drink, and animals to the gods. Rituals and sacrifices played an important role in RELIGION throughout the ancient Near East.

Rituals. Most rituals in the ancient Near East were connected to religious beliefs. In ancient temples throughout the region, PRIESTS AND PRIESTESSES enacted various rituals as part of daily worship. Most of these rituals involved taking care of the needs of the gods, whose presence on earth was represented by statues. The priests fed, clothed, washed, and entertained these statues just as if they were alive. Priests also performed special monthly and yearly rituals, which were among the only times that the statue of a god was seen in public. Other important rituals included those that accompanied the construction of temples.

Religious rituals generally involved PRAYER, offerings, and purification ceremonies, all of which played a crucial role in gaining the attention of the gods and in preparing people to honor and serve them. Purification, which often involved washing oneself with water, had a very significant purpose and meaning in religious rituals. Anything connected to the gods had to be pure. Not only was dirt an impurity but so were physical deformities and illegal or immoral acts. Ritual purification symbolized the removal of all impurities, making humans worthy of serving and connecting with their gods. In ancient MESOPOTAMIA, priests ritually washed their hands before approaching the gods in the temples. During the Roman period, Jews purified themselves through immersion in a special ritual bath called a *miqveh*.

In addition to prayers and offerings, rituals often involved specific movements of the body, sometimes in a repetitive manner. Prayer was generally accompanied by such ritual movements as raising the hands to the mouth or standing with the arms at the sides. Ritual movements performed during Hittite religious ceremonies often included running and kneeling. Among the Israelites, the word for *worship* literally meant "to bow down" or "to bend over," and during worship, people often expressed their submission to god by lying flat on their stomachs with their faces touching the ground.

Ancient Near Eastern societies also practiced many rituals that were not connected directly to religious worship. In Mesopotamia, for example, people were concerned about ignorance of the gods' rules. Through such ignorance, people could offend the gods, which could result in dire consequences. To protect themselves from committing a sin of ignorance, Mesopotamians performed general rituals of atonement* that would cover or correct any sin that they might have committed knowingly or otherwise. The ancient HITTITES also had rituals for correcting mistakes caused by ignorance of the gods' rules.

The people of the ancient Near East also performed rituals to ask for assistance from the gods, such as protection in battle and help in combating evil or seeking guidance from oracles*. Many situations in daily life,

Substitute Kings of Mesopotamia

In ancient Mesopotamia, an eclipse or other heavenly event was a terrible omen, or sign, that meant that the king would soon die a violent death. To protect their ruler, Mesopotamians chose a substitute king who dressed in royal robes and played the part of the king. If this substitute king did not die of natural causes within a certain period of time, he was killed. One substitute king of Isin actually continued to rule after the real king died. Some historians believe that King Esarhaddon used the substitute king ritual at least seven times during his reign.

* **atonement** repayment for an offense or injury

* **oracle** priest or priestess through whom a god is believed to speak; also, the location (such as a shrine) where such utterances are made

such as marriage, childbirth, and illness, called for rituals as well. Death rituals were also very important, especially in ancient Egypt. The Egyptians performed various rituals to prepare the dead for the AFTERLIFE, and Egyptian funeral ceremonies consisted of several ritual activities.

Sacrifice. Sacrifices in the ancient Near East often served simply as food for the gods. This was not their only purpose, however. They might also have been intended as a gift for the gods—often a form of thanks for divine help—or as a means of honoring the deities*. Sacrifices might also have been performed to get the attention of the gods, to earn their goodwill, or to ask a favor.

Sacrifices consisted of offerings such as grain, wine, oil, and other items of food or drink. The daily offerings were intended for the gods, but priests and worshipers who presented them partook from the food once it was consecrated*. In fact, ritual offerings were an important source of food for temple staff. Ritually slaughtered animals were also a common sacrifice in the ancient Near East. The animals most commonly sacrificed included lambs, SHEEP, and GOATS, although bulls, CATTLE, dogs, and other animals were sometimes offered as sacrifices as well. In ancient Greece, for example, dogs were sacrificed to the goddess Hecate because it was believed that she traveled with dogs through the underworld*. In SYRIA during the second millennium B.C.*, donkeys were sacrificed at the conclusion of treaty-making ceremonies.

Eating meat was relatively rare in the ancient Near East and a blood sacrifice—an offering of a ritually slaughtered animal—was usually followed by a feast. Among the Elamites of southwestern IRAN, rams were the most common sacrificial animal, and the most important sacrificial feast was one for the "Lady of the City." During the Israelite sacrificial feast called *zebah shelamim*, the person offering the blood sacrifice would invite family members to the temple to share the rare treat of a meal with meat. Israelites were allowed to sacrifice ruminants, that is, animals that

* **deity** god or goddess

* **consecrate** to declare sacred or holy by means of a religious rite

* **underworld** world of the dead

* **second millennium** B.C. years from 2000 to 1001 B.C.

See color plate 12, vol. 1.

This bronze plate was made for the Elamite king Shilkhak-Inshushinak, who ruled during the 1150s B.C. It depicts a sacrificial ceremony called "rising of the sun." Two naked priests are shown squatting, one about to pour water over the hands of the other as part of the purification ceremonies that took place at the beginning of the day. Also shown on the plate are a table for offerings, temples, and a holy grove.

Rivers

chew their cud, such as goats, sheep, and cattle. Nonruminants, such as pigs and camels, were forbidden as sacrificial animals; hence, they could not be eaten.

Although human sacrifice was rare, there is evidence that a few adults may have been sacrificed at Ur in Mesopotamia and also in Egypt. Other evidence suggests that child sacrifice was performed in ancient CARTHAGE, Phoenicia, and Israel. The Hebrew BIBLE contains a story about the leader Abraham and the near-sacrifice of his son Isaac. Some biblical scholars believe that this story signifies the end of child sacrifice among the ancient Israelites. (*See also* **Death and Burial; Feasts and Festivals; Oracles and Prophecy; Palaces and Temples.**)

RIVERS

See map on inside covers.

* **hieroglyphic** referring to a system of writing that uses pictorial characters, or hieroglyphs, to represent words or ideas

The history of civilization in the Near East is intimately connected to the rivers that flow through the region. The rise of complex urban societies in the region was possible only because of the development of large-scale AGRICULTURE. This development would not have been possible without the reliable sources of WATER provided by such rivers as the Nile and the Euphrates. In the dry Near East, rivers supplied water not only for IRRIGATION but also for drinking, bathing, watering livestock, and the many other needs of a growing population. Rivers also served as principal routes for travel and trade and for connecting cities and kingdoms across long distances.

The Main Rivers. The three most important rivers in the Near East are the Nile, the Euphrates, and the Tigris. It was on the banks of these rivers that the greatest early civilizations of the region arose. The Nile River rises near the equator, flows northward through northeastern Africa, and passes through Egypt before emptying into the Mediterranean Sea. In late summer, the river floods, covering the area along its banks with water containing rich sediments. The water recedes after six to ten weeks, leaving a narrow strip of fertile land amidst the barren Egyptian desert.

Long before the rise of complex civilizations, small bands of people exploited the fertile soil near the Nile for growing crops and raising livestock. By about 3000 B.C., the earliest kings of Egypt united the people living along the Nile into a single country. The regular flooding ensured the prosperity of the land that formed the basis for the wealth of ancient Egypt.

The Nile also served as the highway of ancient Egypt, connecting the northern and southern sections of the country. Because the distances between these two regions was great, the river served as a means of transportation and communication between them and helped unify the kingdom politically. The Nile's importance to transportation is reflected in the Egyptian language. The hieroglyphic* sign for *north* was a ship with its sail folded down, while the sign for *south* was a boat with its sail full of wind.

The Tigris and Euphrates Rivers originate in present-day Turkey (ancient ANATOLIA) and flow southeastward through modern Iraq (ancient MESOPOTAMIA) until they reach the Persian Gulf. Because the regions along

קרשתאבגדהוזחטיכדלמסנןסעפּפצץקרשתאבגד

Roads

the northern reaches of the rivers receive enough rainfall, small-scale farming and livestock and early civilizations were able to thrive. In the south, the early peoples were dependent on the river's annual floods.

The earliest civilizations of Mesopotamia arose on the banks of the southern Euphrates. These included Sumer, Akkad, and later Babylonia, all of which constructed canal networks to store and use the water more efficiently. Early peoples did not establish settlements along the Tigris until the third millennium B.C. (3000–2001 B.C.), because that river runs a steep and swift course that is prone to cause devastating floods. However, by the second millennium B.C.*, several important kingdoms, such as Assyria and Mitanni, had emerged along the banks of the Tigris. These kingdoms also made use of canals to tap the Tigris waters.

The Tigris and Euphrates were just as important to travel in Mesopotamia as the Nile was in Egypt. The rivers connected Mesopotamia to kingdoms in Anatolia and Syria, and the major TRADE ROUTES of the region closely followed the rivers. The Assyrians in particular carried on a major trade with cities in Anatolia that were located along the rivers.

Other Important Rivers. In addition to the Nile, Tigris, and Euphrates, the Near East contains a few other important rivers. Two other major rivers in Iraq are the Diyala and the Khabur. The Diyala, a tributary* of the Tigris River, was the site of many early settlements, including the city-state* of ESH-NUNNA. The area around the Khabur River, in northern Mesopotamia, was heavily settled in the late third and early second millennia B.C. However, the number of settlements along the river declined after about 1500 B.C. This may have been because the region was unsuited to intensive agriculture and because it lay between kingdoms that often engaged in combat.

In the Levant* and IRAN, the climate is very dry, and few rivers run throughout the year. Besides the Jordan River in Canaan and the Karun River in Iran, most other rivers in those regions flow only during the rainy season.

Turkey contains several large rivers, but dangerous rapids make almost all of them unsuited to navigation. The Turkish river that was perhaps the most famous in ancient times was the Meander, which contained many bends along its wandering route through the Turkish countryside, giving rise to the English term *meander,* meaning "to wander." (*See also* **Euphrates River; Geography; Nile River; Shipping Routes; Tigris River; Transportation and Travel.**)

* **second millennium B.C.** years from 2000 to 1001 B.C.

* **tributary** river that flows into another river

* **city-state** independent state consisting of a city and its surrounding territory

* **Levant** lands bordering the eastern shores of the Mediterranean Sea (present-day Syria, Lebanon, and Israel), the West Bank, and Jordan

ROADS

In the ancient Near East, roads were land routes that were cleared, marked, and maintained. Where roads existed, they often offered the best and fastest route of travel for traders and merchants, messengers, armies, and ordinary individuals. They also shaped settlement patterns, because towns and cities developed along roads or where roads crossed. However, only well-organized societies could afford the resources to build and maintain roads. Consequently, as ancient states grew into large and powerful empires, their road-building activities expanded.

Roads

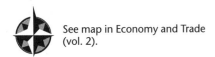

See map in Economy and Trade (vol. 2).

Road Building. In MESOPOTAMIA, most roads were several feet across, and some were wide enough to allow wagons and chariots to pass. The streets in the city of BABYLON varied from 9 to 18 feet in width, while a major route through NINEVEH was nearly 90 feet wide. Some of these ancient roads were paved with a foundation layer of bricks held in place by asphalt and topped by a layer of larger limestone slabs. In the Levant*, remnants of cobbled streets, or streets paved with round or irregular stones, have been excavated by archaeologists*. They have also found a road leading to the gate of the city of MEGIDDO consisting of a layer of hard plaster atop a base layer of crushed stone.

Archaeologists have found no evidence of road signs but have found some roads with markers along the way to keep travelers from losing their way. Cairns, or rocks that have been piled up, lined some Egyptian roads. The Israelites may have used the same method to mark their roads.

Obstacles to Road Building. Although most longer roads were unpaved, they had to be planned, measured, and leveled so that their surfaces would be clear and smooth. The Hebrew BIBLE contains references to Israelite road builders smoothing and leveling the roadways. Road building in Egypt also consisted mostly of scraping a smooth surface. Some roads required more effort, however.

In many regions in the ancient Near East, road builders had to deal with obstacles such as forests and mountains. Building a road wide, smooth, and level enough to carry heavy wagonloads of timber out of mountain ranges usually required workers to use pickaxes to clear a path.

In other regions, such as the plains of southern Mesopotamia, road builders had to contend with swamps and marshes. They also had to build roads and bridges to cross canals, streams, and rivers. Floods often washed away wooden bridges, which had to be replaced. This duty, like most aspects of road maintenance, was the responsibility of the local people, who were supervised by provincial* governors or local leaders.

Imperial Roads. The most ambitious road system of the ancient Near East was that of the Neo-Assyrian empire, which dominated northern Mesopotamia and some surrounding regions from 911 to 609 B.C. The Assyrians created history's first huge, well-administered, and highly centralized empire. Because controlling such a territory required rapid communication between the capital and outlying centers and speedy troop movement, the Assyrians built a large network of roads stretching throughout their empire. The imperial* government controlled the entire road network to ensure that roads existed where needed and were kept in good repair.

Major highways were called royal roads and were measured with great precision so that distances would be accurately known. Segments of the royal roads close to capital cities were paved with stone slabs and lined with stone markers or stelae*, a practice that the Romans would later adopt in their own empire. Road stations were built along the royal roads to serve as stopping places for couriers, marching troops, and civilian travelers.

Less than a century after the fall of the Assyrian empire, the Persians came to dominate the ancient Near East for the next several hundred years. They took over the Assyrian system of royal roads and extended the network to stretch across their empire. The most famous Persian royal road linked the city of SARDIS in Anatolia (present-day Turkey) with Susa, the Persian capital in IRAN. This road was approximately 1,600 miles long, and it took three months to travel it from end to end. The Greek traveler and historian HERODOTUS wrote that he was much impressed by this Persian road, with its stations, inns, swift messenger service, and ferryboats across rivers. (*See also* **Trade Routes; Transportation and Travel.**)

ROSETTA STONE

* **basalt** black or gray stone, often with a glassy surface

* **decipher** to decode and interpret the meaning of

The Rosetta Stone is a slab of black basalt* bearing INSCRIPTIONS that helped scholars decipher* the ancient form of Egyptian writing known as HIEROGLYPHICS. The inscriptions appear in three different scripts: Egyptian hieroglyphics, Greek, and demotic—a popular form of cursive script that was widely used to write the Egyptian language by the 600s B.C. The efforts of those who studied the Rosetta Stone unlocked the secrets of hieroglyphic writing and provided the basis for the decipherment of thousands of hieroglyphic texts.

Discovery and Early Study. The Rosetta Stone was inscribed in 196 B.C. by priests in the Egyptian city of MEMPHIS. The inscription lists the many benefits bestowed on Egypt by King Ptolemy V Epiphanes, who reigned from 205 to 180 B.C. The stone was discovered by members of Napoleon Bonaparte's expedition to Egypt in A.D. 1799. However, the British claimed the stone after the French army in Egypt surrendered to the British shortly thereafter.

Around 1814, the English physicist Thomas Young made the first breakthrough in deciphering the inscriptions. He made a major discovery when he proved that certain hieroglyphs enclosed by oval circles, known as cartouches, indicated the proper name of King Ptolemy. Young's discovery proved other scholars' assumptions that similar cartouches in other inscriptions were royal names. Furthermore, by noting the direction in which animal and bird characters in the hieroglyphs faced, Young determined the direction in which the hieroglyphic script was to be read. Despite Young's pioneering work, he was unable to fully decipher the hieroglyphs. That feat was accomplished a few years later by the French scholar Jean-François Champollion.

Champollion's Triumph. It is fitting that Champollion was the one to break the code of the Rosetta Stone. As a boy, he was fascinated by hieroglyphics, and he studied ancient languages in the hope that one day he would be able to decipher the Egyptian characters found in so many inscriptions and tomb paintings.

Champollion built on the work of previous scholars, especially that of Young. Working from Young's discovery that the cartouches on the

Rosetta Stone

The Rosetta Stone, one of the best-known artifacts from the ancient Near East, has been on display at the British Museum in London since A.D. 1802. Although the stone was discovered by the French, it was given to the British government in 1801 in accordance with the terms of a treaty between England and France.

stone contained the name of Ptolemy, Champollion studied cartouches in other inscriptions. On another monument, he found an inscription in two languages that contained a cartouche bearing the name of CLEOPATRA. He determined that the hieroglyphs in the cartouches were not symbols that stood for ideas or words, as many scholars of the time believed, but instead phonetic elements. That is, they represented consonants and syllables that recorded the sounds of the names in the cartouches.

In 1822, Champollion published his first paper about the stone. In it, he explained his theory and examined many other names from the same period of Egyptian history. However, many scholars maintained that the phonetic elements in the cartouches were only used for Greek and Roman names and that they had no direct equivalent in hieroglyphic Egyptian. In an 1824 paper, Champollion successfully demonstrated that Egyptian words and names could also be written phonetically in the hieroglyphic script.

Champollion also made other important discoveries in his work with the stone. He realized that the Egyptians used different types of hieroglyphic signs. Some were phonetic, some were determinatives (signs following words that placed them in certain categories—for example, proper names, animals, and so on), and some were logograms (signs that conveyed a complete word rather than its pronunciation). He also determined that the Greek inscription had been recorded first, and the hieroglyphic text was a translation from the Greek. Over time, he compiled a full list of hieroglyphic signs and their Greek equivalents. (*See also* **Alphabets; Egypt and the Egyptians; Writing.**)

Sacrifice

See *Rituals and Sacrifice.*

See map in Geography (vol. 2).

The Sahara is the largest desert in the world, covering almost all of northern Africa. Its name comes from the Arabic word *sahra'*, which means "desert." The desert stretches 3,000 miles from east to west and between 800 and 1,200 miles from north to south. Bordered on the north by the Mediterranean Sea, the Sahara stretches east to the Red Sea and west to the Atlantic Ocean. To the south, the Sahara is bordered by the Sahel, a region that stretches from Senegal to southern SUDAN.

The landscape of the Sahara includes huge plateaus covered with gravel, called *serirs* or *regs;* mountains; and areas below sea level, called *chotts* and *dayas*. Almost one-fourth of the Sahara is made up of enormous sand dunes and sand seas called *ergs*. The *ergs* contain huge sand mountains called *draa,* which can rise to a height of 1,000 feet.

Several rivers run through the Sahara. The largest of these is the Nile, which runs along the eastern edge of the desert. In the southwest, the Niger River wanders into the Sahara, and in the south, several rivers empty into Lake Chad. However, the most significant sources of water in the Sahara are not rivers and lakes but wadis, which are the beds of seasonal rivers. Although these riverbeds are normally dry, they run with water, often violently, after a rainstorm or the seasonal melting of highland snow and ice.

The desert, which has existed for more than 5 million years, experienced greater variations in climate in prehistoric times than it does today. However, the grazing of CATTLE during the last 7,000 years has ended these variations and made the region arid. There is evidence that in late prehistory, the Sahara was narrower than it is today and had more water holes and oases*. Consequently, for a short period after the rainy season, large tracts of the desert became pastureland.

The growth of the Sahara is most apparent in the south, where it borders the Sahel. The Sahara began to take over the northern Sahel in ancient times, and the process continues today. This is largely due to overpopulation and excessive farming in the area. The sands of the Sahara continue to expand southward, taking in as much as five miles in years when the region experiences severe droughts*.

There are two main climate zones in the Sahara: the northern dry-subtropical zone and the southern dry-tropical zone. In both zones, the winters can be cold and the summers extremely hot. The hottest temperature ever recorded in the Sahara is 136° Fahrenheit. The change in desert

* **oasis** fertile area in a desert made possible by the presence of a spring or well; *pl.* oases

* **drought** long period of dry weather during which crop yields are lower than usual

temperatures from day into night can also be extreme, with nighttime temperatures sometimes dropping to near freezing. During the rainy season, the northern sections of the desert average about three inches of rain, while the south receives about five inches per year.

Plant life in the Sahara is sparse, but shrubs and grasses do grow there, as do trees in some of the highland areas. Not surprisingly, the region supports few animals. Among the animals that have learned to survive the desert are gerbils, hares, hedgehogs, lizards, hyenas, gazelles, and in the past, elephants. More than 300 different species of birds live in or migrate through the Sahara.

Humans have lived in the Sahara from at least 9000 B.C. Among the people who lived there, the earliest were probably nomadic* hunters, who later became cattle herders. However, by around 1250 B.C., most of the inhabitants from the interior of the Sahara had migrated elsewhere. The most famous civilizations of the ancient Saharan world emerged along the banks of the Nile River, where early refugees from the Sahara came to live alongside the indigenous* people of the Nile Valley. The cultures that developed among the descendants of these people became the Egyptian and Nubian civilizations. (*See also* **Egypt and the Egyptians; Geography; Libyans; Nile River; Nubia and the Nubians.**)

* **nomadic** referring to people who travel from place to place to find food and pasture

* **indigenous** referring to the original inhabitants of a region

See map in Israel and Judah (vol. 3).

* **prophet** one who claims to have received divine messages or insights

* **dynasty** succession of rulers from the same family or group

Samaria was the capital of the northern kingdom of Israel from the early 800s B.C. until the late 700s B.C. Samaria was established by King Omri of Israel, who moved the capital from Tirzah. Before that time, according to the Hebrew Bible, JERUSALEM was the capital of a united Israel and Judah. The people of Jerusalem in Judah felt threatened by Samaria's position as a political and cultural center. This is evident from sections of the Bible in which Samaria and its people are described in a negative light.

The city of Samaria, which also gave its name to the surrounding region, was located about 35 miles north of Jerusalem. It occupied an important strategic site—overlooking the main trade routes between Egypt, Judah, Phoenicia, and southern SYRIA. To make the new capital a royal city, Kings Omri and his son and successor, AHAB, built city walls, a palace, public buildings, storerooms, and large courtyards.

When Ahab married a Phoenician princess named Jezebel, Samaria came under the influence of Phoenician religion and culture. In fact, Jezebel brought the worship of the Phoenician god BAAL to Israel, and Ahab built a temple to Baal in Samaria. Although this association with Phoenicia helped make Israel a major power, it also brought Ahab under much criticism from prophets* who felt Israel was moving away from the worship of the Israelite god YAHWEH. As a result, Omri's dynasty* was overthrown by Jehu in 842 B.C. King Jehu ended the alliance with Phoenicia, and Israel's power subsequently declined.

By the late 700s B.C., the Assyrians had emerged as a major power, and they were expanding their territory. In 722 B.C., Samaria and Israel were conquered by the Assyrians, and many Israelites were sent into captivity in other Assyrian provinces. The Assyrians resettled Israel with peoples from southern Babylonia and Syria. According to their own traditions, the Samaritans believe that they are the descendants of those Israelites who were not sent into captivity. According to Jewish tradition, however, the Samaritans descended from the Israelites who remained behind but intermarried with the people who were resettled in the region from elsewhere in the Assyrian empire.

After the Assyrian conquest, Israel continued to be occupied by the various empires that took control of the ancient Near East. After the Assyrians came the short-lived Neo-Babylonian empire. After the Babylonians, Israel and Samaria were occupied by the Persians, the Macedonians under the Ptolemies and Seleucids, and finally the Romans. During these successive occupations, the city of Samaria remained an important administrative site. (*See also* **Canaan; Hebrews and Israelites; Israel and Judah; Judaism and Jews; Samaritans.**)

SAMARITANS

* **first millennium** B.C. years from 1000 to 1 B.C.

* **sect** group of people with a common leadership who share a distinctive set of religious views and opinions

The Samaritans are a small sect who separated from traditional Judaism. Their name is derived from the region of SAMARIA in present-day Israel and the West Bank, where they have lived since at least the middle of the first millennium B.C.* The history of the Samaritans as a religious group is as unique as it is disputed.

The Samaritans, the Jews, and modern historians each have different versions of the Samaritans' origins. The Samaritan tradition says that they separated from the rest of the Jewish community when the priest Eli settled the group near Shiloh. They also believe that they are the direct descendants of those Israelites who were not deported after the Assyrian conquest of Israel and who remained faithful in their worship of YAHWEH. Jewish history, on the other hand, says that the Samaritans were the descendants of the Israelites who were not deported by the Assyrians but had intermarried with the foreigners who were resettled in the region. Some modern historians believe that the Samaritans were a northern Israelite Judaic sect* who split from traditional Judaism much later, possibly as late as 150 B.C.

According to the Hebrew BIBLE, the Samaritans came into conflict with the Jews in the 530s B.C. In 587 B.C., the Babylonians destroyed JERUSALEM and the Temple of Solomon, the religious center of the Jews. Many Jews were exiled to Babylon, where they maintained a strong Jewish community. When the Persians conquered Babylonia, they allowed those Jews to return to Jerusalem in 538 B.C. to rebuild the temple. The Samaritans wanted to help them, but the Jews refused their offer because they did not consider the Samaritans Jewish. In the 300s B.C., the Samaritans built their own temple on Mount Gerizim in Samaria.

Over the centuries, Samaritans established colonies in DAMASCUS, Egypt, Athens, Rome, Corinth, Delos, and Syracuse. Today the Samaritans are a small sect of about 600 people who live in two communities in Israel and the West Bank. Their main religious text is the TORAH (or Pentateuch). Unlike Jews, they do not recognize the other books of the Hebrew Bible as sacred texts. (*See also* **Hebrews and Israelites; Israel and Judah; Judaism and Jews.**)

Samsu-iluna

SAMSU-ILUNA

ruled ca. 1749–1712 B.C.
King of Babylon

* **city-state** independent state consisting of a city and its surrounding territory

* **dynasty** succession of rulers from the same family or group

Samsu-iluna (SAM•su•i•LOO•nuh) was the son of King HAMMURABI, whom he succeeded to the Babylonian throne. When he came to power, Babylonia was master of southern MESOPOTAMIA. Shortly thereafter, city-states* on the kingdom's northern and southern frontiers began to revolt, forcing Samsu-iluna to spend much of his reign suppressing these rebellions.

In about 1740 B.C., Samsu-iluna defeated the KASSITES on Babylonia's northeastern frontier. The following year, several city-states in southern Mesopotamia banded together under the leadership of Rim-Sin, king of the city of Larsa. Samsu-iluna put down this revolt by changing the course of the EUPHRATES RIVER to deny water to Rim-Sin.

By 1738 B.C., a new dynasty* named Sealand had established itself in southern Mesopotamia. Samsu-iluna twice attacked the Sealanders without success. Meanwhile, the city of ESHNUNNA rebelled but was reconquered in 1730 B.C. Because of the constant threats to his rule, Samsu-iluna built many fortresses along Babylonia's borders. Still, by the end of his reign, Babylonia had lost the entire southern portion of its empire. (*See also* **Babylonia and the Babylonians**.)

SARDINIA

* **Levant** lands bordering the eastern shores of the Mediterranean Sea (present-day Syria, Lebanon, and Israel), the West Bank, and Jordan

* **indigenous** referring to the original inhabitants of a region

* **archaeological** referring to the study of past human cultures, usually by excavating material remains of human activity

* **obsidian** black glass, formed from hardened lava, useful for making sharp blades and tools

* **sixth millennium B.C.** years from 6000 to 5001 B.C.

* **basalt** black or gray stone, often with a glassy surface

* **fortification** structure built to strengthen or protect against attack

The second largest island in the Mediterranean Sea, Sardinia is located west of Italy and north of Tunisia. Its closest neighbor is the island of Corsica, which lies seven miles to the north. Sardinia has been inhabited longer than any other Mediterranean island except CYPRUS.

Not much is known about the Sardinians. Some scholars believe that these people were the Sherden, or Shardanu, one of the mysterious SEA PEOPLES who attacked Egypt and the Levant* in the 1100s B.C. Others believe that the Sherden were not indigenous* Sardinians but simply Phoenicians who had settled on Sardinia.

Whoever the Sardinians were, there is archaeological* evidence that they were involved in obsidian* trade as early as the sixth millennium B.C.* Other evidence suggests that early Sardinian society consisted of small groups who supported themselves through agriculture. The island was also an important source of various metals, including silver and copper, and the site of several metalworking industries.

During the late fifth millennium B.C., Sardinians began to settle more widely, and there are indications that they had contact with the Balkans in southeastern Europe and the eastern Mediterranean. Although they expanded their trade in the early fourth millennium B.C., it appears to have stopped by the early third millennium B.C. However, by about 1400 B.C., the island had again become an important part of the commercial life of the Mediterranean and the ancient Near East.

Phoenician traders arrived on Sardinia around 1000 B.C., and by about 700 B.C., they had established permanent settlements along the coast of the island. Around 200 years later, the Carthaginians, themselves Phoenician colonists from northern Africa, began to settle the interior of the island. In 238 B.C., the Romans took over Sardinia and made it a province of their growing empire. Sardinia remained part of the Roman Empire for the next 700 years and was one of Rome's main suppliers of grain.

זרשתאבגדהוזחטיכדלמסנסעפפצזקרשתאבגד

Sardis

Archaeologists have found nearly 7,000 *nuraghi* towers, such as the one shown here, on the Mediterranean island of Sardinia. While the majority of these *nuraghi* are simple single-tower buildings, about 2,000 of them are complex and multitowered.

The most famous ancient remains on Sardinia are the island's 7,000 stone towers. Called *nuraghi,* these towers were made of basalt* blocks and were built between 1500 and 500 B.C. For years, many archaeologists believed that the *nuraghi* were used only as defense fortifications*. However, they have recently discovered that the *nuraghi* may have been used as homes, either on a permanent basis or specifically in times of danger. (*See also* **Mediterranean Sea, Trade on.**)

SARDIS

* **tributary** river that flows into another river

* **archaeologist** scientist who studies past human cultures, usually by excavating material remains of human activity

* **dynasty** succession of rulers from the same family or group

Sardis was the capital of the kingdom of Lydia in western ANATOLIA (present-day Turkey). After the Persians conquered the Lydians in 546 B.C., Sardis became the western capital of the PERSIAN EMPIRE. It also marked the western end of the Persian royal road that led east to the Persian capital of Susa.

Sardis was located on the Hermos River (present-day Gediz), which flows west into the AEGEAN SEA. The river provided Sardis with one of its major resources—gold. The Pactolus River, a tributary* of the Hermos, carried flakes of gold down from Mount Tmolus, into Sardis.

Archaeologists* have traced human habitation at Sardis back to around 1500 B.C. The city's history after about 680 B.C. is better known, however. This is when the Mermnad dynasty* came to power in Lydia. Under the Mermnads, Sardis became the capital of the Lydian empire. Although Sardis was captured by the Cimmerians—warriors from southern Russia—

47

חרשתאבגדהוזחטיכךלמםנוסעפףצץקרשתאבגד

Sargon I

* **siege** long and persistent effort to force a surrender by surrounding a fortress or city with armed troops, cutting it off from supplies and aid

* **satrapy** portion of Persian-controlled territory under the rule of a satrap, or provincial governor

during the early Mermnad reign, the Lydians had regained the city by 626 B.C. The Persians conquered Sardis when they overcame Croesus, the last Mermnad king, in a siege* at Sardis. As part of the Persian empire, Sardis became the capital of a satrapy*.

In the early 400s B.C., Sardis played a part in the PERSIAN WARS between the Persians and the Greeks. The Greeks seized and burned part of the city in 498 B.C. Sardis was then rebuilt and remained part of Persian territory until 334 B.C., when its people surrendered to ALEXANDER THE GREAT, conqueror of the Persian empire. (*See also* **Lydia and the Lydians; Roads.**)

SARGON I

ruled ca. 2334–2278 B.C.
King of Akkad

* **third millennium B.C.** years from 3000 to 2001 B.C.

* **city-state** independent state consisting of a city and its surrounding territory

 See map in Akkad and the Akkadians (vol. 1).

Sargon I of Akkad created Mesopotamia's first large, organized state. During his 56-year reign, Sargon conquered southern Mesopotamia and parts of Syria, Anatolia (present-day Turkey), and Elam (present-day western Iran). The Akkadian empire that Sargon founded served as a model for later Mesopotamian rulers building their own kingdoms.

Sargon's Rise to Power. Almost no records from the late third millennium B.C.* mention Sargon, so his birth and early life are known mostly through legends written many centuries later. The most famous story says that, shortly after his birth, Sargon was set adrift in a basket on the EUPHRATES RIVER. He was found and raised by a gardener and later rose to an influential position in the court of King Ur-Zababa of the Sumerian city-state* of KISH. Around 2350 B.C., Ur-Zababa was killed or dethroned by Lugalzagesi, king of the city-state of UMMA. Sargon took the throne and became *lugal*—king—of Kish after attacking Lugalzagesi's capital at URUK in about 2334 B.C. It might have been around this time that he took the name Sargon—in Akkadian (Sharrum-kin) it means "the true king"—to convince his subjects that he was the legitimate ruler.

The Growth of Akkad. During his reign, Sargon expanded the empire across the Near East. He captured several cities first conquered by Lugalzagesi before turning to the east and defeating the Elamites. He then extended the empire to the north and west, taking the city-states of MARI and EBLA. Some inscriptions indicate that he pushed the borders of the empire into present-day Lebanon and the Taurus Mountains of southeastern Turkey.

Sargon adopted several new policies to deal with the lands he conquered. After defeating a city, he would destroy its walls to ensure that his rivals could not use it as a fortress. If the local city officials swore loyalty to him, Sargon allowed them to keep their positions. If not, he brought in his own subjects to rule. In this way, he ensured that power remained centrally controlled by Akkad. To retain military control of his empire, Sargon established the world's first permanent army. He also set up military outposts throughout the kingdom. As a reward to his troops (and to ensure their loyalty), he seized or bought large tracts of land and distributed them among the SOLDIERS. Sargon also established a wide-ranging trade network. MERCHANTS came from as far away as the OMAN PENINSULA, Afghanistan, and India, to Akkad, the capital city Sargon founded.

Sargon, however, did not completely do away with the old traditions of the places he conquered. For example, he made his daughter Enkheduanna a high priestess of the patron* god in the city of UR. In this way, Sargon showed that he recognized and accepted the power of the existing local deities and beliefs. By the end of Sargon's reign, many of the areas he conquered had begun to rebel against Akkadian control. As a result, Sargon's successors had to spend much time and energy struggling to maintain control over the empire he had built. (*See also* **Akkad and the Akkadians; Elam and the Elamites.**)

* **patron** special guardian, protector, or supporter

SARGON II

ruled 721–705 B.C.
King of Assyria

* **dynasty** succession of rulers from the same family or group

* **Levant** lands bordering the eastern shores of the Mediterranean Sea (present-day Syria, Lebanon, and Israel), the West Bank, and Jordan

* **imperial** pertaining to an emperor or an empire

* **siege** long and persistent effort to force a surrender by surrounding a fortress or city with armed troops, cutting it off from supplies and aid

* **city-state** independent state consisting of a city and its surrounding territory

* **sack** to loot a captured city

See color plate 7, vol. 3.

* **tribute** payment made by a smaller or weaker party to a more powerful one, often under the threat of force

One of Assyria's greatest kings, Sargon II ruled the Assyrian empire during the last century of its history. The son of TIGLATH-PILESER III and the brother of SHALMANESER V, Sargon consolidated the conquests of his predecessors, extended Assyrian power, and founded the last great Assyrian dynasty*. He also built a new capital city at Khorsabad.

Sargon succeeded Shalmaneser on the throne in 721 B.C., either because the king died or was overthrown in a revolt. Sargon faced several problems during the early years of his reign. The most pressing threats were from the kingdom of URARTU in the north, the rebellious Chaldeans and ARAMAEANS in Babylonia to the south, and the regions of SYRIA and the Levant* in the west. Although these territories and peoples had been conquered earlier by his father, it was up to Sargon II to consolidate his conquests, improve imperial* administration, and increase the stability of the empire.

During the first year of his reign, Sargon moved against Syria and the Levant. He completed a siege* of SAMARIA and destroyed that northern Israelite kingdom, deporting many of its inhabitants. Having secured control and stability in the Levant, Sargon opened a harbor near the SINAI PENINSULA and established a commercial settlement to facilitate trade with Egypt. In 717 B.C., he incorporated the Syrian city-state* of KARKAMISH as a province of the Assyrian empire.

Three years later, Sargon began to deal with the problems in Urartu by raiding that kingdom. Despite the difficult mountainous terrain, his troops defeated the Urartians, forced King Rusa of Urartu and his armies to flee the capital, and sacked* the city of Musasir and its temples. This victory removed much of the threat from Urartu and allowed Sargon to concentrate his energies on Babylonia.

In Babylonia, Sargon faced problems with the rebellious Chaldeans. Their leader, Marduk-apla-iddina II, had earlier joined forces with the Elamites and become king of Babylonia in 721 B.C. Sargon seized control of the TIGRIS RIVER, driving a wedge between the Chaldeans and the Elamites. He then gained the support of cities in northern Babylonia, overthrew the Chaldean leader, and named himself king of BABYLON. To further ensure the stability of the region, Sargon deported thousands of Chaldeans and Aramaeans from the region. Meanwhile, Marduk-apla-iddina fled farther south and agreed to pay tribute* to Assyria in exchange for control of his tribal territory there.

With these conquests behind him, Sargon looked toward ANATOLIA (present-day Turkey), where the Cimmerians had begun to wield great

Satraps

power. When Sargon led his armies into that region, the Cimmerians moved into interior Anatolia ahead of the Assyrian advance. Thereafter, Sargon's main enemy in the region became the Phrygians, led by King Midas. Perhaps threatened by the Cimmerians, the Phrygians proposed a peace settlement with Sargon, who decided to meet King Midas in person. During this trip, Sargon was killed in battle, probably while fighting the Cimmerians. His death ended the Assyrian hope of extending power into Anatolia. Furthermore, Sargon's body could not be found after the battle and given a proper burial, which was a terrible blow to Assyrian morale. (*See also* **Assyria and the Assyrians; Babylonia and the Babylonians; Chaldea and the Chaldeans.**)

SATRAPS

* **provincial** having to do with the provinces, outlying districts, administrative divisions, or conquered territories of a country or empire

The term *satraps* refers to governors appointed by the king during the PERSIAN EMPIRE (ca. 550–330 B.C.). The regions that satraps governed—satrapies—were the largest administrative units of the empire. The organization of the Persian empire into satrapies was initiated in the 500s B.C. by CYRUS THE GREAT and was completed later in that century by DARIUS I. The number of satrapies during Darius's reign varied between 20 and 28.

Satraps were generally members of the royal family or of the noble classes, and the position was sometimes inherited. They had extensive powers and ruled almost as local kings. As head of the provincial* administration, a satrap was responsible for collecting taxes, defending the satrapy, and providing troops for the Persian army and navy. Satraps also served as the supreme judges and law enforcers of their provinces.

The satraps were directly responsible to the king and governed on his behalf. Periodic inspections by various royal officials—known as the king's "eyes and ears"—helped ensure that the satraps remained loyal and were fulfilling their responsibilities. This system of inspections also prevented satraps from gaining too much power.

After the mid-400s B.C., the authority of the Persian empire began to weaken. During this time, the satraps enjoyed a great deal of independence. When ALEXANDER THE GREAT conquered the Persian empire in the 330s B.C., he kept the system of satrapies but reformed it by replacing Persian satraps with Macedonian officials and by limiting their powers. (*See also* **Government.**)

Scarabs

See *Seals.*

SCHOOLS

Schools in the ancient Near East helped students prepare for a useful, respected, and financially comfortable future, just as schools do today. Unlike the modern world, however, the ancient Near East had no concept of schooling for all. Although some boys from humble backgrounds attended school, the students were generally male children of

* **scribe** person of a learned class who served as a writer, editor, or teacher

* **apprenticeship** system of training in which an individual learns skills or a profession from an experienced person in that field

* **second millennium B.C.** years from 2000 to 1001 B.C.

* **archaeologist** scientist who studies past human cultures, usually by excavating material remains of human activity

* **cuneiform** world's oldest form of writing, which takes its name from the distinctive wedge-shaped signs pressed into clay tablets

* **third millennium B.C.** years from 3000 to 2001 B.C.

the elite, privileged classes, who would go on to serve the state as scribes*, priests, or other skilled professionals.

Schools were concerned chiefly with improving the reading and writing skills of their students. Other kinds of education—including apprenticeship* training in practical fields, such as building and crafts—took place outside the schools. The best-documented schools were in MESOPOTAMIA and Egypt. There is also some evidence of formal training of scribes among the HITTITES of ANATOLIA (present-day Turkey) and among the Israelites. Literary texts found in the city of Boğazköy suggest that scribal schools existed in Anatolia as early as the second millennium B.C.* In the kingdoms of ISRAEL AND JUDAH, young boys were trained in scribal schools, but girls remained at home with their mothers, who taught them to become good wives and housekeepers.

Mesopotamia. In the remains of ancient Mesopotamian cities such as UR and NIPPUR, archaeologists* have identified several rooms as schools because they contain cuneiform* tablets. Called tablet houses, these schools taught reading and writing (including how to prepare clay tablets), LITERATURE, MATHEMATICS, and music. Students learned by copying documents, lists, and literary works in Sumerian and Akkadian. Sumerian was the language of religion, literature, and education even after it passed out of everyday use. In fact, this is one of the main reasons such a great number of Sumerian texts have survived.

An experienced scribe, called an expert or professor, headed a school and could physically punish a student for tardiness or bad behavior. Advanced students, or "big brothers," assisted the teacher. The youngest students were called sons of the tablet house. Students did not live at the schools but attended them each day, bringing their midday meal from home. The scribal academies reached their greatest importance during the first half of the second millennium B.C. After that time, they died out, and students began to study in scholars' homes or in smaller schools that were attached to temples or governmental offices.

Egypt. The first organized schools, called chambers or departments of instruction, appeared in Egypt in the late third millennium B.C.* The teachers were local scribes, officials of the civil administration, and priests.

When a boy approached the age of ten, his parents might decide to send him to elementary school, which was usually open to the air and attached to a temple or palace. There he would learn to read and write by studying literary classics. When the boy was a partly trained scribe in his teens, he chose how to continue his education, selecting the appropriate school for a career in the military, the civil government, or the priesthood. The advanced phase of his education could last as long as 12 years. In addition to continued language and literary study, the student was exposed to mathematics, accounting, geometry, surveying, and simple engineering.

At a temple school, or House of Life, a student not only studied religious and magical texts but also learned to manage temple lands and personnel. The Houses of Life were Egypt's intellectual centers, where future physicians, astronomers, and magicians were also educated. Some scribes

51

were chosen to be educated at a site outside Egypt, where they would study such LANGUAGES as Akkadian, Hittite, or Canaanite, which then enabled them to participate in and contribute to Egypt's increasing foreign relations. (*See also* **Education; Scribes; Writing.**)

SCIENCE AND TECHNOLOGY

The physical remains of cultures of the ancient Near East testify to the scientific and technological knowledge of these early civilizations. The PYRAMIDS of Egypt, the CANALS of Mesopotamia, and the astronomical records of Babylonia and Assyria are just a few products of that knowledge. Although these cultures left an extensive written record of their scientific knowledge, archaeologists* and historians have also gained much information from artifacts* and ruins.

Foundations of Ancient Science. Both ancient Egyptian and Mesopotamian texts deal with matters of science. Scribes* in both societies carefully observed the world around them and made detailed records and lists of what they saw. In Mesopotamia, these included catalogs of different types of plants, animals, stones and minerals, and parts of the body. These lists formed the main body of knowledge on which ancient scholars based their scientific theories and practices. In Egypt, the experiments were based on observations. The results of these investigations were recorded and later consulted and revised in the light of new information.

Unlike modern scientific enterprise, the goal of these inquiries was not the advancement of knowledge for its own sake. For instance, the Egyptians believed that the gods created a perfect balance in nature, called *maat.* Their science was an attempt to understand *maat* by observing and understanding the world. When scientific knowledge disagreed with religious belief, religion prevailed.

Science was generally the province of scribes, who preserved and passed along their knowledge. However, they were only interested in the pure sciences, such as MATHEMATICS and astronomy, and the natural sciences, such as zoology and botany. Many of the innovations that profoundly changed civilization, such as metalworking and ARCHITECTURE, are almost completely absent from the scribal records. Such knowledge was transmitted by skilled crafts workers through apprenticeships* and not by scribes on their tablets. This was partly because scribes were solely interested in sciences that could only be mastered by scholarly study.

Mathematics and Astronomy. CLAY TABLETS from Mesopotamia dating to about 2200 B.C. contain the earliest references to instruction in mathematics. However, the Mesopotamians clearly developed mathematical principles at a much earlier date. Mesopotamian mathematics employed a sexagesimal system, that is, one based on the number 60. This system formed the basis of the modern system of timekeeping, which divides each hour into 60 minutes and each minute into 60 seconds. It was also adapted to geometry, in which circles are divided into 360° (6 x 60). Hieroglyphic INSCRIPTIONS indicate that well before 2000 B.C., Egyptian mathematicians employed the decimal (base 10) system that is commonly used today. They were also well versed in the use of fractions.

* **archaeologist** scientist who studies past human cultures, usually by excavating material remains of human activity
* **artifact** ornament, tool, weapon, or other object made by humans
* **scribe** person of a learned class who served as a writer, editor, or teacher
* **apprenticeship** system of training in which an individual learns skills or a profession from an experienced person in that field

Mapping the Ancient World

The ancient Babylonians pioneered the technology of mapmaking, creating detailed maps on different scales. They range from local maps of fields to the earliest map of the world. Most local maps were survey maps used to show the size of a field, probably for tax purposes. Larger maps often depicted districts of the country and individual cities. Some of these maps were amazingly accurate. A map of the city of Nippur drawn sometime in the second millennium B.C. was nearly as precise as that drawn by an American archaeological team thousands of years later.

Science and Technology

The mastery of mathematics facilitated the advancement of the science of astronomy. By applying mathematical knowledge to their observations of the heavens, ancient astronomers were able to calculate the movements of STARS and PLANETS, predict the appearance of eclipses, and precisely time the changing of the seasons. This knowledge was essential for planning religious and agricultural activities. The earliest CALENDARS and clocks also owe their invention to the astronomical observations of the Egyptians and the Mesopotamians.

Building Technology. There can be no doubt that both the Egyptians and the Mesopotamians mastered practical architecture, surveying, and various forms of engineering. The Sumerians were clearly familiar with the dome, the arch, and other architectural techniques. They also built massive ziggurats* of sun-dried brick and constructed the first large WALLED CITIES. The extensive canal system of southern Mesopotamia also shows their skill in hydraulic* engineering.

The pyramids and impressive temple complexes bear witness to the architectural and engineering prowess of the Egyptians. However, both societies left later generations with the enduring mystery of how such monumental structures were constructed. In Mesopotamia, some illustrations of tax collectors surveying fields as well as land survey records have survived. However, these only provide clues to the methods involved and do not contain any detailed description of the processes they illustrate. Neither the Egyptians nor the Mesopotamians committed this knowledge to writing, and modern scholars can only guess at the skills employed to create these ancient wonders.

Other Technologies. Metalworking was one of the most important technological developments of the ancient Near East. The ability to work

* **ziggurat** in ancient Mesopotamia, a multistory tower with steps leading to a temple on the top

* **hydraulic** having to do with the movement of fluids under pressure

The people of the ancient Near East developed many techniques that enabled them to move the large and heavy objects used in the construction of palaces, temples, ziggurats, and pyramids. Excavated at King Sennacherib's palace at Nineveh, this relief shows workers moving a colossal stone sculpture with a lever (bottom center).

53

Scribes

with metal and shape it into tools, weapons, and other objects was developed before 3000 B.C. Alloying, the process of combining two or more metals to create a new metal that is superior to the original metals, was invented shortly thereafter. The first practical alloy was bronze, a mixture of copper and one of several other metals, most commonly tin. By 1000 B.C., metalworkers had mastered ironworking.

MEDICINE was another field pioneered by Near Easterners. In Egypt, medicine was a prestigious profession, and the ranks included specialists, such as dentists and surgeons. Knowledge of the body was crude, but doctors were quite skilled at healing fractures, treating wounds, and performing some operations. Both the Egyptians and the Mesopotamians were aware of the medicinal properties of many plants, from which they created a variety of drugs, potions, and ointments. Their ability to combine natural elements to form new substances indicates a knowledge of basic chemistry that was also applied to the creation of PERFUME, glass, and even imitation gemstones. (*See also* **Astronomy and Astronomers; Glass and Glassmaking; Irrigation; Metals and Metalworking; Mining; Textiles; Wheel; Wood and Woodworking.**)

SCRIBES

In the ancient Near East, scribes were educated individuals specially trained in the art of writing. Because most people were illiterate*, scribes served an essential function in society and were highly respected. Their main responsibility was to write documents for governments, temples, and individuals. Scribes also recorded business transactions and taxes and copied literary and religious texts.

* **illiterate** unable to read or write

Scribal Education. Most surviving information about scribal EDUCATION comes from Mesopotamia and Egypt. Although scribal education differed in some ways from culture to culture, the training of scribes in all ancient societies generally shared many common features.

Scribal education was largely restricted to males and to the upper classes of society. While there are some records of female scribes, these were exceptional cases. Sons from poorer families rarely received scribal education, reflecting the social and economic realities of the ancient world. The scribal profession was considered a proper calling for members of the elite, while most poor families simply could not afford to educate their children. For those who could, a scribal education offered a path to greater wealth and social status. Many ancient texts praise the virtues of the scribal profession compared to the difficult life of those in most other occupations.

Students began their education around age six in Mesopotamia and a few years later in Egypt. Formal scribal schools appeared in UR and other Mesopotamian cities as early as 3000 B.C. However, shortly after 2000 B.C., this system of education broke down, and students began to receive scribal training from individual masters. In Egypt, the pattern was reversed. Young scribes originally were trained as apprentices*, either by their fathers or by trained officials, and the state had a great deal of control over scribal education. After about 2100 B.C., however, local officials

* **apprentice** individual who learns skills or a profession from an experienced person in that field

took over the education of scribes, and scribal SCHOOLS emerged in many towns and cities. In both Mesopotamia and Egypt, scribal schools were attached to palaces and temples.

Standard courses of study for scribes in Mesopotamia and Egypt included language, LITERATURE, and MATHEMATICS. Mesopotamian students also studied music, while Egyptian students could take advanced courses in specialized subjects after completing their basic education. Scribal training began with learning the meanings of the symbols of the writing system and mastering vocabulary lists. Students later progressed to copying passages written by instructors, taking dictation, and writing material from memory. Advanced students learned technical vocabulary associated with various disciplines and professions. These students also learned how to prepare writing tools and materials. After they had completed their education, scribes either entered private practice or served in official state positions.

The Scribe's Tools. Because pencils and paper were unknown in ancient times, scribes used materials readily available to them. Mesopotamian scribes used a reed tool called a stylus to press wedge-shaped CUNEIFORM characters into soft clay tablets. Mistakes were rubbed out by hand while the clay was still soft. Writing boards made of wood or ivory covered with wax also served as notepads as well as student practice tablets. Scribes wrote on the boards by impressing or scratching characters into the wax. The wax could be melted or removed, allowing the board to be used repeatedly.

In Egypt, scribes generally wrote on papyrus*, using a reed brush and ink made from natural substances, such as charcoal or red ocher (impure iron used as pigment). Scribes mixed dried cakes of ink with water to produce liquid ink that was handled much like present-day watercolors. Erasures were made by washing away the mistake with a damp rag, and a smooth pebble or special tool of wood or ivory was used to polish the writing surface and make it smooth. After 1200 B.C., scribes in Syria, the Levant*, and Mesopotamia scratched inscriptions in clay or stone with a stylus or wrote on papyrus or prepared animal skins with a brush and ink. Often these scribes, as well as those in Egypt, made notes or recorded less important documents with a brush and ink on pieces of broken pottery called *ostraca* or on plaster-coated wooden writing boards.

Scribal Duties. Scribes worked for the state, the temple, and private enterprise, and they played a crucial role in many aspects of society. When engaged in business and legal activities, they wrote all contracts, bills of sale, loans, and other documents. Occasionally, they served as witnesses to these documents.

Duties of scribes employed by the state included surveying land and estimating the production of farmers' fields. This latter duty was very important because taxes—generally paid in grain or other produce—were based on estimated crop yields. Scribes collected and recorded the taxes as well. Scribes also served as secretaries to kings and other high officials, recording state correspondence, including laws and treaties. They also supervised the activities of public workers and the operation of certain

Scribal Titles and Duties

Official scribes employed by the state or temple generally had titles that reflected either the material on which they wrote or some aspect of their duties. Among the titles of Sumerian and Akkadian scribes are the following: field scribe, inscriber of stone, military scribe, scribe of the property of the temple, judge's scribe, and scribe of the *naditu* (cloistered) women. In Egypt, the word for scribe, *zakhau*, meant "one who uses the brush," not only to write but also to draw and paint. Thus, a "scribe of contours" referred to a draftsman skilled at drawing outlines on walls, whereas a "column scribe" was skilled at painting columns or pillars.

* **papyrus** writing material made by pressing together thin strips of the inner stem of the papyrus plant; *pl.* papyri

* **Levant** lands bordering the eastern shores of the Mediterranean Sea (present-day Syria, Lebanon, and Israel), the West Bank, and Jordan

A Month at School

Scribal students in Mesopotamia generally attended classes each day from sunrise to sunset. Scholars have discovered little information about vacations or time off. One ancient Sumerian school text, however, contains writing in which a pupil explains his monthly schedule:

The reckoning of my monthly stay in the tablet house is [as follows]:
My days of freedom are three per month,
Its festivals are three days per month.
Within it, twenty-four days per month
[Is the time of] my living in the tablet house. They are long days.

public institutions, such as granaries. Scribes who knew more than one language acted as interpreters and translators.

Many scribes worked for temples, where they served primarily as administrators. Their responsibilities included receiving and recording religious offerings, classifying temple records, and supervising the construction of temples, tombs, and shrines. They also copied texts and occasionally wrote HYMNS and other religious works.

Using their skills, scribes helped preserve knowledge of specialized fields such as astrology, astronomy, MEDICINE, and MAGIC. Some scribes even wrote literature and POETRY, although this was more common in Mesopotamia than in Egypt, where most surviving works deal with religion and funeral practices. (*See also* **Alphabets; Books and Manuscripts; Clay Tablets; Hieroglyphics; Inscriptions; Libraries and Archives; Record Keeping; Writing.**)

SCULPTURE

* **stylized** referring to art style in which figures are portrayed in simplified ways that exaggerate certain features, not realistically

* **relief** sculpture in which material is cut away to show figures raised from the background

* **canon** set of approved standards or criteria

* **literate** able to read and write

* **city-state** independent state consisting of a city and its surrounding territory

* **artisan** skilled craftsperson

* **third millennium B.C.** years from 3000 to 2001 B.C.

In the ancient Near East, sculpture, with its stylized* poses, faces, and themes, whether carved in relief* or in the round, served mainly political, social, and religious functions. Sculpture was not displayed in museums. Instead, most sculpture appeared in temples, palaces, tombs, or on such structures as city GATES.

The subject and method of representation of ancient Near Eastern sculpture were in accordance with artistic canons* set by a society's elite. Images were idealized in sculpture—they showed their subjects the way society expected them to be, rather than as they really were. For example, the face on a statue of a king might be emotionless and stern to show that the king was strict but fair. Whether the king himself actually possessed those qualities or even looked like the statue was irrelevant. Rather, sculpture was meant to convey the values of the ruling classes and to reinforce the existing order of society. Thus, kings were usually portrayed in a regal manner, gods were pictured bestowing blessings on the ruler and the country, and workers were shown dutifully performing their tasks. The size of the subjects also represented how important they were in relation to the other subjects portrayed, not their actual sizes.

Mesopotamian Sculpture. Idealized figures and themes were common in Mesopotamian sculpture, but differences existed among the cultures that occupied the region. Before the emergence of the earliest literate* city-states* in Mesopotamia (ca. 3300 B.C.), the most common sculptures produced throughout the Near East were small figurines of nude women, made of clay, bone, ivory, or stone. Such figurines, usually associated with fertility, remained popular even into the Roman period. During the period from 3300 to 2900 B.C., when the Sumerians and their neighbors, the Elamites of Iran, were forming the first literate urban cultures, artisans* produced sculptures depicting kings, priests, heroes, goddesses, worshipers, workers, and domestic and wild animals.

During the third millennium B.C.*, relief sculpture in Mesopotamia consisted of scenes with members of royalty and gods. Statues in Sumer were usually figures of men and women, most of whom are shown

Sculpture

Dating from the 600s B.C., this basalt relief from Kefkalesi in Urartu depicts guardian spirits and lions in mirror image standing in a fortress. The tree in the middle of the relief is the tree of life. The spirits are holding pinecones and making a gesture of fruitfulness toward the tree. Relief sculptures are rare in Urartian art.

See color plate 7, vol. 3.

dressed in tufted skirts. These statues were small because stone had to be imported into southern Mesopotamia. Many of these figures have clasped hands, a sign of respect to the gods. Bulls and LIONS, animals sacred to the Mesopotamians, were also commonly sculpted figures.

With the rise of the Akkadian empire around 2300 B.C., larger pieces of stone became available, and larger statues gained popularity. A black stone called diorite—possibly imported from an island in the Persian Gulf called Magan (in present-day Oman)—became a favorite material. Statues of gods were common in Mesopotamia after 2000 B.C., and they typically are shown wearing miters (headdresses) with one or more pairs of horns. The horns symbolized the divinity of the gods. Lifelike lion statues in baked clay were also common. They served as guardians of the temples and palaces.

After 1000 B.C., Assyrian power was on the rise and sculpture there was intended to convey that message to the viewer. The interior walls of Assyrian palaces were covered with reliefs. Some depicted the king with his gods or displayed his bravery in combat with wild animals and on the battlefield. The reliefs also depicted the might of the Assyrian army and the terror it inspired through its cruelty and violence. The palace entrances were guarded by colossal figures of winged bulls with human heads, winged gods, and heroes. These guardian figures were attached to the walls, but they were carved in such high relief that they appear to be stepping out to confront the viewer.

Reliefs also figured prominently in Babylonian art during the first millennium B.C. (years from 1000 to 1 B.C.). For example, in the 500s B.C., the Ishtar Gate in Babylon was constructed and contained reliefs of bulls

Sculpture

and dragons. Reliefs of lions lined the walls on either side of the main processional road leading from the gate.

Egyptian Sculpture. Art in Egypt was created in accordance with canons set by members of the elite. As a result, people, gods, animals, and other subjects were portrayed in the same manner whether painted or sculpted.

The ancient Egyptians carved reliefs on stelae*, sarcophagi*, and tomb and temple walls. These carvings showed scenes of royalty, the gods, and daily life. The earliest examples of Egyptian sculpture are clay and stone figurines from the late fifth millennium B.C.* From the late fourth millennium B.C. (years from 4000 to 3001 B.C.), many qualities in Egyptian sculpture became standardized, emphasizing certain features over others. In nearly all Egyptian reliefs, the king and the gods are usually much taller than anyone else in the scene. The king is usually shown as youthful and vigorous, without the signs of old age seen in statues of other nobles. In statues where the figures are standing, a man's left foot is placed ahead of his right foot as if he is striding forward; women usually stand with their feet together. Other statues might show people seated, kneeling, or squatting on their heels.

At several points in Egyptian history, artisans were permitted to vary the representations. During the 1900s B.C., kings were depicted more realistically—they might show signs of aging. During the 1400s B.C., naturalism in the representation of the king and royal family became almost caricature.

A form of sculpture common during the New Kingdom (ca. 1539–1075 B.C.) was the standard-bearing statue, which often showed the king holding a religious object. Later, during the Third Intermediate period (ca. 1075–606 B.C.), block statues—sculptures featuring seated figures who seem to emerge from the block of stone—were common. After about 1000 B.C., images of local officials presenting small statues of gods became popular. This reflects the fact that, by that time, most areas of Egypt were ruled locally, not controlled by the pharaohs*.

Egyptian sculpture was not limited to human and divine subjects, however. The pillars at the temple of LUXOR, constructed around 1375 B.C., were sculpted in the shape of the buds of the papyrus plant. Also, one of the most famous Egyptian statues is that of the Great Sphinx* located near the PYRAMIDS at GIZA, dating to the 2500s B.C.

Anatolia. Very few sculpted works from ANATOLIA (present-day Turkey) before the second millennium B.C. (years from 2000 to 1001 B.C.) are known. Early Anatolian figures of humans and animals show a standard form with large breasts, buttocks, and thighs that were probably fertility images.

Much more sculpture, in the form of reliefs, is known from the period of the Hittite empire (ca. 1400–1200 B.C.). Figures carved in very high relief—gods, lions, sphinxes—guarded the entrances to palaces. One of the best known examples of Hittite sculpture comes from reliefs carved in the rock at Yazilikaya, near ancient KHATTUSHA. The reliefs in these chambers portray the Hittite gods and goddesses, and the chief deities* are shown standing on animals that represent them. Rock reliefs are quite common throughout Anatolia, both in the Hittite and Neo-Hittite periods.

Egyptian Puzzle Sculptures

Egyptian sculpture often included hieroglyphic symbols, and sometimes the symbols were arranged to form puns. By using hieroglyphs in this manner, sculptors created works that could be interpreted in different ways. A good example is a statue of the sculptor Senenmut, who is shown kneeling and offering an image of the cobra goddess Renenutet to the god Montu. Several elements of the offering are also hieroglyphs. When viewed from the front, they spell out one of the names of the former ruler Hapshetsut—suggesting that Senenmut wanted to affirm his loyalty to her rather than express devotion to Montu.

* **stela** stone slab or pillar that has been carved or engraved and serves as a monument; *pl.* stelae

* **sarcophagus** ornamental coffin, usually made of stone; *pl.* sarcophagi

* **fifth millennium** B.C. years from 5000 to 4001 B.C.

* **pharaoh** king of ancient Egypt

* **sphinx** imaginary creature with a lion's body and a human head

See color plate 12, vol. 3.

* **deity** god or goddess

* **Levant** lands bordering the eastern shores of the Mediterranean Sea (present-day Syria, Lebanon, and Israel), the West Bank, and Jordan

* **basalt** black or gray stone, often with a glassy surface

See color plate 4, vol. 1.

* **hieroglyphics** system of writing that uses pictorial characters, or hieroglyphs, to represent words or ideas

Syria and the Levant. As in Anatolia, few freestanding sculptures from Syria and the Levant* have survived. During the fourth millennium B.C., ivory was used, although limestone and basalt* were also sometimes used. The art of the Levant borrowed from other ancient Near Eastern regions. Sculpture in Syria before 2000 B.C. shows strong Mesopotamian influences, featuring people worshiping gods or carrying OFFERINGS.

After 2000 B.C., Egyptian artistic traditions became dominant, and statues of kings, local rulers, and national gods appear with more regularity. Perhaps the most characteristic sculptures of the Levant were bronze statues of gods and goddesses to which offerings were made. Images included both male and female gods dressed in a variety of costumes, as well as figures of bulls representing the storm god BAAL. The rarity of sculpture in Israel may be due in part to the religion of the Israelites, which forbade images of their god and any other living things.

Iran. From the late fourth millennium B.C. (years from 4000 to 3001 B.C.) through the middle of the first millennium B.C., Iranian art, especially in the southwest in Elam, strongly resembled that of its western neighbor, Mesopotamia. However, when the Persians, who were newcomers to Iran, formed their empire in the 500s B.C., they borrowed styles from regions throughout the ancient Near East. For example, a guardian figure carved for the site of Cyrus the Great's palace has four wings in the Assyrian fashion and wears an Egyptian crown, an Elamite robe, and a Persian beard. A statue of Persian king Darius I discovered at the city of SUSA shows him wearing a Greek-style garment and standing in a pose typical of Egyptian sculpture. The type of stone used and the Egyptian hieroglyphics* carved on the base suggest that the statue of Darius was manufactured in Egypt and later sent to Susa.

Perhaps the most famous example of Persian sculpture is the BEHISTUN INSCRIPTION—a relief and inscription carved into a mountainside in western Iran. The relief celebrates Darius's victory over rebels and depicts the Persian god AHURA MAZDA holding out the ring of kingship toward Darius. Other famous reliefs are found on the walls of the palaces at PERSEPOLIS, a city founded by Darius. (*See also* **Animals in Art; Art, Artisans, and Artists; Bas-Reliefs; Human Form in Art.**)

SCYTHIA AND THE SCYTHIANS

* **nomadic** referring to people who travel from place to place to find food and pasture

A nomadic* people of CENTRAL ASIA, the Scythians (SI•thee•uhnz) migrated to present-day southern Russia in the 700s and 600s B.C. There they founded a powerful empire called Scythia (SI•thee•uh). Located north of the Black Sea and centered on the Crimean peninsula, Scythia flourished from the 700s to the 300s B.C. During this time, the Scythians often came into conflict with the peoples of the ancient Near East.

HISTORY

Much of what is known about the history of Scythia and the Scythians comes from the ancient Greek historian HERODOTUS, who visited Scythia

Scythia and the Scythians

* **archaeologist** scientist who studies past human cultures, usually by excavating material remains of human activity

Legendary Origins

According to the Greek historian Herodotus, two ancient legends explained the mysterious origin of the Scythians. Both stories claimed that the Royal Scyths were descended from a man named Skythes. In one story, Skythes was a son of Targitaos, the first man (whose father was the god Zeus and mother was the daughter of a river in Central Asia). Skythes had two older brothers, but only he had the power to touch four golden objects that had fallen from the sky. In the other legend, Skythes and his brothers were the sons of the great hero Hercules. Because only Skythes could successfully handle his father's great bow, it was he who became the ancestor of the Royal Scyths.

* **second millennium** B.C. years from 2000 to 1001 B.C.

* **Levant** lands bordering the eastern shores of the Mediterranean Sea (present-day Syria, Lebanon, and Israel), the West Bank, and Jordan

* **plunder** to steal property by force, usually after a conquest

* **prophet** one who claims to have received divine messages or insights

in the 400s B.C. Modern archaeologists* have also discovered clues to Scythian history from various BURIAL SITES AND TOMBS they have excavated in regions once inhabited by the Scythians.

Migration and Settlement of Scythia. The origin of the Scythians is a subject of controversy. Most scholars believe that they arrived in Central Asia early in the second millennium B.C.*, probably from the east. From that time until the 700s B.C., little is known about their activities.

Large-scale migrations of Central Asian peoples probably began around 800 B.C. in response to events in China, where the Chinese emperor drove warlike peoples from the borders of his empire. This set in motion a chain reaction as, one after another, nomadic tribes moved westward and pushed other groups before them. In the late 700s B.C., a people known as the Massagetae attacked the Scythians, forcing them westward into the region around the Black and Caspian Seas that had been controlled by the Cimmerians.

In a series of wars that lasted about 30 years, the Scythians drove the Cimmerians into ANATOLIA (present-day Turkey) and established themselves in the territories that became Scythia. From their centers north of the Black Sea, the Scythians then began pushing south through the CAUCASUS region, which brought them into contact with both the Assyrian empire and the kingdom of URARTU. In the late 700s B.C., the Scythians allied with the Cimmerians against King SARGON II of Assyria.

Rise of Scythian Power. Numerous conflicts erupted between Scythia, Assyria, and Urartu in the early 600s B.C. However, in 673 B.C., Assyrian king ESARHADDON arranged a marriage between his daughter and Bartatua, the Scythian king, to form an alliance with Scythia against Urartu and the MEDES of IRAN.

Scythia reached the height of its power by about 630 B.C. Taking advantage of a decline in Assyrian power at that time, the Scythians launched devastating invasions of SYRIA and the Levant* and plundered* these regions. They even led raids into Egypt. The savagery of Scythian raids in the Levant made a great impact on the ancient Judeans, and images of these campaigns appeared in the visions of Jewish prophets,* such as ISAIAH and JEREMIAH.

In the late 600s B.C., the Assyrians were attacked by the allied forces of the Medes and Babylonians. At first, the Scythians helped Assyria defend itself, but they soon switched sides and joined in the attack against their former ally. These attacks led to the collapse of the Assyrian empire. The Scythians also played a role in the fall of Urartu in the early 500s B.C.

After the collapse of Assyria and Urartu, the Scythians began to experience trouble from the Medes, whose power was increasing. Attacks by the Medes in the early 500s B.C. forced most Scythians out of Assyrian territory and back into the Caucasus and Scythia, which remained the core of their empire. Blocked from further expansion in the south, the Scythians launched raids westward into Europe in the 500s B.C., reaching as far as present-day Austria and Poland.

See map on inside covers.

Decline and Fall of Scythia. By the late 500s B.C., the Scythians began to lose some of their power. Still, in 512 B.C., they were able to repel an attack by the Persians under DARIUS I. During the 400s B.C., the Scythians remained a relatively strong military power. Their power increased again in the next century, reaching a peak during the reign of King Ateas, who expanded Scythian power into the Balkan region of Europe. In 339 B.C., King Ateas was killed in battle while fighting the armies of King Philip II of MACEDONIA, the father of ALEXANDER THE GREAT. Although the Scythians managed to resist another attack by the Macedonians several years later, their power had begun to decline dramatically.

During the 200s B.C., the Scythians lost most of their territory in Russia to a people known as the Sarmatians. The Scythian kingdom was confined to part of the Crimean peninsula and a narrow coastal strip along the Black Sea. The Scythians maintained a gradually weakening presence in these regions until the A.D. 200s, when they disappeared from the historical record.

PEOPLE AND CULTURE

A group of closely related nomadic tribes, the Scythians spoke an Indo-Iranian language related to Persian, but they had no system of writing. Some evidence suggests that, at different times in their history, they intermingled with other Central Asian peoples, such as the Mongols and the Huns. Some aspects of Scythian culture were similar to those of the Cimmerians, another nomadic people of Central Asia. However, the Scythians also developed a distinct culture of their own.

Horsemanship and Warfare. Feared and respected for their skill in warfare, the Scythians were famous in the ancient world for their horsemanship. They were among the earliest peoples to master the skill of horseback riding, and they applied that skill to the art of war. Mounted archers formed the core of Scythian military forces, and the mobility of Scythian warriors astonished their neighbors and opponents.

The Scythians were also known for their ferocity. They sometimes scalped and beheaded enemies killed in battle and carved out the skulls for use as drinking cups. Scythian armies were made up of freemen who shared in the loot taken from defeated opponents. They received food and clothing for their service but no wages. Some evidence suggests that Scythian women may have fought alongside the men.

Economy, Government, and Society. Scythian society and economy were based on the grazing of CATTLE and on AGRICULTURE, which included the cultivation of wheat. True nomads, most Scythians followed their herds of cattle in seasonal migrations across the vast grasslands of southern Russia, traveling in horse-drawn wagons.

As they conquered new territories, some Scythians settled down to farm, and permanent settlements developed near cultivated lands. Many Scythian settlements were heavily fortified, including that of Kamenka on the Dnieper River in present-day Russia, which was established in the 400s B.C. and which became the center of a Scythian kingdom.

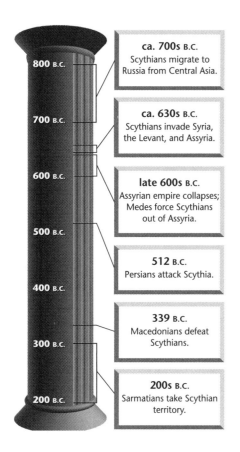

800 B.C.

ca. 700s B.C.
Scythians migrate to Russia from Central Asia.

700 B.C.

ca. 630s B.C.
Scythians invade Syria, the Levant, and Assyria.

600 B.C.

late 600s B.C.
Assyrian empire collapses; Medes force Scythians out of Assyria.

500 B.C.

512 B.C.
Persians attack Scythia.

400 B.C.

339 B.C.
Macedonians defeat Scythians.

300 B.C.

200s B.C.
Sarmatians take Scythian territory.

200 B.C.

Scythia and the Scythians

* **tribute** payment made by a smaller or weaker party to a more powerful one, often under the threat of force

* **artifact** ornament, tool, weapon, or other object made by humans

* **artisan** skilled craftsperson

* **city-state** independent state consisting of a city and its surrounding territory

* **deity** god or goddess

Scythian society was headed by a group of powerful and wealthy tribal chieftains known as the Royal Scyths. This group of chieftains came from the warrior tribes of Scythian society. Other tribes were subject to their rule. The Royal Scyths were led by a king, and the kingship passed from father to son. Territories under the control of the Royal Scyths frequently paid tribute* to the king.

The Scythians practiced polygamy, and it was a common custom for sons to inherit the wives of their fathers when they died. However, the favorite wife of a man generally was killed and buried along with her husband, in a ceremony that was often very elaborate. Kings and other men of high rank often were buried in large tombs with several rooms filled with food, wine, clothing, jewels, and spectacular gold and silver objects. Sometimes, horses and servants were sacrificed and buried as well as part of funeral rituals.

Metalworking and Art. Many of the objects found in Scythian tombs reveal that the Scythians were highly skilled metalworkers. This is also evident from Scythian swords and various iron and bronze weaponry and other implements discovered by archaeologists.

In addition to their metalwork, the Scythians produced decorative objects from a variety of other materials, many of which display superb skill and workmanship. Artifacts* from Scythian tombs include items made of wood, leather, bone, felt, and other textiles. Scythian wall hangings and rugs often featured intricate and colorful designs. Pictorial representations of Scythian men show them wearing very distinctive CLOTHING that included tight trousers, high boots, and hooded jackets. Women may have worn long robes and headdresses with veils. Many garments had colorful, embroidered designs.

Scythian art is essentially realistic in its representation of people, animals, and objects. Much of the art features real and imaginary animals, alone or in combat. Scythian art shows strong Greek influences, and some artworks may actually have been made by Greek artisans*. Some scholars believe that pieces from the golden age of Scythian art, which occurred in the 300s B.C., were created by Scythian artists trained in Macedonia and the Greek city-state* of Athens. The quality of Scythian art from that period was unsurpassed in Central Asia. Most Scythian decorative objects were small in size, which was typical of a nomadic people who moved about frequently.

Religion. The Scythians worshiped many gods. However, they did not build temples or establish elaborate systems of ritual and worship. One of their chief deities* was the fire goddess Tabiti. Often depicted in art with wild animals, she may also have been worshiped as a fertility or mother goddess. Another important deity was the god Papoeus, whom ancient Greek historians associated with their god Zeus. The Scythians also had gods of the earth, sun, and moon, as well as a god of war to whom they sacrificed humans captured in battle. (*See also* **Armies; Assyria and the Assyrians; Burial Sites and Tombs; Metals and Metalworking; Nomads and Nomadism; Persian Empire.**)

Sea Peoples

* **relief** sculpture in which material is cut away to show figures raised from the background

* **Egyptologist** person who studies ancient Egypt

* **archaeological** referring to the study of past human cultures, usually by excavating material remains of human activity

* **Levant** lands bordering the eastern shores of the Mediterranean Sea (present-day Syria, Lebanon, and Israel), the West Bank, and Jordan

* **mercenary** soldier who is hired to fight, often for a foreign country

Ancient Egyptian reliefs* depict in spectacular detail an attempted invasion of Egypt by an alliance of peoples in the eighth year of the reign of Ramses III (ca. 1187–1156 B.C.). The reliefs show two dramatic battles. One battle shows the Egyptian army defeating the invaders on land, while the other shows them destroying the enemy navy. In the latter battle, Ramses is depicted standing on the shore leading his archers as they rain arrows on the enemy ships. Although these are some of the most detailed battle scenes known from ancient Egypt, the identity of the invaders remains mysterious. For convenience they are generally called the "Sea Peoples," a term coined by the French Egyptologist* Gaston Maspero in A.D. 1873.

The texts accompanying these reliefs appear to state that the invaders, before attacking Egypt, had defeated the Hittites, who had dominated ANATOLIA (present-day Turkey) and SYRIA during the Late Bronze Age (ca. 1600–1200 B.C.). In fact, many archaeological* sites in this region show signs of destruction (such as burning) that date to about 1200 B.C. Moreover, some of the Sea Peoples' names, as given by the Egyptians, sound like tribal or place-names from farther west in the Mediterranean. For instance, the Denyen mentioned in the Ramses reliefs have been identified with the Danaoi, a name used for the Greek warriors who fought at TROY; the Shekelesh have been linked with the island of Sicily; and the Shardana with SARDINIA. Using such comparisons, many archaeologists concluded that Ramses was describing a massive migration of "barbarian" peoples from the Mediterranean, who had marched through Anatolia and the Levant*, destroying everything in their path.

Best known of all the Sea Peoples are the Peleset, the leaders of the attempted invasion. They appear to be the PHILISTINES, who, according to the Hebrew BIBLE and Assyrian texts, inhabited the coastal regions of the southern Levant during the Iron Age (ca. 1200–500 B.C.). In fact, the Iron Age pottery from these cities is a locally made version of the Mycenaean (Late Bronze Age) pottery of Greece—a fact that appears to reinforce the theory of the Sea Peoples' migration from the Mediterranean.

In recent years, archaeologists have begun to exercise more caution about the idea of a large-scale Sea Peoples invasion. It is possible that some scholars who were seeking a convenient explanation for the collapse of Late Bronze Age civilization in the Eastern Mediterranean may have exaggerated the whole episode.

In reexamining the records, modern archaeologists have found that Ramses described the Philistines and their allies as "Asiatics," a term that the Egyptians had always used to refer to the peoples of the Levant. Moreover, Ramses claimed to have destroyed the towns and orchards of the Philistines and conquered their land. All of this would be very unlikely if the Philistines had just arrived from the Mediterranean. Moreover, no records describe the Philistines as a seafaring people.

Many Egyptian sources show that other Sea Peoples, including the Lukka and the Shardana, were present in the region even before Ramses III came to the throne. According to the Amarna letters, the Lukka, a people well known as sea-raiders from Lycia, in southwestern Anatolia, were already raiding the coasts of Cyprus in the mid-1300s B.C. The Shardana, who almost certainly had some connection with Sardinia, were friendly mercenaries* in Phoenicia. These early Sea Peoples had allied with the

63

Seals

This drawing of a relief from the memorial temple of Ramses III at Medinet Habu depicts the king engaged in battle with the Sea Peoples in the 1100s B.C. During his reign, Ramses led the Egyptians to crush the Sea Peoples' fleet by drawing them into the narrow channels of the Nile River delta and destroying their ships there. Ramses also defeated those Sea Peoples who attacked by land.

* **pharaoh** king of ancient Egypt

Libyans in their war with pharaoh* Merneptah in the late 1200s B.C. Consequently, they were present in the region much earlier than the time of Ramses III.

In light of the limited evidence, there remains a controversy over the Sea Peoples and their origins. One new view is that the Philistines may already have been present in the Levant when they attempted to invade the borders of Egypt. To help them launch a sea attack they took the assistance of allies and mercenaries from the Mediterranean. However, their invasion failed, and Ramses claims that he captured the invaders, resettling them as mercenaries in Egypt. As for the destroyed cities throughout the Near East around 1200 B.C., scholars believe there could have been many causes, including local wars and rebellions. They are also increasingly considering earthquakes, rather than a Sea Peoples invasion, as the cause of some Late Bronze Age destruction in the region. (*See also* **Lycia and the Lycians; Mycenae and the Mycenaeans; Phoenicia and the Phoenicians.**)

SEALS

A seal is a device with an engraved or raised design, symbol, or word that is used to make a unique mark on other materials. Seals are typically used to certify that a document is authentic or has been approved by some authority. They are also sometimes used to physically close or seal an object, such as an envelope. In the ancient world, seals were extremely important. A variety of people owned and used seals, from kings and court officials to priests, scribes*, craftsmen, and even servants. Both

* **scribe** person of a learned class who served as a writer, editor, or teacher
* **amulet** small object thought to have supernatural or magical powers

men and women owned seals, although it was rarer for women to own them. Seals also had an importance apart from their official functions—they were used as charms or amulets*. Some seals were kept in a family for generations, and some people collected them because of their beauty and value.

Many thousands of seals have survived because they were generally small, hard, and durable objects manufactured in large numbers. Because seals were used so often in ancient times, many thousands of seal impressions on CLAY TABLETS as well as on other clay objects have also survived. However, there are only about half a dozen examples of ancient seal impressions where the original seals have also been recovered.

USES OF SEALS

Seals had several uses in the ancient Near East. In a practical sense, they served to authenticate documents and to seal rooms or objects, such as jars, restricting access to their contents. They also served a spiritual purpose when used as charms and as religious OFFERINGS.

Seals as Security. By 5000 B.C., people in the Near East were using seals to restrict access to rooms or objects. For example, they secured doors by tying a rope around the handle and impressing a seal into a lump of clay surrounding a knot in the rope. Seals were used in the same way to securely close jars, pots, or other objects. Because each seal was unique, its impression could serve to identify the sealer personally, or the authority he represented. More importantly, the presence of the seal impression on the clay served to show that the contents sealed had not been tampered with. Seal impressions were also set on the clay balls (bullae) that contained the tokens used in early RECORD KEEPING.

* **cuneiform** world's oldest form of writing, which takes its name from the distinctive wedge-shaped signs pressed into clay tablets
* **fourth millennium** B.C. years from 4000 to 3001 B.C.

Seals as Authentication. Soon, sealed bullae and tokens gave way to the use of clay tablets and cuneiform* writing. In the late fourth millennium B.C.*, seals were mainly used to certify documents inscribed on clay tablets. They were created to make a recognizable mark that could be associated with a particular person or an office. The presence of seals on a document assured anyone who looked at it that the owners of the seals had approved its contents.

Sealing practices—what types of documents were sealed and by whom they were sealed—varied greatly throughout the ancient Near East. Nevertheless, the most commonly sealed items were receipts and legal documents. When goods were sold, the buyer might place his seal on a document to acknowledge that he had received the items listed in the document. When ownership of property was legally transferred to another person, the original owner sealed the document to indicate that she was willingly giving up her right of ownership to the receiving party. Loans were sealed by the borrower or by a third person who guaranteed payment of the loan if the borrower did not repay it on time. If a legal agreement involved obligations by several parties (such as a marriage or the division of shared property), each affixed their seals to it. Occasionally, the scribe who

See color plate 5, vol. 2.

Killer Seals

According to an ancient text, there were two Akkadian kings who were killed with cylinder seals. Although there is no way to verify this story, modern scholars believe that the instrument of death was not the seal itself. Ancient Near Easterners often wore seals like jewelry, and these particular kings might have been killed by large pins that were used to attach seals to their wearers' garments.

* **deity** god or goddess

See color plate 14, vol. 2.

recorded the transaction also sealed the documents. Many types of transactions required the presence of witnesses, any or all of whom might seal the document. Their seal impressions were intended to serve as a visual reminder of the fact that they had witnessed the agreement should they be called to court to testify.

Sealed documents were placed in a clay envelope. The outside of the envelope contained either all or part of the text of the document inside, as well as the seals of the parties involved. If a dispute over the document arose, the envelope was broken, and it was taken to a judge along with the document inside. Witnesses were required to be present to answer any questions, after which the judge made his ruling. By about 500 B.C., envelopes were generally no longer used. Instead, copies of the document were made and one was given to each party. A similar system is used today for contracts and other legal agreements.

Religious Uses. Seals, often made from the same types of stones used for amulets and charms, were considered to have magical or special powers. Many people wore them as charms, much as a person today might wear a religious medal. Many ancient tombs contain seals that belonged to their inhabitants, emphasizing their importance and suggesting that seals were considered valuable to a person in the AFTERLIFE. Such seals might be inscribed with a prayer, typically intended to ensure long life or health for the seal owner or the king. Unlike other images on seals, prayers were not usually carved in reverse writing so that they could be read when impressed onto a surface. Instead, they were carved so that they could be read by looking at the seal itself. Known as votive (devotional) seals, they were often presented as temple offerings to local deities*. By presenting the seal, the owner aimed to ensure that the prayer would be offered to the god forever.

TYPES OF SEALS

The two basic types of seals are the stamp seal and the cylinder seal, and both types were used throughout the ancient Near East. The type of seal a particular culture preferred depended on how its people planned to use it as well as on their system of WRITING.

Stamp Seals. A stamp seal has a flat or slightly convex surface into which a design is carved. When pressed into a soft material, such as clay or wax, it leaves a reverse impression of the carved design. The earliest examples of ancient Near Eastern stamp seals—by far the oldest type of seal—were found in present-day northern Iraq (ancient MESOPOTAMIA) and date to about 5500 B.C. The images carved on these early stamp seals were simple patterns of fine, closely placed lines. By about 4500 B.C., simple compositions of animal and human figures were carved into stamp seals. The seals themselves came in a variety of shapes including hands, feet, crescents, and geometric patterns, such as circles or squares. Stamp seals were used in southern Mesopotamia until about 3300 B.C., after which they were largely replaced by cylinder seals.

Cylinder Seals. As its name implies, a cylinder seal is a cylinder-shaped object containing a carved impression. The image is carved along the curved face of the cylinder. Although more challenging to the engraver, a cylinder seal has a unique capability—when rolled across the face of a document, it leaves a continuous impression that repeats itself after each full rotation. In this manner, the seal can cover the entire width of a document, rather than just occupying a small space on it. Moreover, engravers can fit more images or characters on cylinder seals, making them more elaborate than stamp seals. This was particularly advantageous for cultures that used a cuneiform system of writing, in part because cylinder seals had more room for long cuneiform INSCRIPTIONS than did stamp seals.

The earliest evidence of cylinder seals comes from a site in IRAN dating to about 3700 B.C. Shortly thereafter, they appear in EGYPT and in the Levant*, where they seem to have been used only to decorate clay vessels. In general, most societies that had adopted the cuneiform writing system preferred cylinder seals to stamp seals. As alphabetic scripts written on prepared animal skins or papyrus* began to replace cuneiform around 1000 B.C., cylinder seals gradually fell out of use. Only in Mesopotamia, where the Assyrians and Babylonians retained the cuneiform system, did cylinder seals remain in use after this time. Cylinder seals, as well as stone stamp seals, were no longer produced or used during the early years of the SELEUCID EMPIRE (312–64 B.C.), when Greek-style engraved metal finger rings came into widespread use.

Although cylinder seals had become the dominant form throughout much of the Near East, several cultures—such as the Anatolians—

* **Levant** lands bordering the eastern shores of the Mediterranean Sea (present-day Syria, Lebanon, and Israel), the West Bank, and Jordan

* **papyrus** writing material made by pressing together thin strips of the inner stem of the papyrus plant; *pl.* papyri

---

Cylinder seals offered several advantages over stamp seals. First, the rolling action enabled the seal maker to cover a large area of sealing material with images. Furthermore, because cylinder seals left a continuous impression whose limit was determined only by the sealing surface, they had both narrative and decorative potential. The cylinder seal shown here depicts a king wearing a knee-length kilt standing among deities.

Seals

* **scarab** representation of the dung beetle, held as sacred by Egyptians

* **Hellenistic** referring to the Greek-influenced culture of the Mediterranean world and western Asia during the three centuries after the death of Alexander the Great in 323 B.C.

* **archaeological** referring to the study of past human cultures, usually by excavating material remains of human activity

* **artisan** skilled craftsperson

An Early Writing

Before the development of writing, people in the ancient Near East used small, hollow balls of clay called bullae to record economic transactions. These clay balls contained small tokens that were marked and had specific shapes for representing units of goods. After the tokens were enclosed within the bulla, cylinder seals were rolled across the soft clay. Other tokens were then pressed into the surface of the bulla. This told anyone handling a bulla that it was secure, how many tokens were inside, and what they represented.

continued to prefer stamp seals. In Egypt, cylinder seals were replaced by the scarab* seal—originally an amulet—shortly after 2000 B.C. When Egypt was under Hellenistic* and Roman rule (305 B.C.–A.D. 642), stone stamp seals were replaced by engraved metal finger rings that bore the owner's personal stamp.

SEAL MAKING AND SEAL IMAGERY

Seals were made from many different materials, including clay, wood, IVORY, bone, and metal. Most often, however, they were made from STONE. The thousands of seals recovered from archaeological* sites in the Near East give some insight into how seals were made and the range of images they bore. So far, however, archaeologists have uncovered few clues as to why a certain image was chosen for a particular seal.

Seal Making. The fact that so many seals share similar styles and imagery suggests that many of them were made in workshops that produced standard designs. Like other artisans*, seal cutters may have occasionally traveled from place to place to practice their craft.

Seal cutters used different tools depending on the material being carved. For softer stones such as limestone, they used stone chips or copper tools; by around 2000 B.C., bronze tools had also come into use. One specialized seal-cutting instrument was the bow drill, which consisted of a bow similar to that used by archers. The bowstring was wrapped around thin posts, or spindles, which had drill bits mounted on their cutting ends. By moving the bow back and forth, the spindles rotated horizontally, enabling the drill bits to cut into the stone, which was placed on a flat surface. By using a bow drill, the seal cutter could make several cuts in the seal simultaneously.

Early Mesopotamian seals were made mostly from dark green or gray stones, such as steatite or serpentine. White, pink, and green limestones and calcites were also popular materials. LAPIS LAZULI became popular around 2500 B.C. because of its beautiful deep blue color and associated magical properties. During the Akkadian empire (ca. 2350–2193 B.C.), hard stones of green and red jasper or striped agate were favorites. From about 2100 to 1600 B.C., the most common material used was a hard gray stone called hematite, which is found in the Zagros Mountains of Iran. While these types of stones were the most popular in ancient times, many others were also used.

Seal Images. Early seal images on Mesopotamian cylinder seals might include scenes of food or textile production. Between 2900 and 2400 B.C., combat and banquet scenes dominated seal imagery. Gods first appeared on seals after about 2400 B.C. They were sometimes depicted in scenes showing the building of structures or in presentation scenes, where a minor deity is seen introducing the king to a god or goddess seated on a throne. The latter image remained popular for many years and was modified over time. After 2000 B.C., the person on the seal might be shown being presented to a deified* king rather than to a god or goddess. The

* **deified** transformed into a god or goddess

* **erotic** related to sexual excitement or pleasure

presentation scene was eventually replaced during the Old Babylonian period (ca. 1900–1600 B.C.) by images of standing deities accompanied by different divine symbols.

In Anatolia, seals contained many of the same images found in Mesopotamia, as well as images of local gods, animals, and hunting and banquet scenes. Persian seals also show hunting scenes as well as scenes of court life, human and animal figures, and abstract designs. In Egypt, a collection of large scarab seals, made from about 1400 to 1350 B.C., celebrated important events in the reign of King AMENHOTEP III. After about 1800 B.C., heart scarabs, which were used as amulets for the dead, appeared. They contained an inscription from the BOOK OF THE DEAD, instructing the heart of the deceased how to behave after death. Erotic* scenes were also found on ancient Near Eastern seals. Some scholars have suggested that these seals refer to the Mesopotamian New Year's festival in which the king and the high priestess engaged in ritual sexual intercourse—the "sacred marriage" ceremony—to ensure the fertility of the kingdom in the coming year. Generally, however, it is difficult for scholars to determine why a particular image was chosen for a seal. (*See also* **Amulets and Charms; Art, Artisans, and Artists.**)

SELEUCID EMPIRE

* **Hellenistic** referring to the Greek-influenced culture of the Mediterranean world and western Asia during the three centuries after the death of Alexander the Great in 323 B.C.

* **cede** to yield or surrender, usually by treaty

See map in Alexander the Great (vol. 1).

Stretching from western ANATOLIA (present-day Turkey) to the border of present-day India, the Seleucid empire was an important center of the Hellenistic* world. From 312 to 64 B.C., the empire sought to blend Greek-style culture and traditions with older native Near Eastern traditions. It dominated commerce and trade throughout the region.

The Seleucid empire was formed from the remains of the vast empire of ALEXANDER THE GREAT. After Alexander's death in 323 B.C., a power struggle erupted among his Macedonian generals for control of his empire. One of these men, Seleucus, gained control of Babylonia and founded the Seleucid empire. He then consolidated his power and expanded Seleucid territory. By the end of his rule in 281 B.C., the empire stretched from present-day India in the east to SYRIA, Anatolia, and southern Thrace, east of Greece, in the west.

Although Seleucid kings ruled the largest empire in the ancient Near East, their power did not go unchallenged. In the 200s B.C., the Seleucids competed with Egypt—primarily for control of Syria—in a series of conflicts known as the Syrian Wars. They also faced internal struggles, including uprisings in Judah. Beginning in the 200s B.C., the size and power of the empire declined steadily as outlying regions gained independence or were ceded* to other Hellenistic rulers. In the east, the Parthians first seized Iran from the Seleucids around 260 B.C. and later, in the 140s B.C., all of southern Mesopotamia. Continual warfare eventually weakened the empire, and the remaining Syrian portion of the kingdom was finally conquered by the Romans in 64 B.C.

The Seleucids blended Hellenistic culture with Near Eastern, but Greek-speaking nobles tended to dominate the ruling classes. Initially, the Seleucids were tolerant of the indigenous cultures and generally allowed the local people to maintain their own traditions, customs, and religious beliefs.

Semiramis

Later, when the Romans began to enter the Near East, they became less tolerant and forcefully imposed Hellenistic culture on the Near Easterners. (*See also* **Egypt and the Egyptians; Parthia; Ptolemy I.**)

SEMIRAMIS

lived 800s B.C.
Legendary queen of Assyria

* **regent** person appointed to govern while the rightful monarch is too young or unable to rule

* **stela** stone slab or pillar that has been carved or engraved and serves as a monument; *pl.* stelae

Semiramis (si•MIR•uh•mis) was a mythical Assyrian queen celebrated for her great wisdom and beauty. She is said to have conquered many lands and is also credited with founding the city of BABYLON. According to legend, she had a lengthy and prosperous reign. At her death, she was believed to have left earth in the form of a dove. Thereafter, she was worshiped as a goddess, with many of the same characteristics as the goddess ISHTAR. The legend of Semiramis was shaped primarily by the Greek historians HERODOTUS and Diodorus Siculus.

Although the story of Semiramis is legend, her character was probably based on a historical figure named Shammu-ramat. The wife of Assyrian king Shamshi-Adad V, Shammu-ramat served briefly as regent* after the death of her husband in about 811 B.C. She ruled Assyria for four years until her son, Adad-nirari III, was old enough to take the throne. A stone stela* dedicated to Shammu-ramat from the city of ASHUR and INSCRIPTIONS at the city of Nimrud provide evidence of her reign. The fact that Shammu-ramat wielded considerable power was perhaps a factor in the development of the legend of Semiramis, because women rarely played such a major role in any Mesopotamian government.

The first known mention of Semiramis was by Herodotus in the 400s B.C. About 300 years later, Diodorus Siculus wrote about her in his history of the world and created an entire legend about her. The legend of Semiramis inspired a number of later writers and composers, including the French writer Voltaire, who wrote a play called *Semiramis* (1748), and the Italian composer Gioacchino Rossini, whose opera *Semiramide* (1823) was based on the legendary queen. (*See also* **Assyria and the Assyrians; Mythology; Queens.**)

SEMITES

* **nomadic** referring to people who travel from place to place to find food and pasture

* **millennium** period of 1,000 years; *pl.* millennia

The term *Semites* refers to members of any of a number of groups in the ancient Near East, including the Akkadians, Arabs, Amorites, Aramaeans, Canaanites, Israelites (Hebrews), and Phoenicians. No one knows their exact origins, but the most common theory is that the Semites were nomadic* tribesmen who, over the millennia*, migrated to and settled most of Mesopotamia, Syria, and the Levant*.

Mesopotamia. Scholars have speculated on who the first Semites in Mesopotamia were and whether they were indigenous*. There is evidence that during the third millennium B.C.*, there were Semitic groups with a common culture living in Mesopotamia. Some of these people lived in the city of EBLA in Syria, others in the kingdom of MARI on the northern Euphrates River, and still others in the city-state* of KISH located on the southern Euphrates. In fact, the Sumerian KING LIST records Semitic names

* **Levant** lands bordering the eastern shores of the Mediterranean Sea (present-day Syria, Lebanon, and Israel), the West Bank, and Jordan

* **indigenous** referring to the original inhabitants of a region

* **third millennium B.C.** years from 3000 to 2001 B.C.

* **city-state** independent state consisting of a city and its surrounding territory

for the early rulers of Kish. Semites may have even lived in Assyria to the north and along the banks of the Diyala River to the east.

With the exception of the Sumerians, ancient Mesopotamia was dominated by Semitic people. The most famous of the early Semitic tribes were the Akkadians in southern Mesopotamia. Led by King SARGON I, they invaded northern Mesopotamia and northern Syria around 2350 B.C. and established the Akkadian empire, which lasted about 200 years. By about 2000 B.C., another Semitic group, the AMORITES from northern Syria, had settled throughout Mesopotamia. During the next 200 years, they assumed power over much of Syria and Mesopotamia, founding several small kingdoms and city-states. In Mesopotamia, Akkadian-speaking dynasties ruled Assyria in the north and Babylonia in the south until the coming of the Medes and Persians from Iran.

Syria and the Levant. Throughout their histories, Syria and the Levant have been dominated by Semitic peoples. Ancient Ebla, which thrived between 2400 and 2250 B.C., was a powerful Syrian Semitic kingdom. Following the destruction of Ebla by the Akkadians and the collapse of the Akkadian empire, the Amorites rose to power in Syria and migrated into Mesopotamia. By around 1200 B.C., the Aramaeans, members of nomadic tribes that lived on the edges of Syria, had started forming small kingdoms in Syria and began taking over more territories and coming into conflict with the Assyrians. In terms of the spread of language, the Aramaeans may have had the farthest-reaching influence in the ancient Near East. By 600 B.C., Aramaic was accepted as the common language of the Neo-Assyrian empire, and later, it became the official language of the PERSIAN EMPIRE.

Almost all the tribes of CANAAN were Semitic, including the Phoenicians, the Moabites, and the Israelites (the PHILISTINES, however, were not Semites). No one knows the specific origins of the Israelites. According to the Hebrew BIBLE, their ancestor, Abraham, migrated to Canaan from Mesopotamia. His descendants then traveled to Egypt, where they remained enslaved until MOSES led them to freedom. They then returned to Canaan, the Promised Land. No one knows whether this biblical version of events is historically true. However, most historians believe that the Israelites entered Canaan around 1200 B.C.

Egypt. Egypt had less Semitic influence in ancient times than either Mesopotamia or the Levant. There is some evidence, however, of a very early Semitic presence in Egypt. Similarities between Levantine and Egyptian pottery and tools dating from the fourth millennium B.C. (years from 4000 to 3001 B.C.) suggest that Semites may have entered Egypt. During the 1800s B.C., Canaanites began to travel to Egypt for trade, many eventually settling down in the eastern Nile Delta, where they became a powerful presence. In the 1630s B.C., the HYKSOS invaded Egypt and established a dynasty* there. Some historians believe the Hyksos were Amorites who came from the Levant. (*See also* **Akkad and the Akkadians; Arabia and the Arabs; Assyria and the Assyrians; Babylonia and the Babylonians; Ethnic and Language Groups; Phoenicia and the Phoenicians; Semitic Languages.**)

* **dynasty** succession of rulers from the same family or group

71

Semitic Languages

SEMITIC LANGUAGES

* **nomadic** referring to people who travel from place to place to find food and pasture

* **Levant** lands bordering the eastern shores of the Mediterranean Sea (present-day Syria, Lebanon, and Israel), the West Bank, and Jordan

* **dialect** regional form of a spoken language with distinct pronunciation, vocabulary, and grammar

* **third millennium B.C.** years from 3000 to 2001 B.C.

* **city-state** independent state consisting of a city and its surrounding territory

* **archaeologist** scientist who studies past human cultures, usually by excavating material remains of human activity

Some languages spoken in North Africa and the Near East belong to the Afro-Asiatic family of languages. This family, also known as the Hamito-Semitic or Semito-Hamitic languages, consists of five branches, the largest of which contains the Semitic languages. Language experts divide Semitic languages into two subbranches: East Semitic and West Semitic. These subbranches include such languages as Akkadian, Arabic, Aramaean, Hebrew, Phoenician, and Ugaritic.

In ancient times, Semitic languages were spoken by the members of various nomadic* tribes that spread across the region. Over time, these languages were adopted by the peoples they came into contact with or conquered in regions such as Mesopotamia and the Levant*.

East Semitic Languages. The various dialects* of Akkadian were the most widely spoken of the East Semitic languages. The first written evidence of Akkadian dates to the 2500s B.C. Use of the old Akkadian dialect expanded with the formation of the Akkadian empire (ca. 2350–2193 B.C.). Thereafter, Akkadian dialects became the lingua franca—a language that is widely used for communication among speakers of different languages—in the ancient Near East. After the third millennium B.C.*, there were two distinct Akkadian dialects: Assyrian and Babylonian.

Some scholars consider Eblaite an East Semitic language related to Akkadian. Eblaite tablets dating back to the 2300s B.C. were discovered in the A.D. 1970s at the site of the ancient city-state* of EBLA in SYRIA.

West Semitic Languages. The languages that belong to the West Semitic subbranch can be divided into Central Semitic and South Semitic languages. Central Semitic includes the Northwest Semitic (Amorite, Canaanite, Aramaic) and North Arabian languages. Amorite is one of the oldest known West Semitic languages. It was spoken in present-day northern Syria. The language spread into Mesopotamia with the Amorite invasions beginning in the 2100s B.C. However, no Amorite texts have been found—the language is only known from personal names—and its place within Semitic languages has been debated.

The oldest examples of Canaanite date from around 1400 B.C. Later examples of Canaanite include the Moabite, Phoenician, and Hebrew languages. So far, archaeologists* have found only one major example of Moabite writing, which they believe was written around 850 B.C. The Canaanite aleph-beth (a writing system that contains symbols for consonants but not for vowels) was also adopted by many cultures of the ancient Near East and formed the basis for the Greek, Etruscan, and Roman alphabets and, therefore, the modern European alphabets.

The oldest evidence of Phoenician writing is usually dated around 1000 B.C. Because Phoenicians were among the most powerful traders in the Mediterranean, several Phoenician words were adopted by the Greeks, the Romans, the Akkadians, and the Egyptians.

Hebrew is the best-known Canaanite language, and its development can be divided into four stages. The first is called Classical Hebrew or Biblical Hebrew, which is the language of the Hebrew BIBLE. Classical Hebrew was spoken by the Israelites and Judeans until the 500s B.C., when it began to be replaced in everyday life by Aramaic. Hebrew was still used for religious rituals, however.

The next stage of the Hebrew language was Rabbinic (or Mishnaic) Hebrew, which was used for writing. Its name is taken from the Mishna, a book of the oral traditions and laws of Judaism, written in the A.D. 100s. The third stage is called Medieval Hebrew, which lasted from about the A.D. 500s to the 1200s. The final stage is Modern Hebrew, which is the national language of present-day Israel.

Aramaic is one of the most important of the ancient Semitic languages. The first written evidence of Aramaic comes from Syria and dates to the 800s B.C. Within the next 100 years, when the Assyrians conquered Syria, they encountered the Syrian version of the simple 22-letter alephbeth that was first developed by the Canaanites. The Assyrians adopted the script, along with Aramaic, the language of Syria, and both spread throughout the Assyrian empire, becoming second in use only to Assyrian. By the 500s B.C., Aramaean had been accepted as the lingua franca of the ancient Near East. It became the official language of the PERSIAN EMPIRE and was the main language of the Jews from the 500s B.C. Some parts of the Hebrew Bible are written in Aramaic.

Another major Central Semitic language is Arabic, a North Arabian language that scholars believe originated in the Syrian and northern Arabian deserts. The earliest Arabic writings date to the 500s B.C. This early Arabic is called Old Northern Arabic. The next period in the development of the language produced Classical Arabic. This is the language of the Muslim holy book, the Koran, which was written in the A.D. 600s. Modern Arabic dialects are spoken today throughout the Near East and North Africa.

The two main divisions of the South Semitic languages are South Arabian and Ethiopian. South Arabian was spoken in the region that comprised present-day Yemen and Oman. The oldest writing in South Arabian is from the 700s B.C. The oldest evidence of an Ethiopian Semitic language, called Geez, dates from around the A.D. 300s. Some modern languages of the region, such as Amharic and Tigrinya, belong to the Ethiopian sub-branch of the Semitic language family. Amharic is an official language of Ethiopia, and Tigrinya is one of the official languages of Eritrea. (*See also* **Alphabets; Ethnic and Language Groups; Languages; Semites; Ugarit.**)

SENNACHERIB

ruled 704–681 B.C.
King of Assyria

* **Levant** lands bordering the eastern shores of the Mediterranean Sea (present-day Syria, Lebanon, and Israel), the West Bank, and Jordan

The son and successor of King SARGON II, Sennacherib (suh•NAK•er•ib) ruled Assyria for almost a quarter of a century. His reign is noted primarily for numerous military campaigns to put down uprisings and consolidate power in Babylonia and the Levant*. Yet Sennacherib's most enduring accomplishment was rebuilding the ancient city of NINEVEH.

Throughout his reign, Sennacherib was plagued by political instability in Babylonia, caused largely by the growing power of the ARAMAEANS and Chaldeans and by the interference of the Elamites of Iran. At one point, he placed his eldest son on the Babylonian throne, but the Elamites captured and killed him. Infuriated at the death of his son, Sennacherib finally defeated his enemies in 689 B.C. and destroyed the city of BABYLON. During his campaign to put down uprisings in the Levant, he destroyed many

Servants

cities in the region. After a long siege* of the city of JERUSALEM, Sennacherib also forced King Hezekiah of Judah to pay tribute* to Assyria.

During his reign, Sennacherib moved the capital of Assyria from Dur-Sharrukin to Nineveh. He enlarged and beautified the city, widened and paved the streets, built aqueducts and canals, and constructed a magnificent new palace and imposing city walls. Toward the end of his reign, Sennacherib chose his son ESARHADDON as his heir. This decision angered Esarhaddon's older brothers, who led a conspiracy against their father that led to his assassination in 681 B.C. (*See also* **Assyria and the Assyrians; Babylonia and the Babylonians; Chaldea and the Chaldeans; Elam and the Elamites; Kings.**)

SERVANTS

Texts and artworks from the ancient Near East contain many references to servants, the men and women who waited on banquet guests, cleaned temples, and performed all the many tasks of elite estates. It is unclear whether the servants were free and working for pay, semifree, unfree and bound to their employers, or perhaps even enslaved.

Although the terms *servant* and *slave* mean very different things in the modern world, it is not always easy for historians to draw a clear distinction between them in the context of the Near East. Egyptian texts, for example, mention many groups of people whose freedom was limited to some degree: dependents, forced laborers, workers, servants, royal servants, prisoners of war, and slaves. However, these texts generally do not provide exact definitions for such classifications. Even when descriptions exist, they do not always reflect the servants' title. For example, the label "royal servant" referred not to a high-ranking servant of the king but to an Egyptian who had become a foreign slave.

Undoubtedly, many of the individuals called servants in texts from Egypt and other places were hired workers, while others were actually slaves. Their identification as servants had more to do with the work they did than with their precise legal status. In Egypt, the term also referred to people who had given up their rights, probably due to personal and economic constraints or legal problems. Whatever their status, servants played an important role in the everyday life of ancient Near Eastern societies and performed several functions that were indispensable in both public and private life.

Servants in Public Life. Documents from ancient Egypt and MESOPOTAMIA contain references to servants' roles in the smooth operation of such institutions as palaces and temples. Some of these individuals were officials or administrators, servants in the same sense that people who work for the government today are called civil servants. For example, *The Story of Sinuhe* is an account of a palace servant who fled from Eygpt to the Levant* for fear of getting involved in a revolt. Sinuhe could also be described as a courtier (member of the royal court).

In ancient times, Egyptian society consisted of a large number of people who were dependent workers performing tasks on land owned by the king or the state. Most of their work was agricultural, but sometimes they

Instructions for Hittite Servants

In Hittite Anatolia, servants working in the palaces and temples were expected to follow specific instructions that were inscribed on tablets. One such tablet reads:

When a servant is to stand before his master, he is bathed and clothed in clean [garments]; he either gives him his food, or he gives him his beverage. And because he, his master, eats [and] drinks, he is relaxed in spirit and feels one with him. But if he [the servant] is ever remiss, [if] he is inattentive, his mind is alien to him.

Members of nobility in the ancient Near East had servants who served them in many capacities. This Egyptian relief from a sarcophagus dates from around 1975 B.C. and depicts a servant attending to a noble-woman named Kawit, seated at right. The servant holds a fan in her right hand, and offers a bowl of ointment to Kawit with her left. The servant is clothed more simply than Kawit, wears no jewelry, and sports a simpler hairstyle, reflecting the differences in their social statuses.

* **Levant** lands bordering the eastern shores of the Mediterranean Sea (present-day Syria, Lebanon, and Israel), the West Bank, and Jordan

performed forced labor of other sorts, such as building the pyramids or serving as soldiers. Although they were not entirely free, these workers were distinguished from slaves.

Mesopotamia, like Egypt, had a class of people whose status fell somewhere between free workers and slaves. These dependent workers, who were not free to leave their jobs but sometimes escaped, provided much of the agricultural labor needed to sustain society. A similar class of bound workers also existed in ancient Israel. Babylonian society included a group known as temple servants, bound to service in the cities' temples. Although they could not leave their jobs, they could marry, have families, and leave property to their heirs.

Servants in Private Life. Throughout the ancient Near East, the comfortable, even luxurious, lives of the rich and noble depended on the labor of servants. Some performed personal services, acting as maids or attendants to members of the household. Others worked at such tasks as cooking, baking, brewing beer, laundering, cleaning, manufacturing textiles, and sewing. On a country estate, servants labored in fields, gardens, and workshops.

Seth

* **scribe** person of a learned class who served as a writer, editor, or teacher

Many servants had highly specialized duties. Individuals with the proper training served as scribes*, healers, midwives, musicians, or dancers. However, it is unclear whether such individuals were paid employees, bound workers who received some pay, or slaves. (*See also* **Labor and Laborers; Slaves and Slavery.**)

SETH

* **archaeologist** scientist who studies past human cultures, usually by excavating material remains of human activity

* **cult** system of religious beliefs and rituals; group following these beliefs

* **Levant** lands bordering the eastern shores of the Mediterranean Sea (present-day Syria, Lebanon, and Israel), the West Bank, and Jordan

* **dynasty** succession of rulers from the same family or group

* **pharaoh** king of ancient Egypt

* **pantheon** all the gods of a particular culture

Seth was the Egyptian god of chaos, storms, and war. Throughout ancient Egyptian history, he was also associated with foreigners and foreign aggression. In art, Seth was most often depicted with a human body and an animal-like head resembling that of an anteater, with square ears and a long, almost beaklike snout. Most archaeologists* believe that Seth's head was not based on a real animal but was a mythical creation.

Seth was the son of the sky goddess Nut. He was the brother of OSIRIS, the king of the gods, and ISIS, the mother goddess. According to Egyptian mythology, Seth is believed to have killed Osiris in order to become king. After Osiris died, Isis, who was Osiris's wife, bore him a son named HORUS. Horus then battled Seth many times to avenge his father's death and ultimately triumphed over Seth.

Despite Seth's reputation for evil, he was worshiped by many Egyptians. The center of the cult* devoted to him was at Naqada, a city near THEBES. He was also worshiped as a predominant god in northeastern Egypt. The HYKSOS, who invaded Egypt from SYRIA or the Levant* adopted the worship of Seth when they established their dynasty* at Avaris in northern Egypt in the 1600s B.C. This may have been because Seth closely resembled the Canaanite god BAAL.

Seth's name was adopted by pharaohs* such as Seth Peribsen of the Second Dynasty and Sety I and Sethnakhte of the Nineteenth and Twentieth Dynasties. However, by the time of the Twenty-first Dynasty (ca. 1075–945 B.C.), Seth's position in the pantheon* changed, and he came to be considered an evil and dangerous figure. (*See also* **Egypt and the Egyptians; Gods and Goddesses; Mythology; Religion.**)

SETY I

ruled ca. 1294–1279 B.C.
Egyptian pharaoh

* **dynasty** succession of rulers from the same family or group

The son of Ramses I, Sety I ruled Egypt alongside his father, who also founded the Nineteenth Dynasty. Because he began his reign as a co-regent, his succession to the throne was secure. Sometimes considered the greatest king of his dynasty*, Sety was named after the god SETH.

Sety was a successful military leader. During his reign, he fought the Libyans and the HITTITES of Anatolia (present-day Turkey) and maintained Egypt's domination of the Levant*. For a brief period, he ruled the city of Qadesh in southern SYRIA.

Notwithstanding his military abilities, Sety is better known for his domestic policies. He secured Egypt's frontiers, established mines and quarries, and repaired many temples and sacred places. He also continued work on the monuments at Karnak that were begun by his father. His

* **Levant** lands bordering the eastern shores of the Mediterranean Sea (present-day Syria, Lebanon, and Israel), the West Bank, and Jordan

* **relief** sculpture in which material is cut away to show figures raised from the background

own tomb is one of the largest and most beautiful in the VALLEY OF THE KINGS. Sety's mortuary temple at ABYDOS is considered his greatest memorial. It is decorated with many WALL PAINTINGS and reliefs* that are considered among the finest examples of ancient Egyptian art.

Although Sety's reign lasted only about 14 years, he left behind a stable and healthy kingdom. He was succeeded by his son RAMSES II. (*See also* **Egypt and the Egyptians; Pharaohs; Ramses II.**)

SHALMANESER III

ruled 858–823 B.C.
King of Assyria

* **city-state** independent state consisting of a city and its surrounding territory

* **tribute** payment made by a smaller or weaker party to a more powerful one, often under the threat of force

* **artifact** ornament, tool, weapon, or other object made by humans

The son of King ASHURBANIPAL II, Shalmaneser III (shal•man•E•ser) took the throne of Assyria when the empire's power was on the rise. He continued his father's efforts to expand Assyrian rule in the Near East and to gain control over vital trade routes in the region.

In 858 B.C., Shalmaneser defeated the city-state* of KARKAMISH near the Syrian border and conquered several other small states in the area. Five years later, he launched a major campaign against the united forces of the cities of DAMASCUS and Hamath and against the kingdom of Israel. Although he claimed victory at the battle of Qarqar, the outcome was indecisive. Other campaigns in the region followed, but no significant territorial gains were made.

Shalmaneser had greater success elsewhere. In 841 B.C., he marched armies to the Mediterranean coast and forced the Israelite city of SAMARIA and the Phoenician cities of TYRE and SIDON to pay him tribute*. By 832 B.C., he had invaded and conquered Cilicia in ANATOLIA (present-day Turkey) and made that region an Assyrian province.

During his reign, Shalmaneser also concluded a number of building projects begun by his father. This included construction of a new capital at KALKHU (present-day Nimrud), with massive city walls, a magnificent palace, and several temples. One of the best-known artifacts* from his reign is the Black Obelisk, a monument excavated at Nimrud that contains various scenes of the king receiving tribute and INSCRIPTIONS describing the extent of his empire. (*See also* **Assyria and the Assyrians; Hebrews and Israelites; Kings.**)

SHALMANESER V

ruled 726–722 B.C.
King of Assyria

* **Levant** lands bordering the eastern shores of the Mediterranean Sea (present-day Syria, Lebanon, and Israel), the West Bank, and Jordan

The son of King TIGLATH-PILESER III, Shalmaneser V (shal•man•E•ser) took the throne of Assyria after the death of his father in 726 B.C. He also ruled as king of Babylonia, which was controlled by Assyria at that time. Shalmaneser ruled for only five years, and little is known about him or his reign. There are no known royal INSCRIPTIONS from his reign, and the Babylonian Chronicle makes little mention of his activities.

Shalmaneser is mentioned, however, in the Hebrew BIBLE in the Book of 2 Kings. The text tells how he marched Assyrian troops into the Levant* to put down a rebellion led by King Hoshea of Israel. He also attacked the Phoenician city of TYRE and began a long siege* of the city of SAMARIA, the capital of Israel. Shalmaneser died before the siege of Samaria ended,

Shamshi-Adad I

and his successor, SARGON II, claimed credit for the capture of the city. Nevertheless, the military campaigns of Shalmaneser led to the end of the northern kingdom of Israel, which became a province of Assyria. (*See also* **Assyria and the Assyrians.**)

SHAMSHI-ADAD I

ruled ca. 1830–1776 B.C.
First king of Assyria

Shamshi-Adad I (SHAM•shi•A•dad) was an Amorite ruler who gained control of a number of cities and states in northern MESOPOTAMIA. A contemporary of King HAMMURABI of Babylon, Shamshi-Adad achieved enormous prestige.

In about 1836 B.C., Shamshi-Adad succeeded his father and brother as king of Ekallatum, a city located on the TIGRIS RIVER in northern Mesopotamia. However, around 1818 B.C., he was forced to flee to Babylon when Naram-Sin, the king of ESHNUNNA, captured Ekallatum and the city of ASHUR. Shamshi-Adad remained in exile in Babylon until the death of Naram-Sin in about 1811 B.C., after which he returned to Ekallatum. Three years later, he conquered Ashur and then began to expand his territory, capturing MARI and other kingdoms and city-states* in Mesoptamia.

At the height of his power, Shamshi-Adad controlled most of northern Mesopotamia. He governed his kingdom as a collection of city-states. Although he united them all under a single kingship, he also allowed each to maintain its local traditions. In his old age, Shamshi-Adad divided control of his kingdom among himself and his two sons. While he lived, this system of government functioned quite well. After his death, however, his sons allowed the kingdom to collapse, and all the areas absorbed by Shamshi-Adad regained their independence. (*See also* **Amorites; Assyria and the Assyrians; Kings.**)

SHEEP

Sheep and GOATS were the first grazing ANIMALS to be domesticated* in the ancient Near East, probably around 7000 B.C. Domesticated sheep were descended from wild sheep, which were abundant in ANATOLIA (present-day Turkey), MESOPOTAMIA, and IRAN.

Sheep were ideal grazing animals for settled societies that practiced AGRICULTURE. Sheep could graze on the plants that grew naturally in fallow* fields, and their droppings fertilized the ground for the next growing season. They could also graze on vegetation on land just outside cultivated areas. During the summer, shepherds had to herd sheep across long distances so that the sheep could find enough food to sustain themselves. These shepherds were often members of a farmer's family or were hired professionals.

In ancient times, sheep may have been slaughtered for meat or as OFFERINGS or raised to provide milk. More importantly, they were also kept for their wool, the most common TEXTILE used for clothing in the ancient Near East. In the Syrian city-state* of EBLA, which had a large textile industry, the palace owned large flocks of sheep. The Mesopotamian city-state of UR also had a textile industry. There the wool from the sheep was brought to temple workshops where it was woven into fabric to clothe the population. Textiles were also important exports and were sent to foreign lands in exchange for metals and other resources not available in Mesopotamia. Records from Ur show that the temples not only raised sheep but also practiced selective breeding to produce traits such as finer wool. (*See also* **Animals, Domestication of.**)

SHIPPING ROUTES

* **archaeologist** scientist who studies past human cultures, usually by excavating material remains of human activity

* **fourth millennium B.C.** years from 4000 to 3001 B.C.

* **cataract** steep waterfall

* **artifact** ornament, tool, weapon, or other object made by humans

* **commodity** article of trade

In ancient times, the RIVERS and seas of the Near East served as the region's highways, allowing distant cultures to communicate and trade with each other. River travel probably occurred long before the rise of settled civilizations. In fact, archaeologists* have found evidence of sea travel that predates the fourth millennium B.C.*

The primary inland shipping routes in MESOPOTAMIA followed the TIGRIS RIVER or the EUPHRATES RIVER. Because of strong southerly currents, most of the ships on these rivers traveled south from ANATOLIA (present-day Turkey) to Mesopotamia. Small boats were sometimes towed upstream against the current, but the journey took about four times as long as the same trip going downstream. River travel was particularly useful for shipping heavy or bulky cargoes, such as timber or stone. The Mesopotamians also built an extensive series of CANALS, which further aided them in commerce.

The NILE RIVER was the main water artery linking Upper and Lower Egypt. Unlike the Tigris and Euphrates, the Nile permitted easy travel in both directions. Boats traveling north rode the current to the Mediterranean, while southbound craft were driven by winds that blew in from the sea. The main obstacle to southward travel was the cataracts* near the southern city of Aswan. However, a series of channels dug just after 2300 B.C. enabled ships to sail around the cataracts.

Archaeological sites throughout the Near East indicate that coastal and open sea travel both developed around 3000 B.C. A sea route from Mesopotamia around Arabia and into the RED SEA was navigated at about this time. Shortly thereafter, records show that the Sumerians conducted active seaborne trade with states along the coast of the Persian Gulf. Remains of some artifacts* in the region have been traced to early Indian civilizations along the Arabian Sea.

Farther west, the most important shipping routes crossed the eastern Mediterranean Sea between SYRIA, Egypt, Anatolia, and the islands of CYPRUS and CRETE. The northern Syrian city of UGARIT, which was the connecting point for many land routes from Anatolia, Syria, and Mesopotamia, was also an important seaport in the Mediterranean, with close ties with the island of Cyprus.

When the Hittite empire fell in about 1200 B.C., Ugarit and other north Syrian and Anatolian seaports declined, and Phoenician ports in the south —TYRE, SIDON, and BYBLOS—came to dominate Mediterranean shipping.

The Phoenicians were the greatest seafarers in the ancient world, carrying trade goods throughout the Mediterranean and establishing colonies as far away as Spain and Morocco. According to the Greek historian HERODOTUS, a Phoenician fleet even sailed around Africa and returned through the Strait of Gibraltar after a three-year voyage.

Egypt was one of the most important destinations for Mediterranean shipping. The land was rich in grain, a particularly valuable commodity* in

קרשתאבגדהוזחטיכדלמסנוסעפפצצזקרשתאבגד

Ships and Boats

such places as Greece and Anatolia, which lacked good farmland. Ships from Egypt carried grain and precious items such as jewelry, gold, and incense to ports in Syria and Phoenicia. In return, ships bound for Egypt brought back much-needed timber as well as olive oil and wine. Egypt developed sea trade with not only its northern neighbors but also those to the south. Egyptian ships sailed down the Red Sea to the land of Punt, believed to have been on the eastern African coast. However, the Egyptians were much more cautious sailors than the Phoenicians, Greeks, and other peoples of the Mediterranean, rarely sailing out of sight of land. (*See also* **Economy and Trade; Mediterranean Sea, Trade on; Phoenicia and the Phoenicians; Ships and Boats; Trade Routes; Transportation and Travel.**)

SHIPS AND BOATS

The peoples of the ancient Near East often relied on water transport to move goods and establish communications over long distances. From an early date, their ships and boats turned the rivers and seas of the region into watery highways.

River Craft. Among the earliest watercraft in Mesopotamia and Egypt were simple reed rafts propelled by paddles or by poles pushed against the bottom of rivers or marshes. The Mesopotamians also used inflated animal skins as flotation devices. The Assyrian king SHAMSHI-ADAD I issued such skins to his soldiers for use in crossing rivers.

A Mesopotamian river craft called the *kelek* combined these two technologies. It consisted of between four and several hundred inflated animal skins fastened together beneath a framework of poles and reeds to form a raft. Well suited to shallows and rapids along rivers, the *kelek* could float even if several skins were lost or deflated. Cargo-carrying *keleks* traveled downstream with the current. Once they reached their destination, they were taken apart, the wood was sold, and the skins were carried back upstream for use on future trips.

Another early Mesopotamian river craft was a type of coracle, a round, flat-bottomed basket with a frame of twigs and reeds covered with animal hides. Such craft were used by many ancient cultures at different periods. In Mesopotamia, the coracles were paddled or rowed by a crew of two to four men. River craft similar to both *keleks* and coracles are still used in parts of the Near East today.

Boats made from wooden planks were also used on the TIGRIS RIVER and the EUPHRATES RIVER of Mesopotamia and on the NILE RIVER of Egypt. Ancient clay models show that early Mesopotamian wooden vessels had high sides, upturned bows (fronts) and sterns (rears), and deep keels (wooden frameworks running the length of the ship at the base of the hull, or body, of the vessel). These boats were paddled or rowed. Sailboats were rarely used on Mesopotamian rivers because the wind generally blows in the same direction as the currents flow.

Early wooden boats in Egypt were shallow vessels with hulls that curved upward at both bow and stern. Unlike their Mesopotamian counterparts, many Egyptian river craft had sails to catch the wind and propel them south on the Nile River against the current. When ships flowed with

Boats of the Gods

The ancient Mesopotamians built boats to carry statues representing their gods. These boats of the gods were generally full-sized vessels with a crew of rowers to propel them over rivers and canals. During religious festivals, the statues of gods made ritual journeys aboard their boats to visit each other. When not being used to carry a god's statue, a boat was stored in a temple dedicated to the deity, and the god's statue and some treasures from the temple might be placed in the boat to display to worshipers. Each boat had a name, and the vessels were an important part of Mesopotamian culture.

the current on northbound journeys, the sails were lowered, and the boats were paddled or rowed. Early Egyptian sailboats had a single tall, narrow sail roughly triangular in shape; by about 2000 B.C., the sails were squarer.

Egyptian craft usually had a movable cabin of cloth stretched over a wooden framework. A large oar at the stern connected to a pole, or tiller, was used to steer the craft. The ships had crews of up to 20 men, most of whom were rowers. The records of one ship indicate that it held between 26 and 40 people, some of whom were probably passengers.

Seagoing Vessels. Scholars know that the Mesopotamians sailed on the Persian Gulf and Arabian Sea as early as the third millennium B.C.*, but no detailed descriptions of their seagoing vessels survive. However, there is ample evidence of seagoing ships from ancient Egypt, SYRIA, and CANAAN that sailed on the Mediterranean Sea.

Although larger than river craft, Egyptian seagoing vessels were similar in many ways. They used the same types of sails and were steered by means of three oars (rather than one) at the stern. The vessels had a thick rope that ran from one end of the ship to the other above the hull, which prevented the bow and stern from sagging when the ship passed over large waves at sea.

Seagoing ships from Syria and Canaan were short, wide vessels with broad sails and wood or reed fencing along the sides of the hull to prevent water from spraying onto the deck. These ships were the first to have crow's nests, or observation platforms mounted high on the masts.

The sails on early seagoing vessels could not be adjusted to change the amount of sail that caught the wind. If wind conditions required less sail, the crew had to remove the sail entirely and replace it with a smaller one. Around 1200 B.C., Mediterranean ships began to be fitted with an improved sail design by which crews could adjust the size of the sail using a series of ropes and lines.

Seagoing sailing ships generally were equipped with oars so that they could travel against the wind or when the winds were calm. Such ships became known as galleys. Early galleys had a single set of oarsmen who sat inside the ship's hull. Later galleys had several sets of oarsmen, one of

* **third millennium** B.C. years from 3000 to 2001 B.C.

Shown here is one of the six funerary boats excavated from the pyramid of the Twelfth Dynasty Egyptian king Sesostris III. These boats were intended for the king to use on his afterlife journey to meet the sun god. Measuring 33 feet long and 9 feet wide, these boats were made with planks and fastened with mortise-and-tenon joints.

Shulgi

See
color plate 12,
vol. 4.

which would often be seated on deck. On early Phoenician ships, a row of shields was mounted along the rail to protect the rowers and other crew members on deck.

Most seagoing vessels were cargo ships, but ships also became important for military purposes. The earliest naval ships were used solely to transport troops. Naval combat tactics involved sailing close enough to an enemy craft so that soldiers could board it. The soldiers then fought what was essentially a land battle aboard ship.

By the 700s B.C., many naval vessels were equipped with rams—metal or wooden projections mounted at the waterline on the bows of ships—which turned the ships into weapons. When a ship was rowed into an enemy vessel at high speed, the ram would strike its hull and open a hole, enabling water to enter and sink the ship or make it inoperable.

Shipbuilding Techniques. Because of the importance of ships and boats for trade, transportation, and warfare, shipbuilding became an important industry in the ancient Near East. Almost all ancient wooden ships were constructed using a so-called "shell-first" construction, in which a shipbuilder first laid the keel and then attached planks to it to form the hull. Supporting frames were then placed inside the completed hull. By contrast, modern shipbuilders attach the frame to the keel and then build the hull around it.

The planking of ancient ships was held together with a series of mortise-and-tenon joints. These joints consisted of mortises, or notches, cut into the edge of planks and tenons, or pegs, driven into the mortises. Planks set on top of each other were joined by fitting the mortises of one plank over the tenons of another and pounding the planks together with a hammer. Additional wooden pegs were often driven into the joints from inside the hull to lock them firmly in place.

When the wooden planks came in contact with water, they expanded, sealing the seams between them. Ancient records show that the Mesopotamians also used a tarlike substance called bitumen to seal the seams between planks. In addition to mortise-and-tenon construction, the planks on some ships were lashed together with ropes or fibers.

These ancient designs remained in use for thousands of years. In fact, the basic river craft of ancient times is in use in some parts of the world today. (*See also* **Naval Power; Transportation and Travel.**)

SHULGI

**ruled ca. 2094–2047 B.C.
King of Ur**

* **city-state** independent state consisting of a city and its surrounding territory

Shulgi was the son of King UR-NAMMU, founder of the Third Dynasty of the city-state* of UR. As the most important ruler of the dynasty, Shulgi not only expanded his empire but also launched extensive reforms within his kingdom.

Shulgi was most likely quite young when he assumed the throne following his father's unexpected death in battle against the Gutians, a group of nomads from the Zagros Mountains region of present-day Iran. The first 20 or so years of his reign were uneventful. However, in his twentieth year as king, he began a massive reorganization of the empire. He divided the lands of southern and northern Babylonia into provinces and placed them under the control of members of the local elite. To ensure central control, he also assigned a military commander to each province. Areas outside the "core" provinces were settled and run by military officers. Both the core and the outer areas paid taxes consisting of agricultural goods, livestock, and other items of value. These goods were then redistributed to the royal household, temples, and other provinces as needed.

Shulgi also established schools to standardize the training of scribes* and other royal officials. He created a uniform system of weights and measures and a new calendar. About halfway through his reign, Shulgi declared himself a god. He then built a large standing army and used it to greatly expand the empire into present-day southwestern Iran. During Shulgi's nearly 50-year reign, Ur became the dominant power in MESOPO-TAMIA. After his death, Shulgi was succeeded by his sons Amar-Sin, then Shu-Sin. It was not long after the deaths of these two rulers that the Third Dynasty of Ur finally collapsed during an Elamite invasion. (*See also* **Babylonia and the Babylonians.**)

* **scribe** person of a learned class who served as a writer, editor, or teacher

SHUPPILULIUMA I

ruled ca. 1370–1330 B.C.
Hittite king

* **vassal** individual or state that swears loyalty and obedience to a greater power

* **pharaoh** king of ancient Egypt

Shuppiluliuma I (suh•pi•loo•lee•U•mah) was the son of the HITTITE king Tudkhaliya III. A skillful military leader, Shuppiluliuma strengthened the Hittite kingdom in ANATOLIA (present-day Turkey), used his skills to expand his territory, and founded the Hittite empire.

In the early 1300s B.C., Shuppiluliuma served as a general in his father's army during campaigns against Mittani, a HURRIAN kingdom in northern SYRIA. Although the campaigns were largely unsuccessful, Shuppiluliuma gained several minor victories, which earned him a reputation as a leader. When Tudkhaliya died, senior officials murdered his successor, enabling Shuppiluliuma to take the throne.

During the early years of his reign, Shuppiluliuma focused on securing his position, consolidating the kingdom, and establishing a hold on territories to the north and west. Thereafter, he turned his attention to Mitanni. He led his armies as far south as the Lebanon Mountains and subdued several Mitannian territories in Syria. Later he conquered the city of KARKAMISH, an important trade center on the western bank of the Euphrates River. This was a final defeat for Mitanni, which then became a Hittite vassal*.

During his expeditions into Syria, Shuppiluliuma came into conflict with the Egyptians, who had vassals and allies there. However, to Shuppiluliuma's surprise, the widow of the Egyptian king TUTANKHAMEN asked him to send one of his sons to marry her and become Egypt's ruler. When presented with the opportunity to take over his main rival and become the leading power in the Near East, Shuppiluliuma hesitated, thinking the message was a trick. When the Egyptian queen confirmed that the offer was real, Shuppiluliuma sent a son to Egypt to be pharaoh*. However, his son was murdered on his journey, probably by Egyptians opposed to a foreign leader, and Shuppiluliuma lost the chance to expand his territory into Egypt.

Shuppiluliuma sent his troops to subdue minor uprisings in Syria and Anatolia. He also sent an expedition to face Egyptian troops to the south. There the Hittites emerged victorious, but in the end, the campaign was a

Sidon

disaster because the Egyptian prisoners brought a plague into Hittite territory. The plague killed both Shuppiluliuma and his son and successor. Thereafter, Shuppiluliuma's younger son, Murshili II, inherited the throne. The Hittite empire survived until the late 1200s B.C., when it fell after years of unrest and an invasion.

SIDON

* **city-state** independent state consisting of a city and its surrounding territory

* **Semitic** of or relating to a language family that includes Akkadian, Aramaic, Arabic, Hebrew, and Phoenician

* **vassal** individual or state that swears loyalty and obedience to a greater power

* **archaeologist** scientist who studies past human cultures, usually by excavating material remains of human activity

* **sarcophagus** ornamental coffin, usually made of stone; *pl.* sarcophagi

* **relief** sculpture in which material is cut away to show figures raised from the background

Sidon (SY•duhn) was a city-state* in ancient Phoenicia. The present-day city of Saida still exists on the site. It is located on the Mediterranean coast about 27 miles south of present-day Beirut, Lebanon. It is believed that the name *Sidon* is derived from the Semitic* word *sayd*, which means "fishing." Founded sometime between 3000 and 2001 B.C., Sidon, along with the other Phoenician city-states of TYRE and BYBLOS, soon became a successful trading and manufacturing city. Starting in the 600s B.C., Sidon was a vassal* to several ancient Near Eastern empires, including Assyria, Babylonia, and Persia. After the Persian empire fell in 330 B.C., the city was ruled by the Macedonian king ALEXANDER THE GREAT, the Ptolemies, the Seleucids, and the Roman Empire.

Sidon is perhaps best known for its famous purple dye, which was extracted from mollusks, a type of shellfish. In fact, a huge mound of these shells can still be found south of the city. Archeologists* believe that this was where ancient dye manufacturers dumped the shells after the dye had been removed.

Archeologists have found very little evidence of the ancient city because the modern city still exists on top of it. However, an elaborate cemetery containing sarcophagi* from the Phoenician period has been discovered. Also, a temple dedicated to Eshmun—the Phoenician god of healing—has been uncovered. By far the most famous archeological discovery from Sidon is the Alexander Sarcophagus, apparently carved for Alexander's vassal king in Sidon. The reliefs* on the stone sarcophagus show Alexander hunting and fishing. (*See also* **Cities and City-States; Phoenicia and the Phoenicians.**)

Siege Warfare

See *Wars and Warfare.*

Silver

See *Metals and Metalworking.*

SINAI, MOUNT

According to the Hebrew BIBLE, Mount Sinai was where the Hebrew god YAHWEH revealed the set of laws known as the TEN COMMANDMENTS to MOSES. In addition, Moses received numerous other laws and instructions from Yahweh concerning the priesthood and rules for worship, celebration, and sacrifices. Mount Sinai is also where the Israelites entered into their covenant, or solemn agreement, with Yahweh. The Israelites agreed to obey Yahweh's laws and worship him as their only God. Moses and the Israelites came to Mount Sinai during the period of their exodus* from Egypt to CANAAN.

The first reference to Mount Sinai occurs in the Book of Exodus, where the mountain is called Mount Horeb. Its exact location is unknown. Beginning in the A.D. 300s, Christian tradition has identified Mount Sinai with a mountain known in Arabic as Jebel Musa (Mountain of Moses). It is located in the southern SINAI PENINSULA between the Gulf of Suez and the Gulf of Aqaba. This location for Mount Sinai is accepted not only by followers of Judaism but also by those who follow Islam and Christianity. Some modern scholars have proposed other possible locations for Mount Sinai, including sites in Arabia and mountains in the Sinai peninsula but closer to the Mediterranean Sea. (*See also* **Hebrews and Israelites; Judaism and Jews.**)

* **exodus** migration by a large group of people, usually to escape something unpleasant

SINAI PENINSULA

* **archaeologist** scientist who studies past human cultures, usually by excavating material remains of human activity

The Sinai peninsula is a triangle-shaped landmass that lies between Egypt and present-day Israel. The southern part of the peninsula is bordered by the Gulf of Suez on the west and the Gulf of Aqaba on the east. These two bodies of water meet at the southern tip of the peninsula, in the RED SEA. To the north, the peninsula is bounded by the Mediterranean Sea.

Archaeologists* have found evidence of seasonal campsites in the Sinai peninsula dating from prehistoric times. However, the earliest written information about the region comes from Egyptian texts that date from about 3000 B.C. These texts describe Egyptian expeditions that went to the region in search of copper and turquoise. Later the northern Sinai was an important trade route between Egypt and the rest of the ancient Near East. The region was controlled at various times by the Egyptians and later by the Assyrians, Persians, Nabataeans, and Romans. Many of these civilizations established trading posts in the region.

The Sinai is most famous, however, because of references to it in the Hebrew BIBLE. According to the Bible, the Israelites crossed the Sinai peninsula during their exodus* from Egypt to CANAAN. The Sinai is also famous as the site at which the Hebrew god YAHWEH gave MOSES the TEN COMMANDMENTS. Although most scholars do not doubt that the Israelites traveled across the region, no one knows the route they took or on what mountain Moses received the commandments. However, most Christians, Jews, and Muslims believe that the Israelites traveled through the southern part of the peninsula and that Moses received the commandments on Mount Sinai. (*See also* **Sinai, Mount.**)

* **exodus** migration by a large group of people, usually to escape something unpleasant

 See map on inside covers.

SLAVES AND SLAVERY

Slaves and slavery existed throughout the ancient Near East, although their conditions varied. The ancient attitude toward slavery was quite different from that of today, in which it is condemned as a violation of human rights. The concept of human rights was unknown to the ancients, who accepted slavery as a natural part of an existence in which no one was completely free of control by the gods, kings, the state, temples, the elite, or a social class above one's own. Although the fate of

Slaves and Slavery

* **serf** peasant required to work land that he lives on but does not own

slaves was often considered unfortunate, there was little outcry against slavery on moral grounds.

The distinction between free and unfree seems clear today, but the boundaries between slaves, serfs*, and SERVANTS were often blurred in ancient times. Many slaves were foreigners captured in war or raids. Others were citizens of a state who had become slaves because of debt or crime. Some individuals even sold themselves into slavery—perhaps for a limited time—when they could not pay their debts. A parent could sell a child into slavery, and many parents did so. The definition of a slave in ancient times was that he or she was property that could be bought or sold much like any other commodity*.

* **commodity** article of trade

Slavery did not play a significant economic role in any Near Eastern culture. Slave populations were not immense, partly because most Near Eastern cultures did not have the resources to buy and guard them. Outside the palaces, even the richest households probably did not own more than 15 slaves, and 1 to 5 slaves in a household was more common. Slaves tended to be used for indoor or craft work rather than for agricultural labor because it was too easy for them to run away while working in the fields.

* **literacy** ability to read and write

The life of a slave was not necessarily miserable, although the majority of slaves probably led difficult lives. Some slaves, especially those with valuable skills, such as literacy* or knowledge of MEDICINE, gained wealth and status. In some circumstances, slaves could marry, raise families, and gain their freedom. Some acquired political power as advisers to kings and queens. However, this was not the case with most slaves.

Mesopotamia. Slaves were part of Mesopotamian society, although their numbers and economic importance were less in earlier periods than during the Greek and Roman eras. Most slaves were originally prisoners of war. They wore special haircuts, tattoos, or brands to distinguish them from free people. A significant number of slaves were not foreigners but indigenous* residents forced into slavery by economic misfortune, such as debt or poverty. Sometimes such slaves were freed by royal decrees that canceled all private debts.

* **indigenous** referring to the original inhabitants of a region

Most slave owners in Mesopotamia were upper-class families who used their slaves in domestic service. Skilled slaves might either work at crafts for their masters or be hired out for profit. Slave owners sometimes entrusted their slaves with managing estates or operating businesses. Successful or talented slaves belonging to wealthy families might even have been allowed to accumulate their own wealth and spend or invest as they wished.

It was not uncommon for slave owners to give slaves their freedom, and some freed slaves were adopted into the families of their former masters. Female slaves might have borne children to either freemen or slaves, but all such children became the property of their mothers' owners. Some childless slave owners adopted their slaves' children.

Egypt. The lowest social class in ancient Egypt consisted of slaves who worked on royal building projects, in private workshops, and as domestic servants. Slavery was rare in Egypt between about 2700 and 1500 B.C., but it increased significantly after that period.

Foreign slaves entered Egypt through a private slave trade, and some Egyptians sold themselves into slavery. Most slaves, however, were foreign captives, either soldiers taken prisoner in battle or civilians seized during raids of foreign territory. One Egyptian king, Sneferu, claimed to have brought back 7,000 captives from the land of Nubia, south of Egypt. On various occasions, Egyptians raided the deserts west of the Nile River and brought back LIBYANS to serve as slaves.

Egypt's kings did not hesitate to uproot large groups of people under the system of slavery. For example, King RAMSES II sent Nubians to work in the Levant* and Asians to Nubia. The biblical story of the captivity of the Israelites in Egypt and their forced labor is an example of such a policy. Slaves often labored in Egyptian mines and quarries and helped construct the PYRAMIDS, tombs, and temples connected with royal burial sites.

Although many slaves toiled in dreadful conditions, those lucky enough to become domestic slaves had better lives, sometimes becoming trusted family servants. The king controlled all foreign prisoners and could decide to "give" them to individuals. Citizens could also buy slaves from traders.

The Egyptian legal system gave slaves some rights. For example, owners did not have a legal right to have sexual intercourse with their slaves, although many undoubtedly did so. However, children born to slaves out of these relations belonged to the slave owners.

Hittite Anatolia. The HITTITES of ANATOLIA (present-day Turkey) bought and sold slaves just like other commodities. One ancient text lists the price of a slave artisan (such as a potter, carpenter, or weaver) as ten shekels of silver, about what it cost to keep a slave alive during a year of famine*. Some wealthy slave owners probably trained their slaves as skilled craft workers, which increased their usefulness and worth.

Hittite law spelled out the rights and obligations of slaves. For example, runaway slaves could be captured and returned to their masters even if they fled to another country. Slaves could marry free people, but the free individuals became slaves for as long as the marriage lasted. Like free people, slaves could collect damages for personal injuries, but unlike free individuals, slaves were not exempt from physical punishments for certain offenses. For example, a slave caught breaking into a free person's house would have his nose and ears slashed and possibly removed. Hittite law ordered an especially gruesome death for any slave who attacked his master.

Israel. The ancient Israelites developed a complex system of rules to define and govern slaves, most of whom worked for private households rather than for the state. They divided slaves into Israelites and non-Israelites. Non-Israelite slaves were either war captives or people who had sold themselves into slavery (or had been sold by others) because of debt. Such slaves were considered property to be sold and inherited.

Like some non-Israelites, Israelites also sold themselves into slavery to pay off debt. These individuals were often more like hired servants than slaves, and they generally were supposed to serve for only a set number of years. When masters treated Israelite slaves more harshly than the law allowed, the slaves and their free relatives sometimes rebelled. The treatment

* **Levant** lands bordering the eastern shores of the Mediterranean Sea (present-day Syria, Lebanon, and Israel), the West Bank, and Jordan

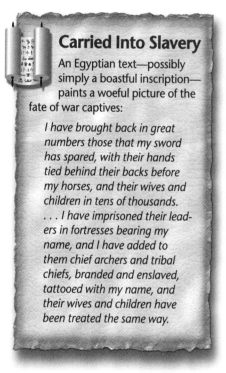

Carried Into Slavery

An Egyptian text—possibly simply a boastful inscription—paints a woeful picture of the fate of war captives:

I have brought back in great numbers those that my sword has spared, with their hands tied behind their backs before my horses, and their wives and children in tens of thousands. . . . I have imprisoned their leaders in fortresses bearing my name, and I have added to them chief archers and tribal chiefs, branded and enslaved, tattooed with my name, and their wives and children have been treated the same way.

* **famine** severe lack of food due to failed crops

Social Institutions

of slaves occasionally led to crises involving the king, the wealthy and powerful masters, and the angry slaves. (*See also* **Eunuchs; Labor and Laborers; Property and Property Rights; Wars and Warfare.**)

SOCIAL INSTITUTIONS

People who live together develop rules that define their rights and responsibilities and determine how they will interact with one another. In every society of the ancient Near East, people existed within a framework, or institutions, that both supported and limited their individual actions. Some of these institutions were direct expressions of RELIGION, GOVERNMENT, and LAW. Others involved the structure of society and aspects of social and private life.

Mesopotamia. The social institutions of the Sumerians and Akkadians who lived in towns and cities of ancient MESOPOTAMIA were based on an urban way of life. City dwellers identified more strongly with the communities where they lived than with relatives by blood or MARRIAGE. The nomads* or partly nomadic livestock herders who lived outside urban areas, however, placed greater importance on clan* and kinship. In the late second millennium B.C.*, many cities began to shrink in size, and villages became the typical settlements. People again began to identify more strongly with tribes or clans.

Mesopotamia was a class-based society. While most people were free, each class had obligations and duties to family, community, and state. The property-owning elite held positions in government, palace administration, military leadership, trade, or the priesthood. One could enter these ranks by birth or by appointment. Other free people who did not own property might work as crafts workers or hired agricultural laborers, for whom there was always a demand. A class called subordinates lived on and worked lands owned by the king. Most slaves were foreign prisoners of war, although Mesopotamians could sell themselves into slavery if they fell into debt.

Justice was one of the fundamental ideas around which Mesopotamian society was organized. Kings presented themselves as serving the gods by enforcing justice and ensuring fairness under the law. They published laws indicating that justice was a public matter, not something left to the whims of kings. Closely linked to justice was religion. In fact, judges often held hearings and swore oaths in a temple. In all classes, from kings to peasants, social institutions reflected the idea that a divine order operated in the universe.

Egypt. The basic social unit of ancient Egyptian society was the nuclear family consisting of parents and children rather than the extended family or clan. One sign of the focus on the nuclear family was that the words for father, mother, brother, and sister were the most common terms for other relationships both inside and outside the family. For example, a student might address his teacher as "Father."

Egyptians lived in communities that varied in size from small villages to large cities. Privacy and individuality—prized by many modern

* **nomad** person who travels from place to place to find food and pasture

* **clan** group of people descended from a common ancestor or united by a common interest

* **second millennium B.C.** years from 2000 to 1001 B.C.

societies—had little place in the culture and everyday life of ancient Egypt. Not only did crowded living quarters offer little physical privacy for most people, but individuals also were generally defined by their roles in larger family and communal groups, such as people working together at the same task.

Egyptian society was divided into three main traditional classes. The nobility consisted of the elite members of the priesthood, the government administration, and the upper ranks of the army. Most members of this class, which probably accounted for less than 5 percent of the total population, were born into it. Commoners called citizens were ordinary free people. Within this large social group, special terms identified individuals who worked on royal, temple, and nonroyal estates. The unfree class included both slaves and peasants compelled to work on land they did not own. The great majority of Egyptians, whether free or unfree, were farmers.

Many social institutions and values of ancient Egyptian culture stemmed from the fact that Egypt was a theocracy—a state in which the government was run by people believed to be guided by or descended from the gods. Whether in temple worship, religious festivals, or public ceremonies, religion played a major role in the lives of people in all social classes. Although Egyptians were united in their devotion to religion, Egypt was an ethnically diverse society. Foreigners frequently entered Egypt and absorbed its culture. Some even rose to high positions in the elite class of society.

Hittite Anatolia. Like most other ancient Near Eastern peoples, the HITTITES of ANATOLIA (present-day Turkey) lived in a state based on kingship. The king was not only the head of government but also the chief priest of the national religion. As the main link between the human and divine worlds, the king was responsible for organizing his people to defend and work the land for the benefit of the gods, who depended on the toil of their human servants. These principles were the basis of Hittite government, law, and religion.

The highest level of Hittite society consisted of the "Great Family"—the king and his extended family. Most major offices of the state were held by individuals from this group. Many members of the landowning elite class belonged to the "Great Family" and had some relationship to the king. Those members of the elite outside the royal family belonged to the upper class simply because they were rich and powerful. The basis of wealth in Hittite society was always land and livestock. Wealthy individuals sometimes paid for entire religious festivals or built, furnished, and staffed village temples.

The lowest rank in Hittite society consisted of slaves, who were bought and sold as commodities*. While many individuals were enslaved for life, some entered into slavery or servitude for a specific period of time in order to pay off debts. Occasionally, rulers demonstrated their godliness by releasing their subjects from debt slavery.

Much of the Hittite population lived in the countryside and worked in AGRICULTURE. These people had to deliver part of their produce to their provincial* governments, which passed it on to the central state authority.

The Wisdom of Experience

The Instruction of Ptahhotep, an Egyptian text written in the 2400s B.C., reflects the importance that Egyptians placed on values and social institutions. In the text, an official asks the king's permission to write instructions on proper conduct for the son who will succeed him in his post:

*May this servant be ordered to make a staff of old age,
So as to tell him the words of those who heard,
The ways of the ancestors,
Who have listened to the gods.
May such be done for you,
So that strife may be banned from the people,
And the Two Shores may serve you!*

* **commodity** article of trade

* **provincial** having to do with the provinces, outlying districts, administrative divisions, or conquered territories of a country or empire

89

Social Institutions

* **Levant** lands bordering the eastern shores of the Mediterranean Sea (present-day Syria, Lebanon, and Israel), the West Bank, and Jordan

* **indigenous** referring to the original inhabitants of a region

* **bureaucracy** system consisting of officials and clerks who perform government functions

* **hierarchy** division of society or an institution into groups with higher and lower rank

* **cult** system of religious beliefs and rituals; group following these beliefs

* **aristocrat** member of the privileged upper class

The central government used these goods to maintain the people who lived and worked within its sphere, to support activities that strengthened royal power (such as military campaigns or the building of palaces), and to distribute to subjects in times of need.

The Canaanites and Israelites. The Canaanites and Israelites were neighbors in the Levant*. Their cultures were similar in many respects, and they shared some social institutions. Both groups divided society into indigenous* inhabitants and foreigners. In Israel, however, there were further categories, such as resident aliens—foreigners who had settled in Israel but were not full citizens. The Israelites also made careful distinctions between free people and slaves.

The king and his bureaucracy* formed the highest level of society in the Levant. In Israel, the king was thought to have been appointed by Yahweh as the shepherd of the people. Although kings were supposed to promote the stability of society, kingship sometimes disrupted social institutions. For example, the establishment of monarchies and the execution of state projects required a central authority to control all resources that had previously been controlled by kinship groups. Still, tribal and clan identity remained very important in Israelite society. People identified themselves first as Israelites, second as members of 1 of 12 tribes, and third as belonging to a clan or extended family called the Father's House. Members of a clan had certain responsibilities toward each other, including avenging murders and buying back land and clan members sold into slavery because of debt.

Both the Canaanites and the Israelites had complex hierarchies* of priests. In Israel, where priests inherited their positions, the structure of the priesthood was thought to mirror the structure of society, with some groups having higher status than others. Status was reflected in such matters as how far into the temple a member of a particular class would be allowed to enter. Yet Israelite religion was never fixed or unified. Different priestly groups often disagreed on practices and organizational principles.

Iran. Much of what is known about the ancient PERSIAN EMPIRE centered in IRAN comes from the writings of the Greek historian HERODOTUS. According to Herodotus, Persian society was divided into tribes of nomads and tribes of farmers. Within each of these categories, some tribes had higher status than others. Tribes were further subdivided into clans. One group in Persian society, the Magians, consisted of specialists in cult* rituals. As with a clan or tribe, status as a Magian was hereditary.

Persian society was also described in economic terms. The Persian king DARIUS III referred to the powerful and the poor, and he considered himself the peacemaker between the two groups. The powerful were aristocrats*, while the poor were free peasants. Within each category were various subcategories and status rankings. There was also a class of people called *kurtash*, whose status was close to that of slaves. The *kurtash* were workers from many parts of the empire who toiled on royal lands and in royal workshops.

The parental authority of fathers set the tone for Persian family life. Families worked together, shared high offices, and passed privileges from generation to generation, but family members could also be punished for another member's crime. Despite such family closeness, young men of the noble class generally spent the time between ages 5 and 20 undergoing tough physical and moral training organized by the king's men. The goal of this training was to make them worthy and faithful subjects of the king.

Persian social values are well expressed in two terms: *arta,* which meant justice and truth, and *drauga,* a lie. In religious terms, *arta* meant worship of the god AHURA MAZDA. In political terms, it meant loyalty to the king. In moral terms, it meant honorable behavior. All these values were intertwined in the Persian understanding of religious, state, and social institutions.

Woven together from laws, rules, customs, and preferences, social institutions of Near Eastern societies gave daily life in each culture its distinctive flavor. (*See also* **Education; Family and Social Life; Priests and Priestesses; Slaves and Slavery; Women, Role of.**)

SOLDIERS

* **scribe** person of a learned class who served as a writer, editor, or teacher

The fates of cities, states, and empires in the ancient Near East were determined in part by their ARMIES. The soldiers who served in these armies ranged from peasants to highly trained and specialized professional troops. While top-ranking officers in Near Eastern armies could achieve wealth, power, and prestige, most ordinary soldiers fared less splendidly. Military service could offer security, but it also offered hardship, discomfort, and danger. An Egyptian scribe* knew well the potentially rough life of the army when he described an infantryman, or common foot soldier, as the "much tormented one" who marches over hills, carries his rations on his shoulders, drinks foul-tasting water, and after facing the enemy in battle is lucky to return to Egypt "full of sickness" and tied to the back of a donkey.

Fighting on Demand. The first armies of the Near East existed only when needed. They consisted of people who came together to fight in a specific campaign, either to defend their homeland or to wage war on foreign soil. These soldiers were either volunteers or citizens required to provide military service to leaders and who therefore had no choice about fighting. In some cases, they were mercenaries—paid soldiers who fought not out of loyalty to king or country but for payment in cash, goods, or items they plundered*.

* **plunder** to steal property by force, usually after a conquest

* **third millennium B.C.** years from 3000 to 2001 B.C.

In MESOPOTAMIA during the third millennium B.C.*, armies grew larger and better organized. One image from the city of LAGASH, dating from about 2500 B.C., portrays a tightly formed phalanx, or rectangular-shaped formation, of foot soldiers with overlapping spears. Such an orderly formation suggests a trained and disciplined fighting force.

For the most part, however, being a soldier was not a full-time profession in Mesopotamia. The terms used to refer to soldiers came from words that described their peacetime activities, such as fisherman, animal herder, or civic official. Many workers had the right to farm state-owned land and to keep a share of the produce, but that right also imposed a certain number of days of military duty.

Soldiers

* **second millennium** B.C. years from 2000 to 1001 B.C.

* **siege** long and persistent effort to force a surrender by surrounding a fortress or city with armed troops, cutting it off from supplies and aid

* **tribute** payment made by a smaller or weaker party to a more powerful one, often under the threat of force

The earliest recorded Egyptian soldiers were local followers of nobles or officials who fought in time of need. However, as early as the third millennium B.C., the Egyptians preferred to have others do their fighting for them. Their armed forces consisted of captured opponents who were made to fight for Egypt and of hired mercenaries. In early times, soldiers from the region of Nubia south of Egypt comprised a significant portion of the Egyptian army. Nubians remained an important element in Egyptian armies throughout ancient times.

Professional Soldiers. During the second millennium B.C.*, warfare in the Near East became more international, and a new kind of fighting force appeared in various Near Eastern states to meet the needs of such conflict. This was the permanent, standing army. The rise of such armies marked the appearance of full-time professional soldiers. The rise of professional soldiers was accompanied by increasing differentiation in rank and function. New levels of officers formed a chain of command between the kings who led the armies and the soldiers who did most of the fighting. Moreover, groups of people within the armies began to specialize in certain types of fighting. In northern Mesopotamia, for example, a chariot-owning aristocracy arose. Charioteers were based in palace lands, and the titles of their officers were identical to those of the court officials. Training and equipping the chariotry was time-consuming and expensive, and the position of charioteer became hereditary, passing from father to son.

Another specialized group was the royal bodyguard, called by a name meaning "men at the king's feet." Other members included archers who used the bow and arrow, shield bearers, engineers who designed and built FORTIFICATIONS and equipment for sieges*, and horsemen who served as messengers and later on the battlefield as CAVALRY. All armies contained large numbers of infantrymen, the backbone of the fighting forces. Professional soldiers might have received pay, goods, or small plots of land in return for their service.

The Hittites of ANATOLIA (present-day Turkey) maintained an army of professional soldiers who campaigned from spring through fall. They spent the winter in quarters, where they were fed by the government and expected to be ready to march at a moment's notice. If the enemy was a major power or if the Hittites faced several conflicts simultaneously, the king would draft additional soldiers from the general population. The king also had agreements with semi-independent outlying districts to supply soldiers and junior officers for the army. Small units of such men were stationed at key points throughout the empire, generally far from their own homes. The Hittites also encouraged their allies to contribute soldiers to their army, and states that paid tribute* were often required to provide troops as well.

During the years from 1000 to 500 B.C., Assyrian professional soldiers established themselves as a highly organized and fierce fighting force. They used new technologies to improve their weapons and armor, chariots, and horse riding equipment. These advances enabled them to successfully expand their empire. Assyrian soldiers were cruel in dealing with their prisoners of war, many of whom were killed, blinded, or mutilated to set an example for other potential Assyrian enemies. Although much

חר שתאבגדהוזחטיכדלמסנסעפפצצקרשתאבגד

Solomon

of the information about the Assyrians' treatment of enemies comes from exaggerated accounts in Assyrian royal INSCRIPTIONS, historians believe the Assyrian army was especially fearsome in the ancient Near East.

A permanent, professional army came into existence in Egypt between about 1500 and 1000 B.C. It included two combat forces, the infantry and the chariotry. Soldiers from western Asia, Nubia, and Libya appear in various WALL PAINTINGS from that period, proving that the Egyptians continued to use foreign soldiers whenever possible. Although foreign-born mercenaries probably fought in all or most ancient Near Eastern armies, they were especially numerous in Egyptian forces. After about 664 B.C., mercenaries from Greece and from Caria in western Anatolia arrived in Egypt to serve as soldiers of fortune. Their military skills made these mercenaries an important element in the Egyptian army that resisted the Assyrians, Babylonians, and Persians. The Carians became so numerous that a Carian colony took root around the Egyptian city of MEMPHIS. The Greek historian HERODOTUS, who may have been part Carian, left a description of the achievements of Carian and Greek mercenaries who fought in the Levant*, Mesopotamia, and Persia as well as in Egypt.

Jewish mercenaries also may have served in Egyptian armies. The Persians were known to have employed Jewish soldiers as well. When the Persians conquered Egypt in 525 B.C., they established a base of Jewish troops at the Egyptian city of Elephantine, which marked the southern frontier of the PERSIAN EMPIRE. Herodotus also wrote that the Persian army often used large numbers of foreign captives as soldiers. He maintained that these foreigners were driven into battle, ahead of the regular Persian troops, by Persians using whips. (*See also* **Caria and the Carians; Chariots; Libyans; Wars and Warfare; Weapons and Armor.**)

* **Levant** lands bordering the eastern shores of the Mediterranean Sea (present-day Syria, Lebanon, and Israel), the West Bank, and Jordan

SOLOMON

ruled ca. 960–932 B.C.
King of Israel

* **prophet** one who claims to have received divine messages or insights

* **concubine** mistress to a married man

* **frankincense and myrrh** fragrant tree resins used to make incense and perfumes

King Solomon is among the most famous of the ancient kings of Israel. Solomon was the son of King DAVID, who united the 12 Israelite tribes and their territories into the kingdom of Israel around 1000 B.C. Almost all that is known of Solomon's life and reign comes from the Hebrew BIBLE. There is no mention of Solomon, David, or Israel in any sources surviving from their own time.

Although he was not David's oldest son, Solomon rose to the throne largely through the efforts of his mother, Bathsheba, and a prophet* called Nathan. Once he became king, Solomon eliminated his opponents and placed men loyal to him in important positions in the military, the government, and the temples.

Solomon also gained stability and power through his marriages. The Bible reports that he had 700 wives and 300 concubines*. Although these numbers are almost certainly exaggerated, it is probable that he made alliances with a number of powerful leaders of the Near East by marrying their female relatives.

One of the famous women with whom Solomon was connected was the queen of Sheba. Sheba was probably a kingdom in southern Arabia that was rich with gold and frankincense and myrrh*. Later legends suggest that the queen and Solomon may have had a child together.

93

Sphinx

* **diplomacy** practice of conducting negotiations between kingdoms, states, or nations

Whether or not this was true, the two leaders had powerful political reasons to work together. Solomon wanted Sheba's products and needed to be able to use trade routes through the queen's land. In turn, the queen of Sheba needed Israel's ports and merchants.

In addition to marriage and diplomacy*, Solomon also used forced labor to develop the wealth of his kingdom. He continued to improve Israel's military, which had already been strengthened by his father. Solomon fortified cities and towns on important trade routes and made changes within Israel. He divided the territory of Israel into 12 administrative regions. Each region was responsible for providing taxes and organizing labor forces to support the central government.

Solomon put the money and labor force to use when he began building his palace and the famous Temple of Solomon in Jerusalem, which became the Israelites' religious center. The men of Israel were required to work for the government for one out of every three months in order to finish these huge projects.

Solomon is famous for his wisdom and goodness. He is credited with writing the Books of Ecclesiastes, Proverbs, and the Song of Solomon in the Hebrew Bible. He is traditionally said to have written many other proverbs and songs. However, most of the sections of the Bible that are credited to him were probably not written by him.

Solomon's son and successor, Rehoboam, not did achieve the amount of success his father had. This was due in part to events that had occurred during Solomon's reign. Solomon had spent much of his country's wealth and may also have angered the people of the northern Israelite tribes by favoring those in the south. These conditions made it difficult for Rehoboam, who only made matters worse when he treated the northern tribes even more severely. As a result, the northern tribes rebelled and formed their own kingdom, which they called Israel. The southern kingdom then became known as Judah, which was the name of Solomon's tribe. (*See also* **Hebrews and Israelites; Israel and Judah; Kings.**)

SPHINX

* **Egyptologist** person who studies ancient Egypt

The sphinx (SFINKS) is an ancient mythical being with the body of an animal—usually a lion, but sometimes a ram or a hawk—and the head of a man, who may wear a royal head cloth. The word *sphinx* probably comes from the Egyptian term *shesep ankh,* which means "living image." Some language scholars believe that the term derives from the Greek word *sphinx,* which means "strangler," but others doubt that the mythical figure of the sphinx is related to this term.

The ancient Egyptians were the first to make stone statues of sphinxes, which they associated with both the king and the god Amun. The most famous sphinx in the world is the Great Sphinx located near the PYRAMIDS at GIZA. With the body of a lion and the head of a king, the Great Sphinx is thought to represent the Fourth Dynasty ruler Khufu, who ruled Egypt from around 2585 to 2560 B.C. However, some Egyptologists* believe that the face of the sphinx is that of Chephren, Khufu's son.

The Great Sphinx is more than 240 feet long and about 65 feet high. It has been covered by the sands of the SAHARA DESERT many times in its

The Great Sphinx at Giza, shown here, is the most famous example of a sphinx. Another famous, although imaginary, sphinx exists in Greek mythology. According to the myth, the people of the Greek city of Thebes were being terrorized by a sphinx who posed a riddle to all passersby and devoured those who were unable to answer. When Prince Oedipus arrived in Thebes, he defeated the sphinx by answering correctly.

See color plate 14, vol. 4.

* **funerary** having to do with funerals or with the handling of the dead

* **pharaoh** king of ancient Egypt

* **Levant** lands bordering the eastern shores of the Mediterranean Sea (present-day Syria, Lebanon, and Israel), the West Bank, and Jordan

long life. It has also been repaired several times over the centuries. As it stands today, the Great Sphinx is missing its nose, beard, and part of its crown. It continues to be worn down by erosion and pollution, but efforts are being made to protect the great statue.

Some Egyptian sphinxes, such as those at the Temple of Amun at KARNAK, do not have human heads. The temple is guarded by rows of sphinxes with the heads of rams. A sphinx at the funerary* temple of Amenhotep III (ca. 1390–1353) was given the tail of a crocodile. Whatever animals they incorporated, Egyptian sphinxes were usually male. Even when a female pharaoh* such as Queen HATSHEPSUT was depicted as a sphinx, she was in her male role as king. The first female sphinxes were depicted in the 1400s B.C., outside Egypt.

From Egypt, the idea of the sphinx traveled to other parts of the ancient Near East, including the Levant*, Anatolia, Greece, and Mesopotamia. In the Levant and Greece, the lion's body of the sphinx was often given wings. In Greek mythology, sphinxes played important parts in the tales of Oedipus and Perseus. Sphinxes did not appear in Mesopotamia until the 1500s B.C., when they were imported from the Levant. (*See also* **Animals in Art; Human Form in Art.**)

Stamp Seals

See *Seals.*

Stars

Long before the establishment of the first settled civilizations, people looked in wonder at the night sky and attempted to understand the meaning of the stars they saw. By around 3000 B.C., the founders of the first cities in MESOPOTAMIA had probably acquired a basic knowledge of astronomy. However, the first recorded systematic observations of the night sky did not occur until after 1800 B.C. These observations were tied to the Mesopotamian religious belief that events in the heavens directly affected events on earth. The Mesopotamians believed that they could determine what would happen on earth by interpreting the signs they saw in the sky. Although knowledge of the stars was originally used to predict the future, it later came to exert a powerful influence over the development of CALENDARS and timekeeping in the Near East.

The Stars and Fate. As early as 3000 B.C., the Babylonians had begun to combine careful observation of the sky with the prediction of earthly occurrences. Thus, in Babylonia, there was no difference between astronomy and astrology. Those who recorded the movements of the stars and PLANETS also interpreted their significance to human affairs.

At first, the signs they saw in the heavens were believed only to be related to the welfare of the state or its ruler. Examples of this can be found in a series of tablets called *Enuma Anu Enlil*, the oldest of which date to before 1200 B.C. One tablet states that if the constellation* Aries is faint, misery or misfortune will befall the king of Subartu. Other predictions relate the color or appearance of certain stars to weather phenomena, peace or war, or the rise and fall of dynasties*.

As astronomical observation became more sophisticated, Mesopotamian astrologers and astronomers refined their system of prediction. By noting the position of constellations throughout the night, they developed the ZODIAC, which divided the sky into 12 equal portions, or houses. Each house was named for the constellation that occupied it. Astrologers began to base their predictions on the arrangement of the planets within each of the houses of the zodiac at a particular date and time. This ultimately led to the casting of individual horoscopes, which related a person's fate to the position of the stars and planets at the time of his or her birth. The observational records used to make these predictions formed the basis of all later scientific astronomy.

Calendars and Timekeeping. Stargazing had practical as well as religious significance to Near Eastern cultures. All civilizations at this time used a calendar based on the phases of the moon, because the time between one full moon and the next is constant. However, 12 lunar months of 29.5 days produce a lunar year of only 354 days instead of the 365-day solar year. This was a problem for agricultural societies, which needed to be able to predict when the planting season began each year. Because they could not calculate this using a lunar calendar, the Egyptians solved the problem through observation of the star Sirius.

In ancient Egypt, there were three basic agricultural seasons of approximately four lunar months each. The first season began when the NILE RIVER started to rise and flood the surrounding land. The second season began when the waters had receded enough to allow planting, and the final

* **constellation** group of stars that is thought to resemble, and is named after, an object, animal, or mythological character

* **dynasty** succession of rulers from the same family or group

season lasted from the harvest to the beginning of the next flood. The Egyptians noted that, for part of the year, Sirius was aligned with the SUN and was invisible. However, shortly before the beginning of the annual flood, Sirius became visible just before sunrise. They used this event—called the heliacal rising of Sirius—to mark the beginning of their new year. By counting the days between heliacal risings of Sirius, they determined the length of a solar year to be 365 days. They then divided the year into 12 equal months of 30 days, with 5 extra days added between the end of one year and the beginning of the next. With this solar calendar, they could accurately predict the cycle of the seasons.

Using other stars that rise heliacally as Sirius does, the Egyptians created star clocks to measure time at night. They divided each month into three 10-day periods called decades. They then identified which stars or constellations rose heliacally on the first day of each decade as well as 11 others that rose after the first one and passed across the sky from sundown to sunrise. These observations allowed the Egyptians to divide the night into 12 units of time. If one looked at the sky and noted how many of these stars or constellations were visible, one could determine how much of the night had passed. Because nights are longer in winter and shorter in summer, the Egyptians eventually had to calculate the total hours of daylight and darkness in different months. However, these calculations always assumed there were 24 hours in a day. This was the origin of the 24-hour day, divided into two 12-hour periods. (*See also* **Astrology and Astrologers; Astronomy and Astronomers; Oracles and Prophecy; Science and Technology.**)

STONE

* **relief** sculpture in which material is cut away to show figures raised from the background
* **artisan** skilled craftsperson

* **quarry** to excavate pieces of stone by cutting, splitting, or (in modern times) blasting

Stone was one of the most widely used materials in the ancient Near East. It was among the primary BUILDING MATERIALS in most Near Eastern societies, especially in monumental ARCHITECTURE. A great deal of the SCULPTURE of the region—both relief* and sculpture in the round—was executed in stone, and artisans* in many societies produced magnificently crafted stone vessels, such as cups, bowls, and vases. Stone was also extensively employed in the manufacture of certain TOOLS, even after metals such as bronze and iron came into widespread use.

Building in Stone. The cultures of the Near East relied on stone to construct their walls and buildings. Before organized societies began to quarry* specific types of stone, people used loose rocks known as fieldstones for building. These were obtained from blocks that had broken off from cliffs or boulders and had become exposed when a river or stream dried up. Small rocks and mud were used to fill spaces between the uncut stones to make the structures sturdy.

The rise of centralized urban cultures around 3000 B.C. made it possible to assemble workers to exploit stone resources in a more systematic way. The Egyptians were probably the first to master these skills. Well before 2500 B.C., Egyptian stonemasons had learned how to cut massive blocks of even the hardest stone and transport them over many miles to building sites. In Mesopotamia, blocks of stone were cut after being quarried to

Stone

* **mud brick** brick made from mud, straw, and water mixed together and baked in the sun

* **Levant** lands bordering the eastern shores of the Mediterranean Sea (present-day Syria, Lebanon, and Israel), the West Bank, and Jordan

Made from a soft stone called chlorite, these vessels were found at Rumeilah, Oman, and date from the first millennium B.C. Hundreds of these locally made vessels have been found in the Oman peninsula, especially at grave sites. The pots were decorated with herringbone, sawtooth, or vertical zigzags and sometimes with stylized animal and floral designs.

make transportation and handling easier. However, because of the scarcity of stone in Mesopotamia, especially in the south, stones were only used for the bases of walls that were regularly made of mud brick*.

Stone construction took several different forms. Many structures, such as the PYRAMIDS of Egypt, were built with a core of rough, unfinished stone of poorer quality that was then covered with a casing of finely worked blocks of granite or limestone. Some city walls consisted entirely of dressed stone, or stones whose edges were cut so smoothly that they could be fitted together very precisely and required no mortar to hold them together. More often, however, walls were constructed from rubble and uncut rock, supported at intervals by piers of precisely cut and dressed stones. Often thin slabs of finished stone called orthostats were used to cover the lower portion of walls made of rubble or mud bricks.

Stone Sculpture and Vessels. Besides its practical use as a building material, stone was a favorite medium for sculptors and artisans in the ancient Near East. The Egyptians fashioned many colossal figures and obelisks (tall, four-sided shafts of stone that taper at the top to a pyramidal point) from stone, a large number of which have survived into modern times.

Many buildings throughout the Near East incorporated stone relief sculpture as part of their decoration. Sometimes sculptors would combine relief and sculpture in the round in the same piece. For example, the GATES of the city of KHATTUSHA in ANATOLIA (present-day Turkey) feature lion figures whose bodies are carved in relief but whose heads and front paws emerge from the wall in three dimensions. A similar lion motif can also be found throughout the Levant*. However, much of the stone available in the Levant was either too hard or too soft for carving, and as a result, sculpture in the round is generally rare. Even the Mesopotamians used stone extensively for sculpture, often importing it from distant lands.

* **basalt** black or gray stone, often with a glassy surface

Sculptors were not the only artisans who employed stone in their work. Even before the rise of urban culture, Egyptian stone carvers were fashioning bowls from an extremely hard stone called basalt*. Some of the finest examples of such work date to before 3000 B.C., hundreds of years before the building of the pyramids. Egyptian artisans crafted basalt bowls, vases, jars, and other vessels featuring unbelievably thin walls and complex designs. However, for reasons unknown, this art declined dramatically toward the end of the Old Kingdom period, around 2130 B.C. The hard stones that had been used earlier gave way to softer materials, and the designs became simpler. Evidence of stone vessels has also been found at other sites throughout the Near East, but none of these pieces shows the quality and craftsmanship exhibited by the early Egyptian artisans.

Stone Tools. Stone was widely used in the manufacture of blades for sickles (handheld tools used to harvest grain). Other common stone tools used during this time included scrapers for preparing animal hides, borers or drills to cut holes in hard stone, and grinding stones used to crush grain in order to make flour.

Stone tools were also a basic part of the stonemason's tool kit. Removing hard stones from quarries required the use of tools made of even harder stone. After cutting the stones, masons used stone pounders and grinders to shape and smooth them. Drills with stone bits were used to cut INSCRIPTIONS and create delicate details in sculpture. Sand was used for the final polishing of stones for buildings or artwork. (*See also* **Art, Artisans, and Artists; Bas-Reliefs; Fortifications; Palaces and Temples; Walled Cities.**)

SUDAN

The Sudan is a region that stretches across north central Africa south of the Libyan and Sahara Deserts. The term *Sudan,* which also refers to a present-day country in Africa that lies directly south of Egypt, derives from the Arabic term *bilad as-sudan,* which means "land of the black peoples."

The Sudan extends from the western coast of Africa across the continent to the mountains of Ethiopia. The northernmost part of the Sudan, a region known as the Sahel, borders the Sahara. South of the Sahel, the Sudan extends southward into the rain forests near the equator. The region consists of tropical or subtropical grasslands and high plateaus, which extend across the continent. Temperatures are high throughout the year, and the region experiences a long dry season. However, the southern Sudan receives more rainfall than the north and contains forests with small trees that grow among tall grasses. In the north, the region is arid and desertlike.

* **archaeological** referring to the study of past human cultures, usually by excavating material remains of human activity

Humans have occupied the Sudan since prehistoric times, particularly along the NILE RIVER. Archaeological* expeditions have provided evidence that people in the region were hunting, gathering, and fishing as early as 9000 B.C. In the desert regions of the northwestern Sudan, there is evidence that from around 9500 B.C. until around 3500 B.C., the climate was wetter than it is today. During that period, the predominant

* **fourth millennium** B.C. years from 4000 to 3001 B.C.

mode of subsistence in the region was fishing, supplemented by hunting hippopotamus, rhinoceros, and buffalo.

In ancient times, the Sudan was part of ancient Nubia and home to the Nubians, a people whose history is closely linked with that of ancient Egypt. During the fourth millennium B.C.*, the Egyptians took control of the northern Sudan, a region they called Wawat. Soon the Egyptian armies began to move farther south into the Sudan, conquering a region known as Kush. The Egyptians valued Kush because it was located along TRADE ROUTES that ran to the Red Sea. Around 1000 B.C., the rulers of Kush and the Nubian armies joined forces and regained their independence from Egypt. The Kushites retained control of much of the Sudan until the A.D. 350s, when they were overthrown by invaders from the Ethiopian highlands.

* **deity** god or goddess

Throughout ancient times, the Nubians were influenced by Egyptian cultural practices, but their local culture continued to flourish. They worshiped Egyptian gods but continued to worship their own deities* as well. Like the Egyptians, they constructed PYRAMIDS for their royal tombs but modified the design. After the Assyrians drove them out of Egypt, the Nubians had far less contact with Egypt. Over time, the Sudan was more influenced by the African cultures to its south. (*See also* **Kush and Meroë; Nubia and the Nubians.**)

SUMER AND THE SUMERIANS

Scholars credit the Sumerians with creating the world's first true civilization, and indeed the list of their accomplishments is impressive. Sumer, located in the southernmost region of MESOPOTAMIA (present-day Iraq), is considered the birthplace of WRITING, CITIES AND CITY-STATES, SCHOOLS, the WHEEL, large-scale ARCHITECTURE, and the earliest system of numbers. Sumerian civilization had a major impact on the political and cultural development of the entire Near East.

POLITICAL HISTORY OF SUMER

* **archaeologist** scientist who studies past human cultures, usually by excavating material remains of human activity

Sumer's origins are largely lost to history and can only be guessed at on the basis of the work of archaeologists*. It is clear that an advanced culture was well established in southern Mesopotamia long before the time of the earliest surviving written records (ca. 3300 B.C.). Most theories about the organization of that society are based on knowledge of later Sumerian civilization. While this provides a general picture of the development of Sumerian culture, many gaps remain.

Earliest Roots. The Sumerians probably included people who migrated to Mesopotamia from various places and had different origins. The earliest known settlement in Sumer was established before 5000 B.C. at Tell el-Oueili. Although the oldest remains found at the settlement are unlike other sites excavated in Sumer, the remains of later buildings at the site show strong similarities to architecture at the cities of UR and ERIDU. This suggests that a common culture developed and eventually

During the 3000s B.C., Sumer was the site of many important historical developments, including the urbanization of such sites as Uruk. By the beginning of the 2000s B.C., several cities and city-states had been established in ancient Sumer. These early cities evolved from the small agricultural settlements that had developed along the banks of the Tigris and Euphrates Rivers and the coastline of the Persian Gulf. Since ancient times, however, that coastline has receded.

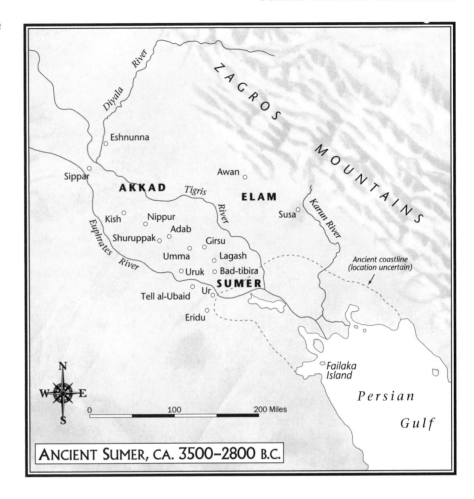

ANCIENT SUMER, CA. 3500–2800 B.C.

* **city-state** independent state consisting of a city and its surrounding land

spread throughout the region. During this early period, agricultural settlements were established along the banks of the Euphrates and Tigris Rivers, and these became the earliest cities. In fact, scholars believe that URUK, in Sumer, was the world's first city.

As the cities grew, they required more agricultural land to support their populations. After a time, larger cities became city-states* by taking control of surrounding territories. This eventually led to conflicts between neighboring city-states competing for territory, and many cities built defensive walls. By around 3000 B.C., Sumer contained about 30 separate city-states that remained independently ruled centers for many years.

Early Dynastic Period. Political conditions in Sumer began to change after about 2900 B.C. The first serious attempts by local rulers to extend their control over neighboring city-states occurred during this period. According to Sumerian texts, KISH was the seat of the first Sumerian kings. The Sumerian KING LIST credits Etana, ruler of Kish, with being the first king to unite the Sumerian city-states around 2800 B.C. However, the first king on the list for whom there is documentation is Enmebaragesi, who ruled Kish in about 2700 B.C.

Kish remained an important Sumerian city-state for several hundred years, although the rulers of the other city-states competed for power. This continued for several centuries until Lugalzagesi, the ruler of Umma,

101

Sumer and the Sumerians

conquered Lagash and secured control over northern Sumer in the 2300s B.C. He then turned south, capturing Ur, Uruk, and Eridu. Lugalzagesi became the first leader to unite all of Sumer. However, his achievement proved short-lived.

Sargon and the Akkadian Empire. In about 2334 B.C., Sargon I became the king of Kish and set out to take control of Sumer. Sargon, a Semite rather than a Sumerian, whose origins are the subject of legend and fable, had held an important position at the court of the king of Kish. When the king died, Sargon succeeded him and moved the capital to the city of Akkad. Sargon first conquered the Elamites, a people living to the east of Mesopotamia in present-day Iran. He then turned south, capturing Lugalzagesi's capital at Uruk and destroying its walls. Sargon next conquered the remaining cities formerly ruled by Lugalzagesi. Having established himself as ruler of Sumer, he then turned his attention north and extended the empire as far as Anatolia (present-day Turkey). In the west, his forces captured city-states in Syria and present-day Lebanon, eventually reaching the Mediterranean Sea. Sargon became the first ruler to exert control over all of Mesopotamia, and his empire encompassed a large part of the ancient Near East.

Sargon died in about 2279 B.C., after a reign of 56 years. His successors, who remained in power for nearly 200 years, continued to expand the empire, although most of their efforts were aimed at securing TRADE ROUTES rather than conquering enemies. Despite the glories of the Akkadian empire, during most of its existence, it was engaged in warfare with cities that challenged Akkadian rule. During the mid-2100s B.C., the empire was weakened by disputes over succession to the throne. This was followed by a series of invasions by the nomadic* Gutians from the northeast. The Akkadians were toppled, and the Gutians controlled much of Sumer for about the next 100 years. Although the Gutians did not settle in Sumer, they ruled the region from outside.

Toward the end of Gutian rule, Lagash became a prominent city-state in Sumer. Its governor, Gudea (ruled ca. 2144–2124 B.C.), was one of the most notable leaders in Sumerian history. He undertook extensive building projects and engaged in trade with such far-off lands as Magan in present-day Oman.

The Third Dynasty of Ur. Around 2120 B.C., the king of Ur, Utu-khegal, defeated the Gutian general Tiriqan and ended Gutian control over Sumer. In doing so, he established the Third Dynasty of Ur. This series of kings, who ruled for more than 100 years, was the last native dynasty* to exercise control over Sumer. Utu-khegal was succeeded by his son Ur-Nammu, who ruled a region extending from the Persian Gulf to central Mesopotamia. During his reign, Ur-Nammu rebuilt many of Sumer's temples and palaces and repaired canals and other important structures that had fallen into disrepair under the Gutians.

After Ur-Nammu's death, the throne passed to his son Shulgi, who completed his father's conquest of the Gutians and continued Ur-Nammu's program of building and restoration. In the twentieth year of his rule, Shulgi undertook a massive reorganization of the kingdom. He

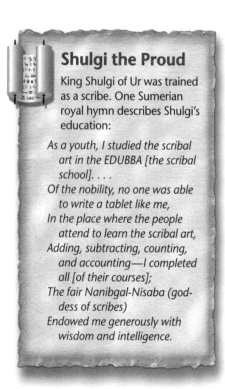

Shulgi the Proud

King Shulgi of Ur was trained as a scribe. One Sumerian royal hymn describes Shulgi's education:

As a youth, I studied the scribal art in the EDUBBA [the scribal school]. . . .
Of the nobility, no one was able to write a tablet like me,
In the place where the people attend to learn the scribal art,
Adding, subtracting, counting, and accounting—I completed all [of their courses];
The fair Nanibgal-Nisaba (goddess of scribes)
Endowed me generously with wisdom and intelligence.

* **nomadic** referring to people who travel from place to place to find food and pasture

* **dynasty** succession of rulers from the same family or group

* **scribe** person of a learned class who served as a writer, editor, or teacher

* **famine** severe lack of food due to failed crops

* **cult** system of religious beliefs and rituals; group following these beliefs
* **deity** god or goddess

* **patron** special guardian, protector, or supporter

* **pantheon** all the gods of a particular culture

restructured the tax system by collecting goods at central points and redistributing them throughout the empire. He also established schools to train the scribes* needed to run this complex system. Shulgi established a permanent army to extend Ur's influence and protect its trading interests. After his almost 50-year reign, however, his successors could not hold the kingdom together. Ur was threatened from two sides: by the nomadic Amorites from the west and the Elamites from the east. Around 2000 B.C., in the twenty-fourth year of the reign of King Ibbi-Sin, the city fell to the Elamites.

After the fall of the Third Dynasty of Ur, Sumer was loosely held together by a series of rulers from the cities of Isin and Larsa. For about the next 100 years, Sumer suffered from famines* and further invasions by the Elamites and other peoples from Iran. The Amorite ruler of the city-state of Larsa captured both Ur and Uruk, and the Elamites captured Isin. For the next 200 years, Sumer remained a patchwork of rival cities with no strong central authority. This marked the end of Sumerian control over southern Mesopotamia.

SUMERIAN SOCIETY

Sumerian government, economics, and religion were woven closely. Rulers held political power by controlling goods produced in fields and in workshops that were owned and managed by the temples. Many kings served as priests of the temple, and a few, such as Shulgi, even declared themselves gods. Most of the people of the Sumerian city-states were thus bound to the king by ties of both religion and economics.

Government. Sumerian city-states were probably originally governed by citizen assemblies rather than kings. The assemblies resolved disputes, authorized construction projects, and dealt with threats from neighboring city-states. They elected leaders who were responsible for ensuring that their decisions were carried out. Over time, these leaders became the most important people in their respective city-states. Political leadership also became associated with the local religious cult*, and rulers claimed to be chosen specifically by their city's deity*. Whether a leader called himself governor or king, he maintained legitimate authority through his ties to the local cult. If a leader was overthrown or defeated by his enemies, the Sumerians believed that he was no longer favored by the city's deity.

Religion. Political and religious power in Sumer were associated in other ways as well. According to Sumerian beliefs, each deity made his or her home in a different city, becoming the patron* god or goddess there. Each city was thus the home of a religious cult dedicated to a local god or goddess.

The Sumerians had a large pantheon* led by ANU, the supreme deity who called Uruk home. Other deities included ENLIL, who was both a god of plenty and a god of harsh justice, and Enki, the god of wisdom and of the sea. Ur was home to Nanna, the moon god; and Utu, the sun god, was worshiped in both Larsa and Sippar. The most important female deity was

Sumer and the Sumerians

See color plate 8, vol. 1.

* **artisan** skilled craftsperson

Inanna, a goddess whose many associations included fertility and war. Myths about these and other Sumerian gods make up an important part of the literature of Sumer.

Economy. The temple was the focus of not only the religious life of a Sumerian city but also its economic life. Temples controlled large amounts of agricultural land outside the city and ran workshops and warehouses within its walls. Temples employed farmers, shepherds, and artisans* in addition to priests and other religious officials. Workers in temple workshops created pottery, wove fabric, produced leather goods, and created sculpture, jewelry, and other works of art. Some of these goods were used in sacrifices to the local deity, while most were distributed to the royal household as well as to ordinary citizens. Many of the finer materials produced were used as trade goods. The Sumerian city-states actively engaged in long-distance trade, establishing colonies as far away as Iran, Syria, and Anatolia. They traded for goods such as timber, metals, and precious stones that were not available locally.

Through the temples, the city provided its inhabitants with the basic necessities of life. In return, the people were required to work every day of the week and to honor the local deity with sacrifices and obedience to the city's ruler. The temple did not control the entire economy, however. There is evidence that some land surrounding each city-state was owned and worked by private individuals. The cities themselves were also centers of private economic production. Pottery making, textile production, metalworking, shipbuilding, carpentry, and other specialized activities flourished in the cities.

The priest-king is a figure associated with the development of urbanization and temple-based administration. These developments first occurred in the city-state of Uruk in ancient Sumer. The cylinder seal impression shown here dates from the late fourth millennium B.C. Uruk and depicts a priest-king wearing a full beard and a calf-length kilt.

ARCHITECTURE, ART, AND LITERATURE

The Sumerians were accomplished architects who built the world's earliest monumental structures. Few identifiable remains still stand because

* **mud brick** brick made from mud, straw, and water mixed together and baked in the sun

* **buttress** brick or stone structure built against a wall to support or reinforce it

See color plate 14, vol. 3.

* **inlay** fine layer of a substance set into wood, metal, or other material as a form of decoration

* **relief** sculpture in which material is cut away to show figures raised from the background

* **epic** long poem about a legendary or historical hero, written in a grand style

buildings in Sumer were not made of stone (a scarce resource there) but of dried mud bricks*, which did not last. The most important buildings were the temples, which were built following a basic plan. Temples sat on raised platforms and their large outside walls were supported with buttresses*. The interiors might be decorated with clay cones set into the wall in patterns. The cones were painted in bright colors, and their tips were often covered in bronze. Murals were sometimes painted on the walls as well. Around 2100 B.C., King Ur-Nammu of Ur constructed the first true ziggurat, or stepped pyramid that supports a temple at the top. Ziggurats are the most famous large Mesopotamian buildings. The largest ziggurats rose some 300 feet high. Scholars know less about ordinary buildings, such as workshops and HOUSES, because few of them remain intact today.

Sumerian art is largely represented by SCULPTURE, which served mainly religious purposes. These works were often beautifully executed and richly decorated with inlays* of precious metals or stones. Carved relief* sculptures were another favored form of decoration on buildings. Sumerians also produced beautifully carved cylinder SEALS containing both decorative patterns and scenes of animals, humans, and gods. These seals were used to make impressions in clay bands used to secure doors and storage jars. The patterns were also impressed in CLAY TABLETS containing business transactions perhaps as a form of personal identification similar to a signature.

The Sumerians' most important cultural contribution was the invention of writing and the SUMERIAN LANGUAGE, which was rarely spoken after about 2000 B.C. The Sumerian script, called CUNEIFORM, consisted of wedge-shaped marks impressed in clay with a reed pen, or stylus. The symbols were originally developed for RECORD KEEPING and evolved into symbols to represent different syllables. The flexibility of this system made it ideal for recording the business of running a city-state. Tens of thousands of clay tablets have been recovered from Sumer, most of which are records of temple business transactions and palace archives.

Many works of Sumerian literature have also survived, including royal HYMNS and epics* celebrating the deeds of a ruler. The best-known Sumerian literature features GILGAMESH, a legendary ruler of Uruk. Among the earliest tales known about Gilgamesh are several Sumerian poems that were probably composed around 2100 B.C. However, the version of Gilgamesh's story that survives today is a rewrite of a version written in the Akkadian language. (*See also* **Languages; Religion; Ziggurats.**)

SUMERIAN LANGUAGE

The early inhabitants of southern MESOPOTAMIA, known as the Sumerians, developed the world's first WRITING sometime before 3000 B.C. Sumerian was written in a CUNEIFORM script, which consisted of wedge-shaped characters that had specific word meanings, and these were pressed into CLAY TABLETS. The written form of the language was based on the spoken form. Although spoken Sumerian faded away as a "living" language by about 1800 B.C., written Sumerian continued to be used by scribes* and priests perhaps as late as the A.D. 200s.

Sumerian Language

* **scribe** person of a learned class who served as a writer, editor, or teacher

* **city-state** independent state consisting of a city and its surrounding territory

* **Semitic** of or relating to a language family that includes Akkadian, Aramaic, Arabic, Hebrew, and Phoenician

* **dynasty** succession of rulers from the same family or group

* **linguist** person who studies languages

History of the Language. The oldest evidence of written Sumerian, called Archaic Sumerian, dates from about 3100 to 2500 B.C. and consists largely of governmental and business documents and also some school exercises. Scholars do not have a good understanding of this language, and the number of texts from this era is quite small. More documents exist in Old or Classical Sumerian, which dates from about 2500 to 2300 B.C. Most examples of Old Sumerian come from the official records of the city-state* of LAGASH. A fairly large number of private letters and INSCRIPTIONS written in Old Sumerian have also been found. The greater quantity of samples has made it easier for scholars to understand Old Sumerian than Archaic Sumerian.

From about 2350 to 2193 B.C., the Akkadians ruled southern Mesopotamia, and their Semitic* language—Akkadian—replaced Sumerian as the main spoken language throughout most of the region. Sumerian was again used as the written language after the Akkadian empire collapsed and the Third Dynasty of Ur (ca. 2112–2004 B.C.) was established. By 2000 B.C., however, this dynasty* was destroyed by invasions by the Elamites, peoples from the east of Mesopotamia. Within the next 200 years, spoken Sumerian vanished completely. The new rulers of Mesopotamia continued to use written Sumerian alongside Akkadian.

Among those who employed written Sumerian were the Babylonians, who established an empire that extended across much of the Near East. They and the empires that succeeded them brought written Sumerian with them into the regions they controlled. This stage of the language's development is called Post-Sumerian because it occurred after the disappearance of spoken Sumerian. As in the earlier stages of its development, Sumerian was used for government and business documents as well as royal inscriptions. It was during this period that most of the great Sumerian works of LITERATURE were recorded in writing. Because written Sumerian was so important as the language of business and government, schools that trained scribes continued to teach it until about A.D. 200. After that time, it was replaced by more modern languages, such as Greek and Latin, and its use—even in written form—ceased altogether.

Characteristics of the Language. Scholars have tried without success to place Sumerian within one of the existing language families. Some linguists* have attempted to relate it to modern languages based on broad similarities between the sounds and meanings of some words. However, these attempts have failed, and most scholars now consider Sumerian a unique language with no close relatives.

The form of written Sumerian most familiar to modern scholars had 4 vowels (a, e, i, and u) and 16 consonants, but it is thought that the language was originally more complex. Based on the information available about written Sumerian, linguists have tried to reconstruct the sound and pronunciation of spoken Sumerian. However, much of this work is based on knowledge of the Akkadian language, which itself depends on knowledge of modern Semitic languages such as Hebrew and Arabic. Given this fact, any modern pronunciation of Sumerian would most likely be vastly different from the original. An ancient Sumerian hearing a modern person speak the language would probably not be able to understand it.

Close study of the existing documents has revealed much about the structure and style of the Sumerian language. Nouns were not classified as masculine or feminine, but were divided into personal and nonpersonal types. Personal nouns included those referring to humans, gods, or (in literature) creatures that had human characteristics. There was no fixed way to indicate amount or the plural form of an inanimate noun. Sometimes a noun was repeated twice to indicate all of one class of objects. For instance *kur* meant "land," while *kur-kur* meant "all the lands." Otherwise, amount could only be determined from the way a word was used. Similarly, verbs had just one form, which might be modified by a prefix, suffix, or infix (an affix appearing in the body of a word) to indicate who was performing an action or when the action occurred.

There were several styles of written Sumerian, depending on the type of material being composed. The writers of business and government documents used certain words and phrases, while the authors of POETRY, prose literature, or HYMNS used different ones. Sumerian even had a separate style called *emesal* used to quote female speech. However, it remains unclear why this variant of the language developed or in what situations it was used. (*See also* **Alphabets; Books and Manuscripts; Decipherment; Ethnic and Language Groups; Languages; Record Keeping; Sumer and the Sumerians.**)

SUN

* **stela** stone slab or pillar that has been carved or engraved and serves as a monument; *pl.* stelae

* **deity** god or goddess

Throughout the ancient Near East, the sun occupied a particularly important place in RELIGION and MYTHOLOGY because of its connection with life, death, and rebirth. It provided the light and warmth that plants, animals, and people needed to survive. Each day it died, sinking below the horizon as it was conquered by the night. However, every morning it was reborn to once again bring light and life to the universe. As the symbol of light and day, the sun represented goodness and life, while night and darkness represented evil and death.

In Mesopotamian society, eclipses of the sun were considered OMENS, or signs that something bad was about to happen. The Mesopotamians worshiped a sun god named Shamash, who represented justice. In this capacity, he is portrayed on a stela* giving the symbols of rulership to King HAMMURABI. Sun gods also held important places in other ancient Near Eastern societies. The Hittites worshiped the sun god of Heaven and the sun goddess of Arinna.

Some of the most powerful Egyptian deities* were sun gods whose names corresponded to their many forms, or manifestations. These names included Ra, ATEN, and HORUS, the falcon god whose eye was associated with the sun. The rising and setting of the sun had profound significance for the Egyptians. Each night the sun god journeyed below the horizon to the underworld on a sacred barge, or raft. His soul traveled along a river that was the underworld's counterpart to the NILE RIVER in Egypt. There his soul was reunited with his body, symbolizing the rebirth of all the souls of the dead. This also signified the joining of Ra and OSIRIS, god of the dead, into a new deity containing aspects of both gods. As morning approached, the sun began its journey back to the sky, signaling the return of life to the

Susa and Susiana

land. Each morning at dawn, a priest lit a ritual torch to signify the sun's triumph over death and its importance to Egypt's welfare and future success. The Egyptians developed a complex series of rituals to ensure the continued order of the universe, represented by the regular reappearance of the sun each day.

The worship of the sun god in Egypt reached its peak during the reign of the pharaoh* Amenhotep IV (ca. 1353–1336 B.C.), also known as AKHENATEN. Amenhotep outlawed the worship of all other gods besides the sun god Aten. He even changed his own name to Akhenaten, which means "he who serves Aten," to signify his devotion to the god. This reform was not accepted by many Egyptians, and Egypt returned to polytheism, or the worship of many gods, after Akhenaten's death. (*See also* **Gods and Goddesses; Rituals and Sacrifice; Theology.**)

* **pharaoh** king of ancient Egypt

* **fourth millennium B.C.** years from 4000 to 3001 B.C.

See map on inside covers.

Susiana was an ancient region in southwestern IRAN. Its major city, Susa, had a long and illustrious history, serving at one time as a capital of Elam and later as a capital of the PERSIAN EMPIRE. Both the region and the city played a significant role in the history of Iran.

By about 7000 B.C., permanent settlements began to be established in many parts of Susiana, and the city of Susa was founded around 4200 B.C. During the late fourth millennium B.C.*, Susa's culture began to resemble that of Sumer, with the use of cylinder seals, counting tokens enclosed in hollow clay balls (bullae), and a cuneiform-like accounting and writing system called Proto-Elamite, which was written on clay tablets. In the late third millennium B.C., Susa and Susiana were dominated both culturally and politically by the Akkadians, who also dominated MESOPOTAMIA.

After the collapse of the Akkadian empire around 2193 B.C., Susa and Susiana fell under the control of the Mesopotamian kingdom of UR. Around 2004 B.C., the Susians allied themselves with the neighboring Elamites, invaded Mesopotamia, and reasserted their independence. Thereafter, the Susians became closely tied to the Elamites, who took control of and ruled Susa and Susiana. For the next 1,400 years, Susiana was an integral part of the Elamite civilization.

As a royal capital and center of commerce, Susa developed into a large and important international city. Around 1500 B.C., for reasons unknown, the city entered a period of decline and was abandoned by most of its occupants. However, Susa regained prominence about 300 years later, when the Elamite empire reached the peak of its power and supremacy.

Around 1110 B.C., Susa was conquered by the Babylonians, marking the beginning of another period of decline. Little is known about Susa or Susiana for the next 300 years except that political unrest and economic disaster plagued the region. In the late 700s B.C., Elamite power reemerged. At that time, Elam and Susiana became allies of the Babylonians and engaged in frequent conflicts with the Assyrians. Thereafter, Susa served primarily as a ceremonial and cultural center rather than a political or economic one.

In about 646 B.C., King ASHURBANIPAL of Assyria renewed attacks on Susiana. He conquered and sacked* the city of Susa and relocated the

* **sack** to loot a captured city

Excavations at Susa have provided archaeologists with a good idea of how that city may have appeared in ancient times. Among their discoveries is the acropolis (shown here), where cultic activities took place. At the foot of the acropolis, archaeologists have found palacelike homes that belonged to prominent individuals.

* **Levant** lands bordering the eastern shores of the Mediterranean Sea (present-day Syria, Lebanon, and Israel), the West Bank, and Jordan

* **satrapy** portion of Persian-controlled territory under the rule of a satrap, or provincial governor

survivors to the Levant*. This effectively ended the history of the Elamite state. Susa and Susiana remained in Assyrian control until Ashurbanipal's death in 630 B.C. Thereafter, Assyrian power in the region began to decline.

By 550 B.C., the Persians had gained control of Susa and Susiana, and the region became a satrapy* of the Persian empire. The Persian king DAR-IUS I fortified Susa and made it one of his capitals. Susa prospered under Persian rule and became one of the most important cities of the empire. It had magnificent palaces and temples and once again served as a great cultural, political, and economic center.

After the conquest of the Persian empire by ALEXANDER THE GREAT in 331 B.C., Susa lost much of its power and dominance, and the city was renamed Selucia on the Eulaeus. With the rise of PARTHIA after 250 B.C., Susa regained its former name and prospered yet again. Although it never regained its former greatness, Susa continued to flourish as a regional center for many centuries afterward. (*See also* **Assyria and the Assyrians; Babylonia and the Babylonians; Elam and the Elamites; Seleucid Empire.**)

Syllabaries

See *Writing*.

SYRIA

* **city-state** independent state consisting of a city and its surrounding territory

Throughout ancient times, Syria was an object of conquest and was often dominated by foreign powers. Along with Mesopotamia and Egypt, Syria was an early center of civilization in the ancient Near East. However, the civilization that developed there was somewhat different from that of the other two regions. Instead of large, unified kingdoms and empires, Syria consisted of small kingdoms and city-states*, many of which were based on loyalty within tribes rather than territory. Consequently, the inhabitants of Syria were never able to achieve any kind of political unity except in small areas of the total region.

Syria

* **Levant** lands bordering the eastern shores of the Mediterranean Sea (present-day Syria, Lebanon, and Israel), the West Bank, and Jordan

* **arable** suitable for growing crops

* **domesticated** adapted or tamed for human use

Located at the crossroads of the ancient Near East, Syria boasts some of the earliest towns and cities of the region, including Ugarit and Ebla. However, because the landscape is relatively open, ancient Syria was vulnerable to invasions by neighboring powers, including those in Mesopotamia, Egypt, and Anatolia. Consequently, throughout ancient times, invaders targeted Syrian cities, resulting in their conquest or destruction.

GEOGRAPHY AND EARLY DEVELOPMENT

Located in the Levant*, ancient Syria was home to many natural land routes that connect western Asia with both Africa and Europe. Although protected by the Mediterranean Sea to the west and the Anatolian plateau to the north, ancient Syria lay exposed to the plains of Mesopotamia to the east and Arabia to the south. These geographic factors left Syria open to invasion and the target of many conquests.

The Syrian landscape consists of mountains, plateaus, fertile grasslands, and desert. The westernmost part is a coastal plain, which in ancient times contained a number of important cities, including UGARIT and the Phoenician city-states of BYBLOS, SIDON, and TYRE. Although Syria had limited natural resources, much of the land was arable*.

Inhabited for thousands of years by people who were hunters and gatherers, Syria later played a significant role in the early development of AGRICULTURE. A number of plants and animals were first domesticated* in Syria—including wheat, barley, rye, SHEEP, CATTLE, GOATS, and PIGS—and their domestication contributed to the development of farming in the region as early as 8300 B.C.

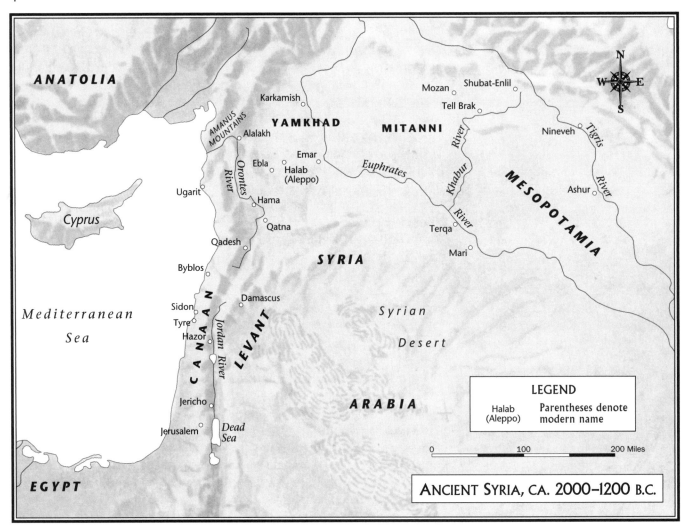

ANCIENT SYRIA, CA. 2000–1200 B.C.

LEGEND

Halab (Aleppo) — Parentheses denote modern name

The development of agriculture supported an increase in population and the spread of village life in Syria. This led, in turn, to the emergence of towns as settlements grew larger and became centers of manufacture and trade. Some of the earliest towns in the ancient Near East were established in Syria, and towns and cities remained the focus of political development throughout much of the region's later history.

Even with the development of larger settlements, many people in Syria continued to live in small villages scattered across the region. In addition, groups of nomads* traveled the area in search of grazing land for their herds of cattle, sheep, and goats. This mix of lifestyles contributed to the development of two different political systems in ancient Syria: centralized states that developed around large cities and decentralized tribal societies that were characteristic of villages and nomadic groups.

HISTORY

Although distinct cultures emerged in Syria, the numerous invasions that occurred in its history left their mark on its people. The people of Syria found themselves under foreign rule many times.

Early History. By the 2500s B.C., an urban culture similar to that of Mesopotamia had emerged in Syria. One of the most important Syrian city-states of this period was EBLA, which dominated much of northern Syria for about 200 years. A number of port cities on Syria's Mediterranean coast traded with Ebla, but they were not politically dependent on it.

In about 2320 B.C., the Sumerian city-state of URUK in Mesopotamia extended its power westward across Syria to the Mediterranean Sea. Uruk's influence over Syria was short-lived, however. Within the next few decades, SARGON I of Akkad and his grandson NARAM-SIN invaded Syria, sacked Ebla, and incorporated the region into the Akkadian empire. Following the collapse of the Akkadian empire, city life in Syria almost disappeared, and most people returned to living in small, temporary settlements. This decline of urban culture in Syria lasted for about a century.

Between about 2100 and 1800 B.C., groups of nomadic peoples known as the AMORITES appeared in Syria and established a number of small kingdoms and city-states. By about 1800 B.C., urban culture was once again flourishing, and many cities had become the centers of small, independent states. One of the most powerful states during this period was Yamkhad, which had its capital at Halab (present-day Aleppo). The kings of Yamkhad dominated a number of minor rulers and tribal leaders in northern Syria, but a few cities remained independent, including KARKAMISH and Qatna. Various tribal societies also continued to exist, and their unruliness and demands for freedom from interference by centralized powers often caused problems for Syrian rulers.

Invasion and Foreign Rule. Around 1600 B.C., parts of northern Syria suffered great destruction at the hands of the invading HITTITES from ANATOLIA (present-day Turkey). Hittite control of northern Syria was short-lived, however. In its wake, a new power—the HURRIANS—gained control of the region.

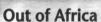
* **nomad** person who travels from place to place to find food and pasture

Out of Africa

Evidence suggests that the ancestors of modern humans migrated out of Africa more than a million years ago. Because of Syria's location at the crossroads of Africa, Asia, and Europe, these ancient ancestors no doubt traveled through the region on their way to other lands. The discovery of primitive stone axes and other tools dating from at least 250,000 years ago provides evidence of early habitation in Syria. Scholars also have evidence that early Neanderthal peoples inhabited Syria almost continuously between about 100,000 and 35,000 years ago.

111

For some time, Hurrian tribes from the mountains of eastern Anatolia and western IRAN migrated to northern Syria and established settlements throughout that region. In many places, they comprised the majority of the population. Soon they gained political control over the Amorites and established Hurrian kingdoms throughout Syria.

The most important Hurrian kingdom was Mitanni, located in upper Mesopotamia and eastern Syria. At the peak of its power, the kingdom of Mitanni ruled almost all of northern and central Syria. Its presence in the region effectively blocked other foreign intruders from entering Syria, at least until Mitanni clashed with Egypt in the mid-1400s B.C.

Conflicts between Mitanni and Egypt ended peacefully when the two powers decided to divide Syria between them. They reached this agreement because of the Hittites, whose renewed strength posed a serious threat to the interests of Egypt and Mitanni. In the mid-1300s B.C., the Hittites defeated Mitanni and pushed the Egyptians back to southern Syria. Ultimately, the Hittites and Egyptians agreed to divide Syria just as Egypt and Mitanni had done earlier.

Under both the Egyptians and the Hittites, most of the small kingdoms and city-states in Syria served as vassals*. Although they had little power to pursue independent foreign policies, local rulers often had significant authority to deal with their internal affairs. However, rivalries among the various Syrian states made it difficult for them to act in unison on any issues.

A PERIOD OF CHANGE

Syria's history continued to be marked by foreign conquests. Sometimes the invaders were large empires acquiring more territories and resources. At other times, migrating peoples and nomadic tribes came to settle in Syria.

Upheaval and Change. In the late 1200s B.C., invasions by the SEA PEOPLES appear to have caused great change and upheaval in Syria and the Levant. In many parts of Syria, urban life declined dramatically as people moved away from cities to the countryside. Some cities, such as Ugarit, disappeared forever. Meanwhile, large numbers of people from Anatolia fled ahead of the invaders and migrated to Syria. These migrants, who became known as NEO-HITTITES, established a number of small states in northern Syria.

In the 1100s B.C., the ARAMAEANS—a group of Semitic* peoples—appeared in Syria. Over the next few centuries, they spread throughout the region and came to play an important role in Syrian history. The rise of Aramaean civilization led to the reintroduction of tribal rule. In time, however, the Aramaeans established centralized states with ruling dynasties* of tribal origin. The principal Aramaean kingdom in Syria was DAMASCUS.

Beginning in the 800s B.C., the fate of Syria became linked with empires to the east: Assyria, Babylonia, and Persia. During the 800s B.C., the Assyrians launched repeated military campaigns against Syria, and by the next century, the entire region had been conquered. Some Syrian kingdoms became vassal states ruled by local kings. Others, including Damascus, were incorporated into the Assyrian empire as provinces governed by Assyrian officials.

* **vassal** individual or state that swears loyalty and obedience to a greater power

* **Semitic** of or relating to people of the Near East or northern Africa, including the Assyrians, Babylonians, Phoenicians, Jews, and Arabs

* **dynasty** succession of rulers from the same family or group

Consistent with Syria's location at the crossroads of the ancient Near East, Syrian art was influenced by that of neighboring cultures. Dating from the 800s B.C., this statue of Aramaean king Addu-yisi from near present-day Tell Halaf displays Syrian, Aramaean, and Assyrian artistic elements.

Although the Assyrians' domination of Syria lasted for less than 150 years, the region forever bore their name, for *Syria* is a shortened form of *Assyria*. Before the end of the 700s B.C., invasions of northern Mesopotamia by the Cimmerians and Scythians from Russia weakened the Assyrians, and in the late 600s B.C., Assyria fell to attacks from the Babylonians and the MEDES of Iran. After the fall of the Assyrian empire, Syria became a battleground in a struggle between Egypt and Babylonia for control of the Levant. In the end, Syria fell under Babylonia's control for about 50 years.

Later History. In 539 B.C., the Persians conquered BABYLON and took control of Syria, which became a satrapy, or province, of the PERSIAN EMPIRE. While local dynasties continued to rule in some coastal cities, most of Syria was governed by loyal Persian officials appointed by the satrap, or provincial governor.

Taharqa

Persian rule of Syria was mostly peaceful, although the Persians occasionally had to put down local revolts. The Persians did not allow political independence, but they permitted the local cultures of Syria to develop with little interference. Syrians could practice their own religion and carry out their own trading activities. Syrian coastal cities were even free to establish colonies along other parts of the Mediterranean coast. As a result of such policies, Persia had little influence on Syrian culture during the 200 years of its rule.

In 331 B.C., ALEXANDER THE GREAT of MACEDONIA conquered the Persian empire and gained control of Syria. After his death in 323 B.C., the region was divided between Alexander's generals and their successors, the Seleucids and the Ptolemies. These two dynasties often competed for control of Syria, and conflicts erupted between them a number of times.

The occupation of Syria by the Seleucids, ruling from Antioch, marked a significant change in Syria's history. For the next several centuries, the fate of the region became increasingly linked to the West instead of the Near East. During the Hellenistic* period, Syrian society was strongly influenced by Greek-style culture. The region also became involved in international political and economic affairs, which brought Syria prosperity and led to urbanization*. Hellenistic culture, prosperity, and urbanization continued under the Romans, who took control of Syria in 64 B.C. and incorporated it as a province of the Roman Empire. (*See also* **Akkad and the Akkadians; Animals, Domestication of; Assyria and the Assyrians; Babylonia and the Babylonians; Cities and City-States; Egypt and the Egyptians; Hellenistic World; Migration and Deportation; Nomads and Nomadism; Phoenicia and the Phoenicians; Scythia and the Scythians; Sumer and the Sumerians; Trade Routes.**)

* **Hellenistic** referring to the Greek-influenced culture of the Mediterranean world and western Asia during the three centuries after the death of Alexander the Great in 323 B.C.

* **urbanization** formation and growth of cities

TAHARQA

**ruled 690–664 B.C.
Egyptian pharaoh**

Taharqa (tuh•HAHR•kuh) was the fifth Nubian king in Egypt's Twenty-fifth Dynasty. He is best known as the king who lost Egypt to the Assyrians. Despite his unsuccessful military leadership, Taharqa is considered the greatest of builders.

Taharqa inherited the thrones of Nubia and Egypt at the age of 32 after the death of his cousin (or nephew) Shebitku. Around 674 B.C., Taharqa fought off the invading Assyrians, led by King ESARHADDON. Three years later, Esarhaddon returned and successfully conquered northern Egypt, including the capital at MEMPHIS. However, Esarhaddon foolishly left the conquered territory in the hands of a few Assyrian military officers, and Taharqa was able to reconquer the region. Nevertheless, in 669 B.C., Esarhaddon's son and successor, ASHURBANIPAL, returned to Egypt and drove Taharqa into Nubia. Taharqa, who was never able to reconquer Egypt, died in Nubia and was buried in a pyramid in the cemetery of Nuri. He was succeeded by his nephew Tantamani.

During his reign, Taharqa sponsored more building projects than any other Nubian ruler. He adorned the Great Temple of Amun at KARNAK with new processional ways and commissioned other buildings nearby. In Nubia, he commissioned several new temples in the Egyptian style in the cities of Sanam, Kawa, and Pnuba. He also built several small temples in the northern province of Kush. (*See also* **Egypt and the Egyptians; Nubia and the Nubians; Sudan.**)

TAXATION

* **tribute** payment made by a smaller or weaker party to a more powerful one, often under the threat of force

* **vassal** individual or state that swears loyalty and obedience to a greater power

* **city-state** independent state consisting of a city and its surrounding territory

* **first millennium** B.C. years from 1000 to 1 B.C.

The rise of centralized states in the ancient Near East required sources of income for GOVERNMENTS, which had to pay for ARMIES and the construction of public works and to supply food to the people in times of need. Loot seized during military campaigns on foreign soil did not provide an income large enough or regular enough to support governments, and neither did tribute* collected from conquered territories or vassal* states. From the earliest days of centralized states, the solution to the financial needs of governments was some form of taxation in which people living in a state paid set amounts to the government. The government then determined how the income from taxes was to be spent or redistributed.

Payment and Collection of Taxes. Throughout much of the ancient period, people paid their taxes in kind, that is, in some form of goods rather than cash. The most direct form of taxation involved giving the government or its representatives a share of one's agricultural or craft production. Such taxes might consist of items such as grain, CATTLE, cloth, or other goods. In MESOPOTAMIA during the Third Dynasty of Ur (ca. 2112–2004 B.C.), the Sumerians maintained a large government animal pen near the city of NIPPUR. This place served as a clearinghouse for all sorts of in-kind payments, from GOATS to JEWELRY. The Mesopotamians also imposed a tax payment called *ishkaru* at NUZI in the 1400s B.C. This consisted primarily of finished goods, such as garments, arrows, chariots, or armor; in Assyria in the 800s B.C., it consisted of silver.

Labor was another kind of payment that could be regarded as a tax. Individuals, households, or villages might owe the government a certain number of days of work each year. Records from throughout Mesopotamia refer to a tax called the *ilku,* which was a labor tax owed by those who worked land owned by a higher authority. A tenant could assign someone else, such as a laborer on his property, to perform the *ilku.* As exchanges of precious metals become more common, some taxes were paid in such metals. For example, as early as the 2300s B.C., one ruler of the Sumerian city-state* of LAGASH required some taxes and fines to be paid in silver.

Governments collected taxes through various means. In some societies, the temples or the army were responsible for gathering or receiving tax payments. Eventually, the office of tax collector emerged and became an important administrative division in all governments. In outlying districts, provincial governors often were responsible for making the appropriate payments to the central government. By the first millennium B.C.*, a practice called tax farming—in which the government sold to the highest bidder the right to collect taxes in a region—had become a basic feature of the Babylonian and Persian administrations. Having paid the tax required by the government, the tax farmer or collector often tried to collect an additional amount from the individuals or communities within his territory and keep it as profit.

Technology

Types of Taxes. Because most ancient Near Eastern economies were based on AGRICULTURE, taxes on land and its products remained a key part of every state's overall income. According to the Hebrew BIBLE, for example, the prophet Samuel warned those Israelites who wanted a king that such a ruler would take a tenth of their crops and orchards.

Some of the most detailed accounts of land taxes come from Egypt, where land was valued and taxed according to the amount of benefit it received from the annual flooding of the NILE RIVER, which enriched the soil. Officials measured each parcel of land carefully to determine how much tax—in the form of grain—its owner owed to the temples or to the government. Priests, however, did not have to pay taxes on the land they owned, and this was true in early Mesopotamia as well.

Taxes paid by those who worked on or rented royal lands comprised a significant part of the income of the Mesopotamian state. One such tax, during the 2100s B.C., was the *gunmada,* a provincial tax owed by military men living on state-owned land on the outskirts of the kingdom. The *gunmada* was paid in cattle, delivered to the livestock pens near Nippur. Land taxes were commonly paid with grain, which served as a medium of exchange similar to money.

Land taxes were not the only taxes paid in the ancient Near East. Trade and commerce were taxed as well. For example, MERCHANTS carrying goods into or out of a state had to pay import or export taxes, or customs duties, on them. Governments also charged fees, tolls, or taxes for the use of canals and roads or for the privilege of traveling through a place or using a harbor. By the Hellenistic* period, Near Eastern governments had developed many forms of taxation. The Babylonians, for example, had a salt tax, a tax on the sale of slaves, a canal tax, and a sort of sales tax that consumers paid when they bought certain other products. The collection of these and other taxes was crucial to the administration of the state. (*See also* **Economy and Trade; Land Use and Ownership; Property and Property Rights; Record Keeping; Scribes.**)

* **Hellenistic** referring to the Greek-influenced culture of the Mediterranean world and western Asia during the three centuries after the death of Alexander the Great in 323 B.C.

| Technology | See *Science and Technology.* |

| Temples | See *Palaces and Temples.* |

TEN COMMANDMENTS

The Ten Commandments, which are recorded in the Hebrew BIBLE, form the ethical basis for Judaism, Christianity, and Islam. According to the Bible, these commandments were revealed to MOSES when YAHWEH spoke to him on Mount SINAI during the Israelites' journey from Egypt to Canaan. The Ten Commandments are also called the Decalogue, from the Greek words *deka* and *logoi,* which mean "ten words," and form the core of the contract between Yahweh and the Israelite people.

התשרקצצפעסנמלכיטחזהדגבאתשרקצצפעסנמלכידחטיטזהדוהגדבגנד

The Ten Commandments are recorded twice in the Hebrew Bible. They are listed in the Books of Exodus (Chapter 20) and Deuteronomy (Chapter 5). Although the circumstances of how Moses received these laws are slightly different depending on which book reports the event, the laws are essentially the same.

In the first two commandments, Yahweh tells the Israelites that he is their only God and that they should not worship other gods. The third and fourth rules state that the Israelites should not use Yahweh's name in a disrespectful manner and should observe the Sabbath (the day of rest and worship). The fifth commandment states that the Israelites should honor their parents. The last five commandments deal with ethics, saying that the Israelites should not murder, steal, commit adultery*, give false testimony, or desire their neighbors' possessions.

No one is certain when the Ten Commandments were written. Some scholars believe that they were composed between the 1500s and 1200s B.C. Others believe that they were written around 750 B.C. It is also possible that they were written even later as a summary of the ancient religious and legal traditions of the Israelites. The Ten Commandments did not carry new ideas except for statements about the uniqueness of God and the holiness of the Sabbath. Similar laws existed in almost all other ancient Near Eastern cultures. (*See also* **Hebrews and Israelites; Judaism and Jews; Law; Mosaic Law; Torah.**)

* **adultery** sexual relations between a married person and someone other than his or her spouse

TESHUB

* **second millennium B.C.** years from 2000 to 1001 B.C.
* **pantheon** all the gods of a particular culture
* **imperial** pertaining to an emperor or an empire

Teshub (TE•shub) was the storm god of the HURRIANS, a group who lived in northern MESOPOTAMIA and SYRIA during the second millennium B.C.* The HITTITES adopted him, as well as his wife KHEPAT, into their large and complex pantheon* and merged him with the traditional Hittite weather god, Tarkhun. During the Hittite imperial* period, which lasted from 1350 to 1200 B.C., Teshub was considered the ruler of the heavens and head of the Hittite pantheon. He was usually portrayed holding a mace (a clublike weapon with a pear-shaped end for striking) and sometimes a lightning bolt as well.

In a group of Hittite myths called the Kumarbi Cycle, Teshub appears as the son and enemy of KUMARBI, king of the Hittite gods. The Hittites adopted the mythology of the Kumarbi Cycle, like Teshub himself, from the Hurrians. The first tale in the cycle, titled *Theogony* (or *Heavenly Kingship*), tells how a series of four gods held the heavenly throne, each overthrowing the one before him. Finally, Teshub rises to power and prepares to overthrow the third king, Kumarbi. Unfortunately, the description of the battle has been lost. In the second tale, titled *Song of Ullikummi,* Kumarbi creates a stone monster named Ullikummi to destroy Teshub, but Teshub descends into the sea in his chariot to defeat the monster. A related myth, called the *Myth of Khedammu,* says that Kumarbi created a dragon named Khedammu, again to challenge Teshub. The dragon begins devouring humanity so that the people can no longer serve the gods. For a time it appears that "Teshub, the powerful king of Kummiya, will have to hold the plow himself." Because the rest of the myth is lost, the

Textiles

ending remains unknown. A later fragment of myth hints that Teshub's pride and violent nature were sources of trouble among the gods. (*See also* **Gods and Goddesses; Mythology.**)

TEXTILES

Textiles are fabrics of fiber or yarn that are made by hand or by machine. The production of textiles—for personal use and as articles of trade—was one of the most important activities in the ancient Near East. Documents from MESOPOTAMIA describe textile workshops that employed thousands of individuals, and textile manufacturing was often depicted in the WALL PAINTINGS and bas-reliefs* of ancient Egyptian tombs.

Despite the importance and extent of textile production in the Near East, few examples of ancient textiles have survived to the present day. Unlike durable materials, such as STONE, metal, and POTTERY, textiles rarely survived thousands of years of burial or exposure to the elements. Only in very dry regions, such as Egypt, have archaeologists* discovered remains of ancient textiles. Nevertheless, from ancient texts, artworks, and remains of weaving equipment from ancient workshops, scholars have gained some insight into the production and uses of textiles in the ancient Near East.

Origins and Use of Textiles. The earliest evidence of textile production in the Near East is a fragment of woven cloth from a site in ANATOLIA (present-day Turkey) dating from about 7000 B.C. Clay balls found in northeastern Mesopotamia dating from about the same time contain impressions of cloth that show the patterns of weaving. The quality of the workmanship evident from those impressions leaves little doubt that weaving was practiced long before that time. Scraps of fabric found at ÇATAL HÜYÜK in Anatolia show that mechanical weaving machines, or looms, were in use in that region by at least 6000 B.C. Evidence of textile production in Egypt suggests that it may have developed later there, perhaps around 4500 B.C.

The earliest textiles were made from linen, a fabric composed of fibers derived from FLAX. Flax grows naturally in many places throughout the region and was first domesticated* around 6000 B.C. Linen fabrics woven earlier than that must have been produced from wild flax. Although flax was the first fiber used for making textiles, wool eventually became the most widely used material in textile production. SHEEP were domesticated around 7000 B.C., but their coats were short and had little usable wool. Around 4000 B.C., breeders began to produce sheep with long woolly coats suitable for textile production.

Other natural textile fabrics were unknown in the Near East until much later. Hemp, used for textiles in northern and central Europe and Asia as early as 5000 B.C., did not reach the Near East until about 1000 B.C. Cotton was probably introduced to the region from India around the same time. Silk, first developed in China in the third millennium B.C.*, did not reach the ancient Near East until about 650 B.C.

Textiles served many functions. CLOTHING, tents, and similar items provided shelter and protection from the elements. Cloth sails helped propel ships, while burial shrouds covered the bodies of the dead. Colorful

Beautiful Old Rugs and Carpets

Perhaps the best-known textile products from the Near East today are beautifully woven rugs and carpets. The finest of these intricately patterned textiles were not woven on a loom but by hand, one knot at a time. In fact, archaeologists have found evidence of such carpets and the tools used to manufacture them in graves in Central Asia dating from about 2000 B.C. The earliest existing example of a pile carpet came from a tomb in Siberia dating from about 450 B.C. Unlike other decorative textiles from the ancient Near East, people from all levels of society probably used carpets.

material is cut away to leave figures projecting slightly from the background

* **archaeologist** scientist who studies past human cultures, usually by excavating material remains of human activity

* **domesticate** to adapt or tame for human use

* **third millennium** B.C. years from 3000 to 2001 B.C.

rugs, furniture coverings, wall hangings, and other textile items beautified palaces, temples, and homes, while textile containers were used to hold and carry everything from foods and personal belongings to weapons and tools. Textiles also served as a means of communicating values, status, and roles. For example, certain patterns, colors, and designs distinguished different groups or individuals.

Weaving and Dyeing. To produce textiles, ancient textile workers first stripped individual fibers from flax or wool and tied their ends together. The fibers were then soaked and softened. These softened fibers were spun into yarn that could be woven into cloth.

The earliest looms in the ancient Near East consisted of two wooden beams placed horizontally above the ground. A series of yarns were stretched between these beams. A weaver then passed bundles of yarn back and forth through those yarns at right angles to them to create a woven fabric of vertical and horizontal threads. By varying the color and arrangement of the yarns, the weaver could create different designs and patterns in the cloth.

Another type of loom, the vertical loom, appeared in Anatolia in the early third millennium B.C. This loom stood upright and relied on small weights of clay, stone, or metal to keep the vertical yarns tight. An even more advanced type of loom was the tapestry loom, which had spread from the CAUCASUS region to SYRIA by the middle of the third millennium B.C. Both vertical and tapestry looms allowed weavers to produce complex patterns and more types of weaves than horizontal looms. Although more difficult to operate, they were less tiring physically because the weaver did not have to squat or bend over to use them.

The earliest evidence of textile dyeing in the Near East dates from about 3000 B.C. The most commonly used coloring agents were natural dyes extracted from plants or animal-based dyes. The most famous and expensive dye was a purple dye obtained from a type of sea snail. Known as Tyrian purple—from the Phoenician city of TYRE where it was produced—the dye was so popular among kings that it became a symbol of

The ancient Iranian textile shown here depicts lions very similar to those decorating the palace of Darius I in Susa. This wool and linen textile, which dates from around the 400s B.C., was exported to Central Asia, where it was mounted on felt and made into a leather chest strap for a horse. This strap and other similar textiles were found at a burial mound in the far reaches of Central Asia.

Thebes

royalty. During Roman times its production was a state secret, and only members of the elite were allowed to own or use the dye.

Textile Industries. Textile production was probably the most important industry in ancient Mesopotamia. Records from the late third millennium B.C. indicate that tens of thousands of people worked in state-run textile workshops in the city of UR. These workshops used the wool from enormous herds of sheep to produce millions of pounds of woolen fabric each year. The palace and temples used some of this, but most was exported to other lands in exchange for goods not available locally.

During the first half of the second millennium B.C.*, the Assyrians traded tin from IRAN and textiles from southern Mesopotamia for precious metals from Anatolia. They produced their own textiles, but these were considered inferior to the high-quality cloth woven in the south. Mesopotamian governments often used wool as a form of payment for workers, and households were expected to weave the clothes they needed and perhaps make extra cloth to meet commercial demand.

Linen was the main textile produced in Egypt because woolly sheep were not raised there until after about 1000 B.C. The Egyptians also organized textile production in workshops, but the industry was less extensive than in Mesopotamia. In Egypt, Mesopotamia, and elsewhere in the ancient Near East, women did most of the spinning and weaving. However, whereas men supervised textile work in Mesopotamia, female overseers predominated in Egypt. After the vertical loom was introduced in Egypt around 1500 B.C., men become more actively involved in textile production. As in Mesopotamia, most Egyptian households wove their own cloth and made their own clothing. (*See also* **Art, Artisans, and Artists; Economy and Trade; Labor and Laborers; Women, Role of.**)

* **second millennium B.C.** years from 2000 to 1001 B.C.

THEBES

See map in Egypt and the Egyptians (vol. 2).

The ancient Egyptian city of Thebes was located on the NILE RIVER, about 400 miles south of present-day Cairo. The city and its surrounding area included the temples of KARNAK and LUXOR, numerous royal burial sites across the river, and the VALLEY OF THE KINGS and the VALLEY OF THE QUEENS. The ancient Egyptians called the city Nowe or Nuwe, which indicates that it was dedicated to the sun god AMUN.

The main part of Thebes was located almost entirely on the east bank of the Nile River, while the burial sites of the kings and queens were located on the west bank. Also located on the west bank were the villages that housed the workers who built the temples and tombs and the houses of the priests who maintained the religious sites.

The oldest monuments in Thebes date from the Eleventh Dynasty (ca. 2081–1938 B.C.). It was during this period that Upper and Lower Egypt were unified and the city became the capital of Egypt. During the Twelfth Dynasty (ca. 1938–1759 B.C.), the royal capital was moved from Thebes to LISHT, closer to Lower Egypt. However, Thebes remained an important site, particularly for temples that honored Amun.

Around 1630 B.C., a nomadic* group from western Asia known as the HYKSOS conquered Egypt, but they were unable to subdue Thebes. The

* **nomadic** referring to people who travel from place to place to find food and pasture

leaders of the city finally succeeded in driving the Hyksos from power in about 1523 B.C. This success marked the beginning of Thebes' greatest period. Grand estates for the country's elite and huge temples in honor of the gods were built in Thebes. On the west bank of the Nile, temples and elaborate tombs were built for the dead. Between 1100 and 950 B.C., the government was controlled by the high priest of Amun in Thebes, as well as a pharaoh* who ruled from the city of Tanis in the Nile Delta. During the early 600s B.C., Nubian pharaohs ruled Egypt from Thebes. In 663 B.C., however, the city was destroyed by the Assyrian king Ashurbanipal, and it never regained its former glory. (*See also* **Cities and City-States; Egypt and the Egyptians; Nubia and the Nubians.**)

* **pharaoh** king of ancient Egypt

THEOLOGY

The term *theology* refers to the systematic study of a religious faith. In ancient times, people did not question or study their beliefs. They were accepted as true, inherited traditions. Priests and temple workers did learn about their religions, but they generally focused on the correct performance of religious rituals. In terms of the ancient Near East, the word *theology* will be used to refer to the people's system of beliefs about the supernatural and their knowledge of the gods and the world.

Modern scholars know about theology in the ancient Near East from several sources, including myths, HYMNS, PRAYERS, and other religious writings. Artifacts, such as religious statues and architectural remains of temples and tombs, also provide insights into the beliefs the peoples of the ancient Near East held about their gods.

Nature of the Supernatural. In many ancient Near Eastern societies, the supernatural—existence beyond what can be seen—was first thought of as living forces. For instance, people felt that living forces permeated the rivers, lakes, wind, and animals. In more sophisticated cultures, the people came to believe that these forces were controlled by supernatural beings—gods. Gods could have animal forms, such as bulls or birds, but more commonly they were presented in human forms, both male and female, although larger and more powerful than normal beings.

* **deity** god or goddess

Once supernatural powers were given human form, there was a tendency to model the behaviors and existences of the deities* on the human world. For example, people assumed that deities had spouses, children, and servants and that they had the same emotions—jealousy, fear, anger, joy—as humans. Some gods, however, exhibited mixed human and animal forms.

Deities were not the only supernatural powers believed to exist in the ancient Near East, however. In some sophisticated theologies, powers, such as "fate" or "norms" (*me* in Sumerian, *ma'at* in Egyptian), gave stability to the cosmos and order to the divine realms. People also believed that some forces became DEMONS, generally evil and irrational beings who caused harm to people for no reason. The dead were also believed to have supernatural powers. The spirits of parents, grandparents, and other ancestors could be either helpful or harmful, depending on how they were treated by their descendants. Because of this belief, the dead were feared and

121

Theology

The Memphite Theology

One of the few theological writings from ancient times is the Memphite Theology, which was inscribed on a monument in the Egyptian city of Memphis around 700 B.C. This theological work was at first said to be a copy of a more ancient Egyptian creation myth. It describes how Ptah, the great city god of Memphis, created everything else in the universe simply through his thoughts and words. The Memphite Theology is now thought to be a fake, written in a deliberate attempt to establish Memphis as an important religious center.

appeased. The Israelites, Mesopotamians, Canaanites, and Egyptians all made offerings to their dead ancestors to gain their favor and support and to avoid their anger. The cult* of the dead was especially important in ancient Egypt.

Regional Theologies. The Mesopotamians, Hittites, Egyptians, and peoples of the Levant* had many gods. According to their theologies, the deities were present in the world in the form of small statues that were kept in temple sanctuaries*. Serving the deities centered on offering their statues food and drink. Failing to serve the deities properly was believed to lead to illness or some other misfortune. It was believed that the gods had created humans to serve them, and as long as the proper rituals, OFFERINGS, and other aspects of worship were carried out, the deities would be satisfied and act kindly toward their human servants.

The theology of the Israelites was at first similar to the theologies of other Near Eastern cultures, with their many deities. However, over time, the Israelites came to believe in one deity, called YAHWEH. The Israelites viewed their place in the universe as a result of a covenant, or agreement, Yahweh had made with them. The covenant was that, in return for proper observance of Yahweh's laws, the Israelites would have a strong nation and just laws.

Most of what is known about Iranian theology comes from the Zoroastrian religion. As taught by the prophet* Zoroaster in the 600s B.C., there was only one god. This god—AHURA MAZDA—created twin brothers, one of whom followed the path of goodness and truth, while the other pursued evil and lies. Over time, Zoroastrianism included other gods, and Ahura Mazda came to be identified with the good twin, while AHRIMAN represented the evil one. Ahura Mazda and Ahriman were believed to be engaged in a battle over the universe, a battle that Ahura Mazda would one day win.

Theology and Government. The theological beliefs of the ancient Near Eastern peoples were reflected in the structures of their governments. Rulers in the ancient Near East were considered chief representatives of the gods. As such, they were responsible for overseeing their communities in accordance with the gods' wishes and for ensuring that the gods were worshiped properly. A community's favor with the gods and its prosperity depended on how well its ruler fulfilled his duties to the gods. The gods had also appointed the king to protect the people of his kingdom. Therefore, it was his responsibility to oversee the administration of the laws the gods had entrusted to him.

Myths. Part of the theology of ancient Near Eastern cultures was communicated through their mythology. Most of the questions ancient people had about their origins and existence were answered in their myths—stories that explained how supernatural forces created and controlled the heavens and earth. All ancient myths were developed to resolve a problem or answer a question. For example, a myth might provide reassurance against a potential disaster, such as a flood, or explain some unknown part of life, such as conception. Myths were a way of making sense of the world, and they provided ancient people with a sense of stability and security.

Most people in the ancient Near East had theogonies—stories about how gods came to be. They also had CREATION MYTHS that answered the question of how the world began. Creation myths from different regions shared certain similarities. For example, all the myths began with some substance that was presumed to have always existed and required no explanation. In Egyptian and Mesopotamian myths, this substance was water. According to Zoroastrianism, the world was created from fire. According to the Israelite religion, before creation there was water, earth, wind, and darkness. In another Israelite story, the universe before creation was a rainless desert.

Judaism and Zoroastrianism are unusual in that their theologies included myths pertaining to the end of the world. According to their beliefs, the immortal human soul receives punishment or reward based on a person's actions in life. There will be a day of judgment at the end of the world when the soul's fate will be decided. (*See also* **Iconography; Judaism and Jews; Mythology; Religion; Rituals and Sacrifice; Zoroaster and Zoroastrianism.**)

THERA

* **archaeologist** scientist who studies past human cultures, usually by excavating material remains of human activity

* **fresco** method of painting in which color is applied to moist plaster so that it becomes chemically bonded to the plaster as it dries; also, a painting done in this manner

* **tsunami** large sea wave caused by a volcanic eruption or earthquake

* **drought** long period of dry weather during which crop yields are lower than usual

* **oracle** priest or priestess through whom a god is believed to speak; also, the location (such as a shrine) where such utterances are made

The island of Thera, also called Santorini, is part of a group of islands known as the Cyclades, which are located in the AEGEAN SEA, an arm of the Mediterranean Sea. Thera was famous for its wine, and in ancient times, it provided an important stop between CRETE and the rest of the Cyclades. Thera is perhaps best known for the enormous volcanic eruption that occurred there. This eruption affected the entire Aegean region.

Humans have lived on Thera since at least 2000 B.C., when the town of Akrotiri was the main settlement on the island. The Minoan civilization was Thera's most important influence. Archaeologists* have uncovered pottery, frescoes*, and other items at Akrotiri exhibiting this influence. Unique multistoried houses have also been found at Thera. Archaeologists believe that the settlement was a major center for the seatrade among the Aegean islands.

History's largest volcanic eruption occurred on the island in about 1500 B.C. (Some scholars date the eruption somewhat earlier, others somewhat later.) The eruption literally blew most of the island away. In fact, the entire Aegean region, especially the southern Aegean and Crete, was affected by the tsunamis*, ash fallout, and EARTHQUAKES caused by the violent eruption. Akrotiri was buried under almost 100 feet of ash, and scientists have even found ash from the volcano as far away as Egypt and Israel. Some scholars believe that the eruption gave rise to the myth of the lost island of Atlantis. Others believe that it was the source for stories in the biblical Book of Exodus.

In about 1000 B.C., the island was resettled by Dorians from the Greek mainland. A drought*, as well as a command from the oracle* at Delphi, prompted many of the citizens of Thera to found a colony on the northern coast of Africa in about 630 B.C. This colony, Cyrene, became one of the islanders' most important achievements. (*See also* **Greece and the Greeks; Mediterranean Sea, Trade on; Volcanoes.**)

Thutmose III

THUTMOSE III

ruled ca. 1479–1425 B.C.
Egyptian king

* **pharaoh** king of ancient Egypt

* **regent** person appointed to govern while the rightful monarch is too young or unable to rule

* **Levant** lands bordering the eastern shores of the Mediterranean Sea (present-day Syria, Lebanon, and Israel), the West Bank, and Jordan

* **diplomacy** practice of conducting negotiations between kingdoms, states, or nations

* **vassal** individual or state that swears loyalty and obedience to a greater power

Thutmose III (thoot•MOH•suh) was a pharaoh* during the Eighteenth Dynasty and is considered one of Egypt's greatest rulers. When his father, Thutmose II, died around 1479 B.C., his young son and heir was not old enough to become king. Therefore, HATSHEPSUT, both wife and half sister of Thutmose II, became regent*. Eventually, however, strong-minded and ambitious Hatshepsut declared herself pharaoh and ruled together with Thutmose III until her death in about 1458 B.C.

When Thutmose finally gained sole power over the Egyptian throne, he began to reestablish the empire that his grandfather Thutmose I had created. First, he marched into the Levant* and subdued a rebellion of local princes. However, he understood the power of diplomacy* far better than his predecessors had; instead of killing his conquered enemies, he took the princes' heirs back to Egypt as hostages. Once a prince died, his heir was returned to assume the throne, having been trained to be an obedient vassal*.

In just 20 years, Thutmose successfully conquered much of the Levant and southern SYRIA. Like his grandfather Thutmose I, he reached the EUPHRATES RIVER, but he was unable to go any farther because of the Mitannians. Thutmose III died around 1425 B.C. and was buried in the VALLEY OF THE KINGS. He was succeeded by his son Amenhotep II. (*See also* **Egypt and the Egyptians; Kings; Pharaohs.**)

TIGLATH-PILESER III

ruled 745–727 B.C.
King of Assyria

* **usurp** to wrongfully occupy a position

* **city-state** independent state consisting of a city and its surrounding territory

* **nomad** person who travels from place to place to find food and pasture

* **tribute** payment made by a smaller or weaker party to a more powerful one, often under the threat of force

* **province** region that forms part of a larger state or empire

Considered one of the most capable rulers in Assyrian history, Tiglath-pileser III (TIG•lath•pi•LAY•zuhr) was the first king of the Neo-Assyrian empire. He led a series of brilliant military campaigns that rapidly expanded the empire and restored it to greatness after decades of decline.

In 745 B.C., while serving as governer of the city of KALKHY, Tiglath-pileser usurped* the throne of Assyria during a rebellion against the weak ruler Ashur-nirari V. After taking power, Tiglath-pileser launched an aggressive policy in the north and west, conquering the kingdom of URARTU, a number of Neo-Hittite kingdoms, and several Phoenician city-states* in SYRIA and CANAAN. He also campaigned against the MEDES in the northeast and helped Babylonia defeat the Aramaean nomads*, who were threatening its borders.

Following these conquests, Tiglath-pileser began to consolidate Assyrian control. Instead of just demanding tribute*, he turned conquered regions into Assyrian provinces*. He also renewed a policy of forced migrations, or deportations, removing thousands of people from conquered territories and replacing them with loyal groups from other parts of the empire.

In 729 B.C., Tiglath-pileser took advantage of unrest in Babylonia and seized the city of BABYLON. He then declared himself king of Babylonia, thus linking the two kingdoms. He died soon afterward, having regained much of Assyria's former greatness and leaving an enormous empire to his son and successor, SHALMANESER V. (*See also* **Aramaeans; Assyria and the Assyrians; Babylonia and the Babylonians; Kings.**)

TIGRIS RIVER

* **tributary** river that flows into another river

See map in Mesopotamia (vol. 3).

Since ancient times, the Tigris River has been one of the most important waterways in the Near East. The earliest civilizations in the region developed between the Tigris and the EUPHRATES RIVER, in a region that was known as MESOPOTAMIA (a Greek word meaning "land between the rivers"). Both rivers originate in the mountains of eastern Turkey and run in a southeasterly direction, emptying into the Persian Gulf.

From its source in Hazar Lake, the Tigris flows steeply downhill through mountainous territory. Most of the water in the river is supplied by winter rains and melting snows from mountains in Turkey. Its upper reaches are fed by four main tributaries* that drain much of eastern Turkey. When the winter rains and spring snow melts are heavy, the Tigris is prone to devastating floods. During these times, because of its steep course, the Tigris is much swifter and deeper than the Euphrates. This makes it more difficult to draw water from the Tigris for use in irrigating fields downstream.

Although most of the early Mesopotamian cities were founded on the banks of the Euphrates, some cities were also built along the Tigris, including NINEVEH, perhaps as early as 7000 B.C., and ASHUR, around 2500 B.C. Both of these cities eventually became part of the Assyrian empire. The Assyrians also built other cities, including KALKHU and Khorsabad, along the Tigris. Among the important cultures that arose in the lands surrounding the Tigris were those of the HURRIANS, the people of Mitanni, and the Urartians. The city of Seleucia, one of the capital cities of the SELEUCID EMPIRE, was built on the Tigris around 300 B.C. After the Parthians captured Mesopotamia in the 140s B.C., they built their capital, Ctesiphon, across the river from Seleucia. (*See also* **Floods; Geography; Rivers; Water.**)

Tin

See *Metals and Metalworking.*

Tombs

See *Burial Sites and Tombs.*

TOOLS

* **artisan** skilled craftsperson
* **artifact** ornament, tool, weapon, or other object made by humans

The laborers and artisans* of the ancient Near East used a wide variety of tools, many of which resemble those used by people today. With their simple tools and implements, ancient workers were able to produce a variety of artifacts* used in everyday life. Their tools—made from wood, stone, copper, bronze, and iron—built the ancient world and allowed the people to take care of themselves.

Tools of Farming and Industry. The earliest tools were stone objects, such as knife blades, spearheads, and arrow points used for hunting. Once an animal was killed, stone blades, choppers, and scrapers were used to cut it up and to remove and process its hide for CLOTHING or shelter. Early farmers used wooden plows to prepare soil for planting and stone sickles to harvest grain. They also used stone grinders to crush the

Tools

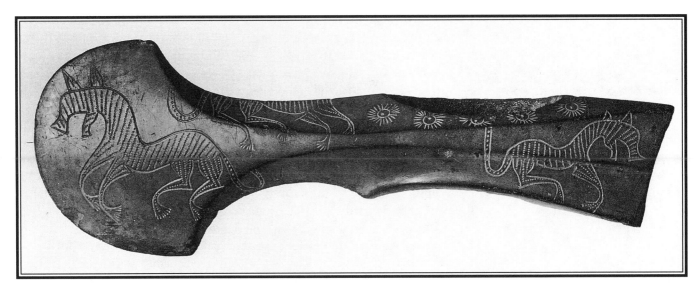

Axes in the ancient Near East served not only as tools but were also turned into weapons for cutting and slashing an opponent. This decorated bronze ax head was excavated at Anoukhva, in the north Caucausus, and dates from the early first millennium B.C.

* **smelt** to heat ore for the purpose of extracting pure material

* **cuneiform** world's oldest form of writing, which takes its name from the distinctive wedge-shaped signs pressed into clay tablets

* **scribe** person of a learned class who served as a writer, editor, or teacher

grain to make flour for bread. Eventually, copper, bronze, and later, iron tools replaced many of those of stone and wood. However, stone was still used for tools many hundreds of years after the use of metals became widespread.

Ancient carpenters used saws, hammers, chisels, planes (for shaving wood), and awls (for punching holes). To bore holes in hard substances, workers used bow drills. The string of the bow (like that used by an archer) was wrapped around one or more thin posts, each tipped with a stone or metal bit at its cutting end. Moving the bow back and forth horizontally rotated the posts, allowing the bit to press down and cut into the material being worked. Builders also used several implements for planning and laying out their projects. The plumb bob, a weighted string hung from the center of one side of a triangular frame, served as the earliest type of level. The frame was placed pointed side down between two beams or other objects on the ground. If the string aligned precisely with the point, the architect knew the surface was level. Other surveying and measuring tools included rulers called cubit sticks and squares that were used to determine whether the corners of a building formed true right angles.

The metalworkers who created many of these measuring tools relied on specific tools of their own. The hammer, tongs, and anvil were part of the metalworking trade from a very early date. The first metalworkers blew through a metal tube to make fires hotter for smelting* metals. This eventually gave way to the bellows, a handheld device that could pump much more air and dramatically increase the heat of a fire.

Tools of Artists and Scientists. Sculptors used many of the same tools employed by builders—hammers, chisels, and adzes (cutting tools)—to shape stone into statues or stone bowls. Artisans used the bow drill to bore holes in JEWELRY, SEALS, and other decorative objects. Scribes used WRITING implements fashioned from reeds. In Mesopotamia, wedge-shaped cuneiform* symbols were pressed into wet CLAY TABLETS with a stylus (writing tool) made from a reed called sedge. Egyptian scribes* used stiff hollow reeds for pens.

Ancient physicians had access to surgical and dental instruments, including scalpels, retractors (instruments for holding open edges of a wound), and needles. Remains of corpses from Egypt show that surgeons often achieved successful results using these very basic devices. Although tools had developed as a means to kill animals, they had also become a means of prolonging and enriching human lives. (*See also* **Art, Artisans, and Artists; Measurement; Metals and Metalworking; Sculpture; Stone; Wood and Woodworking.**)

TORAH

* **exodus** migration by a large group of people, usually to escape something unpleasant

The Hebrew word *torah*, which means "instruction," refers to the first five books, also called the Pentateuch, of the Hebrew BIBLE. The term also came to refer to the oral tradition of laws and customs that interprets the written Torah.

According to Jewish tradition, YAHWEH revealed the Torah and the TEN COMMANDMENTS to the leader MOSES on Mount SINAI. This event occurred during the Israelites' exodus* from Egypt. Modern scholars, however, believe that the Torah was written by different people, possibly under different circumstances and during different times.

The names for the books come from the first line of each book, and the English names summarize the events in each book. *Bereisheet* (Genesis), meaning "In the Beginning," discusses the origins of humankind and the selection of the Israelites as God's chosen people. *Shemot* (Exodus), which means "Names," as in "Now these are the names of the sons of Israel," describes the journey of Moses and the Israelites from Egypt to Canaan. *Va-yikra* (Leviticus), which means "He called," as in "And the Lord called unto Moses," discusses priestly regulations and laws. *Ba-midbar* (Numbers) which means "In the Wilderness," refers to a census or description of the 12 Israelite tribes. *Devarim* (Deuteronomy) which means "Words," as in "These are the words of Moses," is a summary of the laws stated earlier.

The written Torah is the most sacred religious text in Judaism, and parts of it are read weekly during most Jewish services. Today every synagogue houses at least two Torah scrolls, each handwritten on leather. These scrolls are kept in a special box called the ark of the Law. Special ceremonies are performed each time the Torah is removed from and returned to the ark. (*See also* **Hebrews and Israelites; Judaism and Jews; Mosaic Law.**)

Trade

See *Economy and Trade.*

TRADE ROUTES

Trade between distant regions of the ancient Near East was common by the early third millennium B.C.* By studying records and ruins of ancient civilizations, archaeologists* and historians have been able to trace the main routes over which trade was conducted. Despite the danger of bandits and wild animals, most trade goods were carried overland

Trade Routes

* **third millennium B.C.** years from 3000 to 2001 B.C.

* **archaeologist** scientist who studies past human cultures, usually by excavating material remains of human activity

* **fourth millennium B.C.** years from 4000 to 3001 B.C.

* **city-state** independent state consisting of a city and its surrounding territory

* **lapis lazuli** dark blue semiprecious stone

* **first millennium B.C.** years from 1000 to 1 B.C.

* **domestication** process of adapting or taming for human use

See map in Economy and Trade (vol. 2).

* **delta** fan-shaped, lowland plain formed of soil deposited by a river

on ROADS by donkey CARAVANS. Traders also used water routes. Water travel was faster, safer, and more efficient than overland travel, and large cargoes were sent by boat or ship whenever possible.

Mesopotamian Trade Routes. As early as the late fourth millennium B.C.*, the city-states* of URUK and Susa had networks of trade routes. One such route was used to bring lapis lazuli* to Sumer and Elam from present-day Afghanistan. Lapis lazuli was then traded along the Great Khorasan Road that ran southwest from IRAN to MESOPOTAMIA.

Another extensive trade network developed along the Tigris and Euphrates Rivers, connecting southern Mesopotamia to ANATOLIA (present-day Turkey) through northern SYRIA. Most of the trade routes in this region followed the rivers closely where possible. Farther north and west, the routes ran through passes in the rugged mountains of southeastern Anatolia.

The Assyrians opened up trade into central Anatolia, where they had established trading colonies by about 1900 B.C. Two major roads ran west from the Assyrian capital of ASHUR to the important trading colony of Kanesh. During the first millennium B.C.*, the Assyrians constructed and maintained an extensive road system that stretched from northwestern Mesopotamia to the Persian Gulf and east into Iran. After the collapse of the Assyrian empire, the Persians took over and extended the Assyrian road system. Under the Persians, the "royal roads" as they were known reached to the westernmost portions of Anatolia. They eventually linked the cities of the Aegean seacoast to the rest of the Near East.

The domestication* of camels around 1100 B.C. opened new caravan routes across the Syrian Desert between Mesopotamia and the Mediterranean Sea. Tin and precious stones from Iran and Afghanistan and TEXTILES from Mesopotamia were the main goods carried north and west along these routes. The Mesopotamians brought back copper, silver, wool, dyes, and timber. Much of the southbound trade moved via rivers, especially large cargoes such as timber from the Mediterranean region. CANALS in southern Mesopotamia carried most of the trade goods from the northwest that entered Babylonia.

Mesopotamia developed seaborne trade with its southern neighbors of the Persian Gulf by the middle of the third millennium B.C. Sumerian records report a brisk copper trade with the country of Magan, in the present-day OMAN PENINSULA. In the 2200 B.C., the Akkadians imported copper, ivory, turquoise, and exotic animals from MELUKKHA in present-day northwestern India, through the Persian Gulf. Many of these goods were bought and sold on the Persian Gulf island of Dilmun (present-day BAHRAIN). This small kingdom became an important trading center for MERCHANTS from Arabia, southern Mesopotamia, and India.

Egyptian Trade Routes. Egypt had begun to trade with the island of CRETE by at least 2000 B.C. Ships from Egypt sailed the Mediterranean Sea on a current that flowed from the delta* of the NILE RIVER northward to Crete. In summer, a wind from the northwest aided ships on their way back to Egypt. However, seaborne trade in the eastern Mediterranean took place along the coastal cities in Syria. Egypt had a serious need for timber, which it obtained from Syria, along with olive oil and wine.

Egypt also traded with African states to the south, such as Nubia and Punt. Nubia was easily reached by sailing up the Nile (the Nile flows from south to north). Scholars are unsure of the precise location of Punt, but Egyptian records indicate that expeditions to that region traveled on the RED SEA. Punt probably lay along the African coast where the Red Sea flows into the Indian Ocean at present-day Somalia.

The Levant and Arabia. The people of the Levant* played a large role in trade because the region was centrally located in the ancient Near East. Several roads ran in a north-south direction, with crossroads connecting where the terrain allowed.

By 1000 B.C., the main trading cities on the eastern Mediterranean coast had come under the control of the Phoenicians. These seafaring people had developed ships that were able to make sea voyages to places as far away as Spain and possibly England. By the 700s B.C., the Phoenicians were trading with Egypt, Anatolia, Greece, and other locations throughout the Mediterranean.

The people of ancient Arabia used the camel for trade. In fact, these animals were especially important in the opening of trade routes to southern Arabia. Trade goods here included such luxury items as frankincense and myrrh*. Trade routes were also dictated by where traders could stop for water on their journey. (*See also* **Economy and Trade; Mediterranean Sea, Trade on; Phoenicia and the Phoenicians; Shipping Routes; Transportation and Travel.**)

* **Levant** lands bordering the eastern shores of the Mediterranean Sea (present-day Syria, Lebanon, and Israel), the West Bank, and Jordan

* **frankincense and myrrh** fragrant tree resins used to make incense and perfumes

TRANSPORTATION AND TRAVEL

* **diplomat** person who conducts negotiations or relations with foreign kingdoms, states, or nations

The people of the ancient Near East lived in a world that was smaller than today's in many ways. First, they had little or no contact with the peoples of northern Europe, eastern Asia, and southern Africa, which lay beyond their world. Second, traveling long distances for pleasure—as vacationers do today—was probably not done. People traveled only when they had to: to take goods to market, to flee an invading army, to visit a temple in another city, or to lead livestock to new pastures.

MERCHANTS, SOLDIERS, MESSENGERS, and diplomats* were among the best-traveled people of ancient times. Some of them made frequent and long journeys as part of their jobs and responsibilities. However, the great majority of people probably never traveled far from home, although written records suggest that short local journeys—as people visited each other, attended festivals, and engaged in commerce—were common in all periods.

Much of what is known about transportation and travel in the ancient Near East comes from royal records concerned mainly with military matters. However, this material sometimes contains general information about routes and methods of travel. It sheds light on how the people of the ancient Near East moved themselves and their goods from place to place.

Historical Importance of Travel. Three types of long-distance travel helped shape the history and culture of the ancient Near East—those concerned with war, trade, and COMMUNICATION.

Transportation and Travel

Praise for Road Builders

One of the biggest engineering challenges of the ancient Near East was building and maintaining roads that allowed wagon crews to transport huge logs from forests high in the mountains to where they were used to construct palaces and temples. The *Epic of Gilgamesh* says of a mythical mountain guardian, "Where Khumbaba was wont to walk, a trail was set down, roads were straightened, and the going was made good." King Nebuchadnezzar II of Babylonia, who wanted some of the credit for himself, boasted of his road-building achievements in that region: "I cut through steep mountains, I split rocks, opened passages, constructed a straight road for the cedars."

Much of the traffic that moved along the ROADS and waterways of the ancient Near East consisted of ARMIES on the move. Invasions, conquests, retreats, and similar events of long-lasting political and historical significance took place to the drumbeat of soldiers' marching feet and the sound of water lapping the sides of SHIPS AND BOATS.

Traveling merchants comprised the second important category of long-distance travelers. The process of buying goods in one place and selling them in another led to the growth of a network of TRADE ROUTES and a system of organized commercial travel, much of which took place in CARAVANS. Many of the contacts that allowed languages, foods, customs, beliefs, and technology to spread among ancient cultures occurred in the context of trade.

The third significant group of travelers consisted of messengers. Although the ancient Near East lacked formal public postal services, communications could and did travel over great distances. While some messengers traveled on royal or government business, there were also private services that carried messages for a fee. Messengers helped weave a network of cross-cultural connections, as shown by a series of tablets found in the Egyptian city of AMARNA. Dating from the 1300s B.C., these CLAY TABLETS consist of correspondence between Egypt and other states throughout the Near East, all carried by messengers. Similar evidence of communication by messengers exists throughout the region.

Transportation and Travel by Water. The easiest and cheapest way to move large quantities of goods in ancient times was by water. The NILE RIVER in Egypt and the TIGRIS RIVER and EUPHRATES RIVER in Mesopotamia served as vital transportation arteries from very early times.

The oldest known evidence of water transportation in Mesopotamia—a clay model of a sailboat found in a grave in the ancient city of ERIDU—dates from before 4000 B.C. For thousands of years, RIVERS gave the Sumerians, and later the Babylonians, of southern Mesopotamia access to their northern neighbors, Assyria on the Tigris and Syria on the Euphrates. In the flatlands of central and southern Mesopotamia, the rivers flowed slowly enough to allow easy boat travel in both directions. In the north, however, the rivers flowed down out of the hills and mountains, and the current was too swift for upstream travel. Boats could be towed against the current, but this was costly and done only for especially important missions. Usually people sailed downstream only and then returned upstream by land.

In addition to the large rivers, Mesopotamia had an elaborate network of primary and secondary CANALS fed by the rivers. Riverboats could navigate these canals. Waterways were vitally important to the well-being of Mesopotamian states, as King HAMMURABI of BABYLON pointed out in a message to the king of MARI, explaining why he wanted to control the city of Id and its wells of asphalt, a tarlike substance used to make boats watertight. Hammurabi wrote, "The strength of your country consists of donkeys and wagons, but the strength of this country consists of boats."

Transportation and Travel by Land. Although transportation by water was economical, not everyone had access to boats or waterways,

Transportation and Travel

nor were all waterways navigable. Consequently, walking was the most common form of transportation in the ancient world, although women, children, the elderly, and the sick might ride a donkey. Records from the first millennium B.C.* show people riding mules, HORSES, and CAMELS, but such means of transportation remained far less common than walking.

The first wheeled vehicles in the Near East appeared in Mesopotamia around 3000 B.C. Before that time, people and animals had hauled goods on sleds. One common type of early wheeled vehicle was the ox-drawn wagon for carrying goods and sometimes passengers (such as high-ranking men and women). There were also two-wheeled and four-wheeled carts and CHARIOTS pulled by donkeys or horses. Although first used for passengers, chariots quickly acquired military uses throughout the ancient world.

Even with wheeled vehicles, however, most overland transport relied on pack animals. Donkeys were among the first animals used as freight carriers, and they remained the most common pack animal in mountainous regions, where they were prized for their sure footing on narrow paths. After about 1100 B.C., camels also became pack animals. Their ability to endure long stretches without water made them especially valuable in desert areas.

Whether on foot, in a wagon, or on the back of an animal, people who ventured out of familiar territory required roads with clear landmarks because MAPS for travelers did not yet exist. The importance of recognizable points along a route is illustrated in the Mesopotamian story of

* **first millennium** B.C. period between 1000 and 1 B.C.

Wagons were first used as a mode of transport in the ancient Near East around 3000 B.C. Later they were sometimes used in warfare. This baked clay model of a covered wagon (ca. 2400s B.C.) was excavated near Karkamish in northern Syria.

131

Trojan War

GILGAMESH when the hero asks, "Where is the road to Utnapishtim, what are its landmarks?" Magical spells from ancient Mesopotamia speak of angry ghosts who removed landmarks and made travelers go astray. Then as now, getting lost was one of the hazards of a road trip. (*See also* **Migration and Deportation; Nomads and Nomadism; Shipping Routes; Wheel.**)

Trojan War

See *Troy.*

TROY

* **epic** long poem about a legendary or historical hero, written in a grand style

* **archaeologist** scientist who studies past human cultures, usually by excavating material remains of human activity

* **imperial** pertaining to an emperor or an empire

See map in Anatolia (vol. 1).

Troy is one of the most famous cities in history, yet until recently, most people did not believe that it was real place. Located in present-day Turkey (ancient ANATOLIA), the city gained its fame from the Greek poet Homer's epics* the *Iliad* and the *Odyssey.*

The ancient city of Troy was located in northwestern Anatolia near the AEGEAN SEA. Throughout ancient times, Troy was essentially a fort that housed the Trojan king and his court. The city was rebuilt nine times during its 3,000 years of inhabitation. Each time the city was destroyed, the Trojans would level the ruins and build on top of them.

Located along major trade routes in the ancient Near East, Troy quickly grew rich and prosperous. Little else of the city's early history is known. Archaeologists* believe that around 1260 B.C., Troy was destroyed by fire, perhaps during the legendary Trojan War as described in Homer's poems. The survivors of the fire rebuilt the city, but not to its former glory. During the next few hundred years, the city was destroyed and rebuilt several times until the 700s B.C., when the Greeks colonized the area.

The Greeks resettled Troy, which they called Ilion. There they built a temple to Athena, which attracted many visitors and great rulers, including the Persian king XERXES and the Macedonian ruler ALEXANDER THE GREAT. In 85 B.C., the Romans attacked and destroyed Ilion. Shortly thereafter, the city was rebuilt. Over the years, Roman emperors added many imperial* buildings to the city, which they called Ilium. The city continued to flourish until the A.D. 300s, when the Romans founded Constantinople in Turkey. Thereafter, Ilium ceased to be an important city, and ultimately it was abandoned.

The location of Troy was unknown until the early A.D. 1800s, when German archeologist Heinrich Schliemann identified a place in Turkey as the site of the ancient city. In excavating its ruins, archaeologists discovered ten levels of settlements occupied over a period of more than 3,000 years. Archaeologists found massive walls, citadels, gateways, and towers at several levels, indicating that the city was wealthy in ancient times. Other items unearthed during the excavations included jewelry and ornaments of gold, Mycenaean pottery, tools, vessels made of copper and bronze, and weapons.

Although many scholars are unsure whether Homer's account of the Trojan War is based on actual events, archaeological excavations have

Archaeologists conducting excavations at Troy uncovered part of a fortress wall dating from the second half of the second millennium B.C. They believe that a large settlement existed outside these walls. South of the fortress, archaeologists also found a cemetery containing cremation urns. To date, this is the only cemetery found at Troy.

provided evidence that the city of Troy was destroyed around the same time as the war is believed to have occurred. Some historians think that the destruction was caused by an earthquake and fire, while others maintain that the city was destroyed because of the events of the Trojan War. Although archaeology cannot prove whether and where the Trojan War took place, it provides a frame of reference for the events described in Homer's epics. (*See also* **Greece and the Greeks; Mycenae and the Mycenaeans.**)

Turkey

See *Anatolia.*

TUTANKHAMEN

ruled ca. 1332–1322 B.C.
Egyptian pharaoh

* **pharaoh** king of ancient Egypt

* **heretic** person who goes against the established beliefs of a religion

* **deity** god or goddess

Tutankhamen (too-tehng-KAH-muhn), an Eighteenth Dynasty pharaoh*, is one of the most famous rulers in Egyptian history. However, his fame comes not from a long and successful reign or because he had great military victories. Instead, Tutankhamen is famous because his is the best-preserved tomb ever found in the VALLEY OF THE KINGS, a cemetery located near ancient THEBES.

Tutankhamen succeeded the pharaohs Smenkhkare and AKHENATEN. These rulers were considered heretics* because they had tried to make ATEN the sole Egyptian god, whereas the Egyptians worshiped many deities* of whom AMUN was the chief god. Akhenaten had even established a new capital called AKHETATEN in Aten's honor.

Scholars are uncertain about Tutankhamen's ancestry. Some historians believe that Smenkhkare was his brother. Texts from a temple at

Tyre

* **regent** person appointed to govern while the rightful monarch is too young or unable to rule

* **pantheon** all the gods of a particular culture

See color plate 10, vol. 4.

* **archaeologist** scientist who studies past human cultures, usually by excavating material remains of human activity
* **sarcophagus** ornamental coffin, usually made of stone; *pl.* sarcophagi
* **amulet** small object thought to have supernatural or magical powers

TYRE

* **city-state** independent state consisting of a city and its surrounding territory

LUXOR state that Amenhotep III was his father, but it is possible that the word *father* was used to mean ancestor. Notwithstanding the controversy regarding his ancestry, scholars know that Tutankhamen was first named Tutankhaten, meaning "living image of the Aten."

Tutankhamen inherited the throne when he was 9 years old. His main advisers were his regent*, Ay, and the general of the Egyptian armies, Horemheb. These two men advised the young king to distance himself from his Aten-worshiping predecessors. He therefore changed his name to Tutankhamen (in honor of Amun), returned the capital of Egypt to Thebes, and repaired temples and statues dedicated to the old Egyptian pantheon*. He married one of Akhenaten's daughters, Ankhesenpaaten, who also distanced herself from her father by changing her name to Ankhesenamen.

Tutankhamen died when he was about 18 years old and was buried in a tomb in the Valley of the Kings. This tomb was probably originally meant for a minor official, for it did not have the long corridor typical of royal tombs and it only had four small rooms. It is most likely that the tomb actually designed for Tutankhamen was used instead by his regent and adviser, Ay. After Ay died, Tutankhamen's other main adviser, Horemheb, became pharaoh. Although he had made changes favorable to Amun, Tutankhamen later fell into disgrace for being associated with the Aten-worshiping rulers. Consequently, most references to the young king were removed from monuments and temples, and his tomb was forgotten.

During the 1100s B.C., the tomb of Ramses VI was unknowingly constructed above Tutankhamen's tomb. During the construction of this tomb, tons of stone chips fell over the entrance of Tutankhamen's tomb, hiding it for thousands of years.

As a result of his short reign, his later disgrace, and the burial of his tomb, Tutankhamen was forgotten until A.D. 1922, when archaeologist* Howard Carter uncovered his tomb and its treasures, which were totally intact. Tutankhamen's mummy lay inside a sarcophagus* that held a nest of three coffins. The outer two coffins were made of wood with gold coverings. The third coffin was made of solid gold. The king's mummy was dressed with jewelry and amulets*, and his head was covered by a gold mask. The burial chamber also contained four shrines made of wood covered in gold. The other three rooms of the tomb were filled with furniture, clothes, weapons, statues, and a chariot. (*See also* **Burial Sites and Tombs; Death and Burial; Egypt and the Egyptians; Kings; Pharaohs.**)

An important city-state* in ancient Phoenicia, Tyre was built on an island and on its neighboring mainland off the coast of present-day southern Lebanon. According to traditional stories, Tyrian king Hiram I (ruled ca. 969–936 B.C.) enlarged the city by joining two islands with a landfill. Later rulers of the city expanded it even farther to include the mainland portion, which was often known by a different name—Ushu. Some historians believe that Tyre may have been founded as a colony of SIDON, another Phoenician city-state.

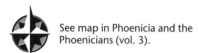

* **archeological** referring to the study of past human cultures, usually by excavating material remains of human activity

See map in Phoenicia and the Phoenicians (vol. 3).

* **siege** long and persistent effort to force a surrender by surrounding a fortress or city with armed troops, cutting it off from supplies and aid

* **Levant** lands bordering the eastern shores of the Mediterranean Sea (present-day Syria, Lebanon, and Israel), the West Bank, and Jordan

* **vassal** individual or state that swears loyalty and obedience to a greater power

Archaeological* excavations at Tyre, undertaken since the A.D. 1800s, have revealed that it was first inhabited from about 2700 B.C. However, there is a gap in the archaeological evidence from 2000 to 1600 B.C., when the city may have been abandoned. From then until the city was rebuilt in the 1400s B.C., the site was used for burials and storage pits. Thereafter, the city began to thrive as a center of trade and commerce. By the 900s B.C., Tyre had become the dominant city-state in Phoenicia and the most important harbor and trading center in the eastern Mediterranean. Tyrians also established colonies throughout the region, including CARTHAGE in North Africa.

According to the Hebrew BIBLE, Tyre also maintained a close relationship with the kingdom of Israel. The most famous king of Tyre, Hiram I, provided SOLOMON of Israel with building materials and plans for his palace and the first Temple of Solomon in JERUSALEM. Jezebel, the daughter of the king of Tyre and Sidon, was married to King AHAB of Israel.

In 572 B.C., King NEBUCHADNEZZAR II laid siege* to Tyre during his attempt to consolidate Babylonian control in the Levant*. The Tyrians successfully held him at bay for 13 years, after which he was forced to withdraw. Although Nebuchadnezzar conquered the mainland portion of the city, he never took the city's island fortress. By 538 B.C., the Persians had driven the Babylonians out of Phoenicia, and Tyre became a Persian vassal*.

In the 300s B.C., when the Macedonians conquered Persia, ALEXANDER THE GREAT became the first to conquer the island portion of Tyre. He achieved this by destroying the mainland portion of the city and using the rubble to build a road to the island. Alexander then invaded Tyre, killed 10,000 of its inhabitants, and sold the rest into slavery. After Alexander, Tyre came under the control of the SELEUCID EMPIRE and later the Roman Empire. (*See also* **Byblos; Phoenicia and the Phoenicians.**)

UGARIT

* **city-state** independent state consisting of a city and its surrounding territory

* **Levant** lands bordering the eastern shores of the Mediterranean Sea (present-day Syria, Lebanon, and Israel), the West Bank, and Jordan

* **artisan** skilled craftsperson

* **scribe** person of a learned class who served as a writer, editor, or teacher

* **second millennium B.C.** years from 2000 to 1001 B.C.

Ugarit (oo•GAH•rit) was an ancient city-state* located at Ras Shamra on the Mediterranean coast of northern SYRIA. The capital of a kingdom of the same name, Ugarit was one of the oldest cities in the ancient Near East. The city had a good harbor, natural defenses, and access to TRADE ROUTES. These features helped it become a center of commerce with extensive trading contacts with Mesopotamia, Anatolia (present-day Turkey), the Levant*, Egypt, Cyprus, Greece, and the Minoans of Crete.

Settled by at least 6500 B.C., Ugarit experienced a period of expansion between 3000 and 2000 B.C., during which it became the center of a prosperous kingdom. Its inhabitants were a mixture of AMORITES, Canaanites, HURRIANS, and other peoples. Ugaritic society consisted of two main groups: free citizens and people employed by the king. While most residents of towns and villages in the kingdom worked as farmers and herders, inhabitants of the city of Ugarit included artisans*, soldiers, priests, scribes*, and other specialized workers.

Early in the second millennium B.C.*, Ugarit formed an alliance with Egypt as protection against invaders from the north and east. Thereafter, the city fell under Egyptian. Still, it continued to flourish, and between

Ugarit

Carved to depict a goddess feeding goats, this Mycenaean-like ivory box lid comes from Minet el Beida, the harbor town of Ugarit, and dates from the 1200s B.C. Large numbers of carved ivory objects have been excavated from tombs and palaces at Ugarit. These objects are evidence of the technical competence and international tastes of the city's craftspeople.

 See map in Syria (vol. 4).

the 1400s and 1200s B.C., Ugarit reached the height of its prosperity. During this period, trade grew tremendously, and the city expanded greatly in size. Royal palaces, temples, libraries, and other public buildings were constructed, while art and literature flourished.

Ugarit remained under Egyptian control until about 1330 B.C., when the HITTITES of Anatolia gained political dominance. The city did not begin to decline until the 1100s B.C., a period marked by numerous pirate raids. Shortly thereafter, the city of Ugarit was destroyed and largely abandoned, leading to the collapse of the kingdom as well. Many scholars believe that the city was destroyed by the SEA PEOPLES, but the chief archaeologist* who excavated Ugarit believed that the city was destroyed by a violent EARTHQUAKE.

Archaeological excavations conducted in the early A.D. 1900s yielded information about the city and its cultural heritage. The most important discoveries include cuneiform* texts written in the Akkadian, Hurrian, and Hittite languages. Archaeologists also excavated cuneiform aleph-beth (script that contains symbols for consonants but not for vowels) texts

* **archaeologist** scientist who studies past human cultures, usually by excavating material remains of human activity

* **cuneiform** world's oldest form of writing, which takes its name from the distinctive wedge-shaped signs pressed into clay tablets

136

ARTS AND CULTURE

Plate 1
Made of ivory, this Phoenician carving of a female head, which is 6¼ inches tall, dates from the 700s B.C. It was found at a palace at Kalkhu (present-day Nimrud) in Assyria, where it was originally attached to a piece of furniture. The Assyrians prized fine furniture and often took it as booty from lands that they conquered.

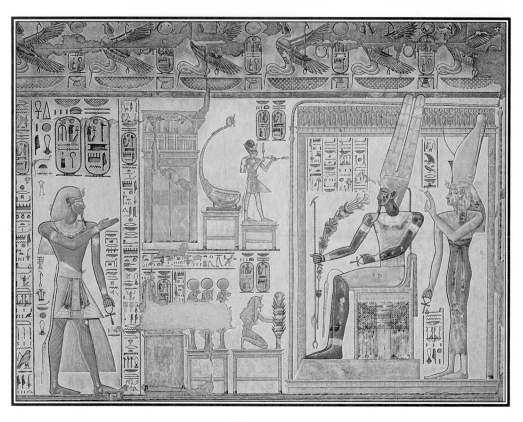

Plate 2

Dating from Egypt's Twentieth Dynasty, this wall painting was found in the funerary temple of Ramses III (ruled ca. 1187–1156) at Medinet Habu. This scene, from the temple treasury, depicts some of the gold, silver, and other precious objects stored there. Ramses III is shown offering ritual furniture to the god Amun, who is seated at the right. Among the other objects being offered are statues, vases, and a harp.

Plate 3

Ancient Near Eastern artisans used silver and other precious metals to make jewelry and luxury and decorative items, such as the vase shown here. Approximately 14 inches tall, this silver vase belonging to King Entemena of Lagash dates from around 2450 B.C. The copper-based vase bears engraved figures of both mythical and real animals. The top of the vase contains an inscription of devotion to the city god of Lagash.

Plate 4

The people of the ancient Near East used amulets as lucky or protective charms. A winged scarab (representation of the dung beetle) made of precious stone sits at the center of this amulet, which was found in the tomb of Eighteenth Dynasty Egyptian king Tutankhamen (reigned ca. 1332–1322 B.C.). The amulet, which is inlaid with lapis lazuli, carnelian, glass, and other stones, may have been worn as a pectoral.

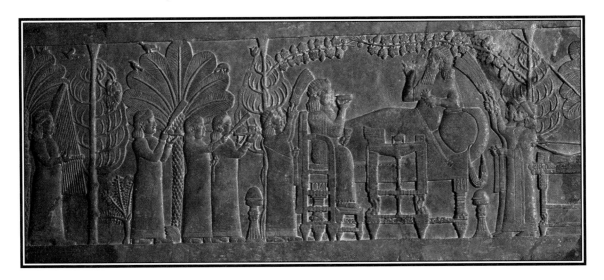

Plate 5

The ancient Near Easterners often used art to depict and commemorate triumphs over enemies. The gypsum relief shown here, which dates from the 600s B.C., depicts a feast at which Assyrian king Ashurbanipal (ruled 668–627 B.C.) and his queen, Ashur-sharrat, celebrate a victory. The object of celebration, which was sent from the battlefield, is the head of Elamite king Teumman, shown hanging from the second tree on the left.

Plate 6
This round bronze sculpture from ancient Luristan (present-day Iran) features water spirits in the center. Dating from around 1850 B.C., the sculpture measures 13 inches in height. Many bronze objects have been found at Luristan.

Plate 7
Bricks were used in the construction of walls in the ancient Near East. People glazed bricks with an enamel coating to give them a much harder surface. These enameled brick panels from a palace at Kalkhu (present-day Nimrud) date from the reign of Assyrian king Shalmaneser III (ruled 858–823 B.C.) They depict two bulls standing on their hind legs, with a tree between them.

Plate 8
Rings were among the most commonly worn jewelry in the ancient Near East. Made of carved gold, silver, bronze, or iron, rings were worn on several fingers and could be plain or engraved. The gold Hittite ring shown here dates to between 1400 and 1200 B.C. It depicts a winged goddess standing between two lions on another lion's back. The rosette in front of the lion on the left is probably a symbol of the goddess.

Plate 9
The 7-inch-high clay vase shown here dates from around 2000 B.C. and was found at Susa in ancient Elam. It resembles a type of vase found in Lagash, reflecting the influence Mesopotamia had on its close neighbor, Elam. Similar vases have also been found in the region of the Diyala River and at Tello, all of which appear to have been made in the same shop, possibly in Susa.

Plate 10

The A.D. 1922 discovery of the tomb of ancient Egyptian king Tutankhamen (ruled ca. 1332–1322 B.C.) in the Valley of the Kings provided modern scholars with many examples of Egyptian art, such as this plastered and painted wooden chest. The scene on its central panel depicts Tutankhamen in his chariot, attacking a group of Nubians. On the ends of the chest, Tutankhamen is shown as a sphinx trampling Egypt's enemies.

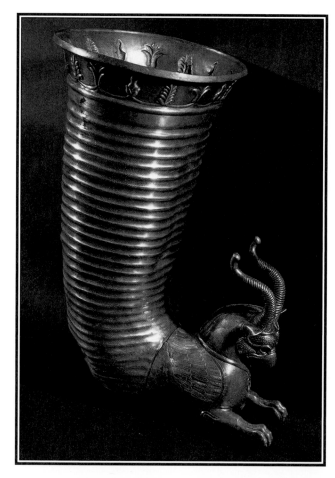

Plate 11

This silver rhyton, or ancient drinking horn, was found in Central Asia and dates from the Achaemenid period (538–331 B.C.). The bottom of the rhyton depicts a mythical beast called a griffin. A small opening on the chest of the griffin indicates where the liquid poured into the rhyton came out.

Plate 12

Ancient Minoan and Cycladic art are known for their colorful frescoes, many examples of which were found on the islands of Crete and Thera. The fresco above depicts a galley ship being rowed through waters where dolphins swim. It comes from Thera and dates from around 1500 B.C.

Plate 13

Animals were portrayed in ancient Near Eastern art for both secular and religious purposes. The gold- and silver-winged ibex shown here forms the handle of a vase. Approximately ten inches long, this ibex is typical of art from the Achaemenid period (538–331 B.C.). The Persians were especially skilled in metalworking, and their gold jewelry is noteworthy for its fine quality.

Plate 14
Although the sphinx originated in Egypt, its use in art spread to other cultures in the ancient Near East, who added their own elements. In Syria and the Levant, the body of the sphinx was often portrayed with wings. Dating from the 700s B.C., this 3-inch-high sphinx was found at Hadatu in northern Syria.

Plate 15
Glassmaking was an important industry in the Levant during ancient times. The Phoenicians were famous in the ancient world for their skill in producing colorful glass beads, such as those in this necklace, which dates from the 500s B.C. The Phoenicians might have learned some of their glassmaking skills from the ancient Egyptians.

* **dialect** regional form of a spoken
language with distinct pronunciation,
vocabulary, and grammar
* **stela** stone slab or pillar that has been
carved or engraved and serves as a
monument; *pl.* stelae

written in the local Ugaritic language, a West Semitic dialect* with many similarities to biblical Hebrew. These texts contain a wealth of information about the cultural and religions traditions as well as the mythologies of the people of Ugarit. Other objects found at the site include carved ivory panels, engraved metal vessels, and carved stone stelae* and statues. (*See also* **Cities and City-States; Cuneiform; Economy and Trade.**)

* **city-state** independent state consisting
of a city and its surrounding territory

 See map in Mesopotamia (vol. 3).

A city-state* in southern MESOPOTAMIA, Umma rose to prominence sometime before 2500 B.C., largely due to a change in the course of the EUPHRATES RIVER. The main channel of the river shifted to the east, causing it to flow away from established cities such as NIPPUR and URUK. Cities lying on the old channel—especially Uruk—suffered a decline in population, while settlements on the new channel—such as Umma—flourished.

As Umma grew, it began to extend its influence into the regions surrounding the city. This brought it into conflict with neighboring city-states, such as LAGASH to the southeast. Umma clashed with Girsu, the capital of Lagash, over a boundary dispute as well as rights to the use of water from the Euphrates River.

Records indicate that Mesilim, the king of KISH, negotiated a settlement and established a formal border between Umma and Lagash. However, Umma broke this agreement, and between 2500 and 2400 B.C., the two city-states engaged in several wars. These battles raged off and on for many years with neither side seizing a decisive advantage. Ultimately, Umma emerged victorious, and its king, Lugalzagezi, conquered Lagash. He then proceeded to attack and subdue major city-states in southern Mesopotamia and established the first large Sumerian state, with its capital at Uruk. Around 2340 B.C., King SARGON I of Akkad attacked and defeated Lugalzagezi and incorporated his former lands, including Umma, into the Akkadian empire. (*See also* **Cities and City-States.**)

* **city-state** independent state consisting
of a city and its surrounding territory
* **patriarch** male leader of a family or
tribe
* **archaeological** referring to the study of
past human cultures, usually by
excavating material remains of human
activity
* **artifact** ornament, tool, weapon, or
other object made by humans

Located in southern MESOPOTAMIA, the city-state* of Ur was the capital of several empires as well as a major trading center connected to the Persian Gulf. Many scholars believe it was also the home of Abraham, one of the patriarchs* of Israel according to the Hebrew BIBLE.

First settled in the fifth millennium B.C. (years from 5000 to 4001 B.C.) by people of the Ubaid culture, Ur developed into one of the region's largest settlements. According to archaeological* evidence, the Ubaid settlement was destroyed by a flood. However, it was resettled in about 3900 B.C. During the next 1,000 years, Ur grew from a prominent town into a walled city. By the 2500s B.C., it was a major Sumerian city-state with impressive art and architecture. This is evident from the excavations conducted in the early A.D. 1900s, which uncovered the Royal Cemetery of Ur. The tombs contained jewelry, weapons, furniture, and other artifacts*, revealing the existence of a complex and accomplished culture.

During the 2400s B.C., the kings of Ur extended their power throughout southern Mesopotamia, and Ur became the capital of the region. This

Ur

* **dynasty** succession of rulers from the same family or group

* **ziggurat** in ancient Mesopotamia, a multistory tower with steps leading to a temple on the top

* **nomadic** referring to people who travel from place to place to find food and pasture

* **sack** to loot a captured city

 See map in Mesopotamia (vol. 3).

period, known as the First Dynasty of Ur, lasted until the city was conquered by Sargon I of Akkad around 2300 B.C. Thereafter, Ur remained under Akkadian rule until that empire collapsed around 2200 B.C. In the late 2100s B.C., King Utu-khegal drove out the Gutians, who had settled in the region, and his successor, Ur-Nammu, established a new dynasty*, the Third Dynasty of Ur, that lasted more than 100 years. During this period, kings undertook several building projects at Ur, including the construction of several ziggurats*. Ur reached the height of its glory under Ur-Nammu's son Shulgi. During his nearly 50-year reign, Shulgi reorganized the empire and conquered new territory. However, around 2000 B.C., while the Amorites, a nomadic* people, invaded from the west, Ur was sacked* by the Elamites from the east.

Ur was rebuilt and became a center of RELIGION and trade. During this period, which lasted about 250 years, Ur fell under the control of the Babylonians. In about 1740 B.C., the Babylonian army destroyed the walls surrounding Ur as well as several homes and public buildings as punishment for the city's participation in a rebellion against Babylonian control. Most residents stayed in the city and had restored their homes and many of the religious buildings by the 1400s B.C. Nevertheless, Ur slowly declined until about 600 B.C., when Babylonian king Nebuchadnezzar, and later Nabonidus, undertook an extensive rebuilding of the city. This marked the last period of Ur's greatness. By the 300s B.C., the Euphrates River had changed course

When Akkadian king Sargon I conquered Ur, he appointed his daughter Enkheduanna as high priestess to that city's patron god. He did so to demonstrate to the people of Ur that he respected their god and their beliefs. Dating from around 2300 B.C., this limestone disk depicts Enkheduanna, third from right, in her role as high priestess to the moon god.

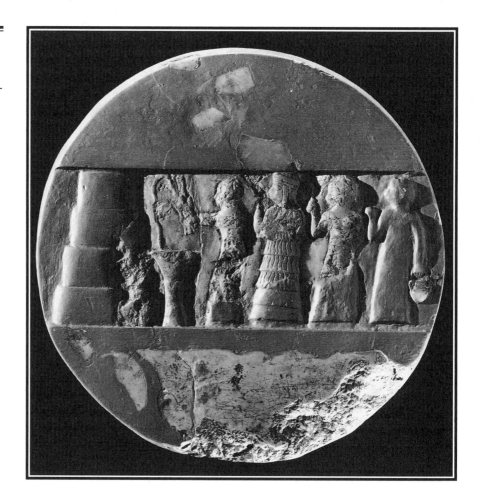

away from the city, leaving it without a ready source of water. Ur was abandoned shortly thereafter. (*See also* **Babylonia and the Babylonians; Burial Sites and Tombs; Walled Cities; Ziggurats.**)

UR-NAMMU

ruled ca. 2112–2094 B.C.
King of Ur

* **diplomacy** practice of conducting negotiations between kingdoms, states, or nations

* **city-state** independent state consisting of a city and its surrounding territory

* **ziggurat** in ancient Mesopotamia, a multistory tower with steps leading to a temple on the top

* **nomadic** referring to people who travel from place to place to find food and pasture

Ur-Nammu was the founder of the Third Dynasty of Ur, a succession of kings who ruled southern MESOPOTAMIA for more than 100 years. Little information exists about Ur-Nammu's life before he became king. Some historians speculate that he was the brother of King Utu-khegal, who ruled UR from around 2119 to 2112 B.C. Others believe that Ur-Nammu was his son. Whatever their relationship, Ur-Nammu served as military governor of Ur under Utu-khegal. When Utu-khegal died, Ur-Nammu succeeded him as king.

Ur-Nammu assumed several titles including Mighty Man, Lord of Uruk, Lord of Ur, and King of Sumer and Akkad. He then set out to live up to those names by extending his influence throughout southern and central Mesopotamia. He did this largely by negotiation and diplomacy* rather than by military force. The only exception involved the city-state* of LAGASH, which he apparently eliminated to redirect trade from the Persian Gulf into Ur. Ur-Nammu also began a large-scale program to rebuild large portions of Ur and repair irrigation CANALS that had been neglected for years. Among his most notable building accomplishments was the completion of the first true ziggurats* in Ur and in other cities under his control. The ziggurat of Ur, which consisted of three platforms topped by a temple, was nearly 50 feet high.

Many scholars consider Ur-Nammu the author of the first recorded set of law codes. (Some, however, credit them to his son SHULGI, who followed him as king.) Although these codes were not used to decide court cases at the time, they were the first attempt to describe various legal situations and set penalties for those who broke the law.

Ur-Nammu's reign ended when he died in combat against the Gutians, a people who had ruled Ur for many years before they were driven out by Utu-khegal. Ur-Nammu's son Shulgi took over as king and during his 50-year reign, greatly expanded the empire to the north and east. However, Shulgi's successors were weak and unable to hold the kingdom together. Around 2004 B.C., a combination of internal weakness, pressure from a nomadic* people called the AMORITES, and an invasion by the Elamites ended the dynasty founded by Ur-Nammu. (*See also* **Dynasties.**)

URARTU

One of the more mysterious civilizations of the ancient Near East, Urartu (u•RAHR•too) was a kingdom in the mountainous CAUCASUS region and flourished for about 600 years, beginning in the 1200s B.C. In the Hebrew BIBLE, the region of Urartu is called Ararat. During the 700s and 600s B.C., the kingdom enjoyed considerable political power, dominating eastern ANATOLIA (present-day Turkey) and competing with the Assyrian empire.

Urbanization

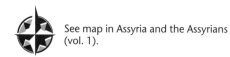

See map in Assyria and the Assyrians (vol. 1).

* **assimilate** to adopt the customs of a society

* **artifact** ornament, tool, weapon, or other object made by humans

* **plunder** to steal property by force, usually after a conquest

Little is known about the early history of Urartu, although evidence suggests that the its cultural heritage was influenced by the HURRIANS of northern Mesopotamia. First mentioned in Assyrian records from the 1200s B.C. as a region of many lands and cities, Urartu may have been unified into a kingdom in the following centuries in response to growing Assyrian power.

In the late 800s B.C., Urartu entered an era of rapid conquest, and this expansion continued into the next century. Throughout this period, Urartu was often at war with Assyria, and the Assyrians exerted a strong influence on the kingdom. The Urartians assimilated* many aspects of Assyrian civilization while also maintaining a distinctive culture of their own. Among the best-known artifacts* of Urartian civilization are POTTERY, SEALS, and metalworks of decorated bronze.

By the early 700s B.C., Urartu had become the most powerful state in eastern Anatolia. Its military success was no doubt aided by a decline in Assyrian power at that time. Within a few decades, however, Assyria began to reassert its power, leading to a number of dramatic military confrontations between the two kingdoms. One of the most famous of these engagements took place in 714 B.C., when SARGON II of Assyria defeated Rusa I of Urartu and plundered* Urartian temples and much of the kingdom.

Despite these victories, the Assyrians never succeeded in conquering Urartu, and it remained powerful and prosperous, dominating the eastern Anatolian landscape. However, Urartu faced more formidable enemies in the 600s and 500s B.C., when repeated invasions by the Cimmerians, Scythians, MEDES, and Persians brought the kingdom to a final, violent end. (*See also* **Scythia and the Scythians.**)

URBANIZATION

* **sixth millennium** B.C. years from 6000 to 5001 B.C.

* **city-state** independent state consisting of a city and its surrounding territory

* **Levant** lands bordering the eastern shores of the Mediterranean Sea (present-day Syria, Lebanon, and Israel), the West Bank, and Jordan

* **domesticate** to adapt or tame for human use

* **scribe** person of a learned class who served as a writer, editor, or teacher

The process of urbanization, the formation and growth of cities, was under way in the ancient Near East as early as the sixth millennium B.C.* Urbanization continued as small village settlements grew into towns and then cities and city-states*. Historians believe that the first large cities arose in MESOPOTAMIA, although urban centers also developed in ANATOLIA (present-day Turkey), Egypt, IRAN, and the Levant*.

Urbanization could not occur until after people had started to domesticate* plants and animals instead of obtaining food through hunting and gathering. AGRICULTURE provided people with a steady food supply that allowed them to settle in one place, usually a location with useful features, such as a good water source. Not all early settlements grew into cities, but those that did became the first political organizations larger than villages.

The shift to urban life brought lasting changes to the ways people lived, worked, and interacted with one another. Some of those changes involved resources and labor. Settled urban populations grew because they could store and stockpile food, sharing and distributing it as needed. This meant that instead of farming, some people could work full-time in crafts, in religious or governmental roles, or in professions such as that of scribe*. This greater variety of WORK in urban settings went hand in hand with other changes in social organization. First, a ruling class emerged,

Uruk

* **bureaucracy** system consisting of officials and clerks who perform government functions

and then bureaucracies* were established to administer such aspects of city life as the gathering and distribution of food and the building of temples, CANALS, and other public structures. The diversification of LABOR also meant that differences in rank and social class became more pronounced in urban societies.

Another development that occurred as a result of urbanization was the appearance of organized, large-scale warfare. Once people began accumulating material goods in central locations, such as the cities, they became targets of others who banded together to steal from them. The Sumerian and Akkadian cities in Mesopotamia, for example, were storehouses for the enormous agricultural wealth produced by the fertile plains around them. This concentrated wealth brought attacks by nonurban peoples from the mountainous countries to the north and east and from the semi-deserts to the west. In addition to defending themselves from attack, cities launched wars of aggression, usually to gain control of territory or access to resources.

* **literacy** ability to read and write

Literacy*, developments in the arts and in techniques such as metal-working, and other features associated with the growth of civilization in the ancient Near East appear to have been linked to urban centers. Not every ancient civilization was urban, however. The Scythians and other nomadic* peoples of CENTRAL ASIA developed arts, crafts, and high levels of military and political organization without becoming city builders. Although urbanization was not the only route to civilization, today's scholars look to the remains of ancient cities for the most complete and best-preserved records of ancient history, culture, and people. (*See also* **Cities and City-states; Egypt and the Egyptians; Scythia and the Scythians; Walled Cities; Wars and Warfare.**)

* **nomadic** referring to people who travel from place to place in search of food and pasture

URUK

* **fifth millennium B.C.** years from 5000 to 4001 B.C.

* **city-state** independent state consisting of a city and its surrounding territory

* **archaeologist** scientist who studies past human cultures, usually by excavating material remains of human activity

Many scholars consider the Sumerian settlement of Uruk (OO•ruk) in southern MESOPOTAMIA to be the world's first true city. Founded during the fifth millennium B.C.*, Uruk grew from an agricultural settlement into an influential city-state* by about 3200 B.C. It retained its importance in Mesopotamia until around 2000 B.C., and it remained occupied for 2,000 years. However, Uruk is not historically significant simply because of its size or the length of time it was occupied. The remains of the city uncovered by archaeologists* contain the earliest evidence of some of the most important cultural developments in human history. For this reason, Uruk has been called the birthplace of civilization.

Uruk probably began as two separate settlements, Uruk and Kullaba, that merged to form one city. Each former settlement became a district in the city of Uruk. Kullaba was the location of the temple of the sky god ANU, while the Uruk district (then called Eanna) housed the temple of Inanna, the goddess of war. The earliest remains of advanced culture were found in the Eanna district. These include many CLAY TABLETS that provide evidence of the world's first system of WRITING. Monumental public ARCHITECTURE and works of fine art were also excavated there.

Uruk expanded rapidly, attracting settlers from the surrounding regions. By about 3200 B.C., it was the largest settlement in the Near East. As

Uruk

This upper part of a statue, possibly of a ruler from Uruk, dates from the late fourth millennium B.C. In keeping with the assertion that Uruk was the world's first city, scholars also believe that the origins of Mesopotamian sculpture, cylinder seals, and architecture can be traced back to ancient Uruk.

 See map in Mesopotamia (vol. 3).

* **dynasty** succession of rulers from the same family or group

the population grew, the government and economy of Uruk also developed. Texts recovered in Uruk show that the city had textile and metalworking industries at a very early date. Because southern Mesopotamia contains no natural sources of metal, it is clear that Uruk had developed an active trade network with other regions of the ancient Near East. There is also evidence that it established colonies in northern Mesopotamia and western IRAN and that the people of Uruk established TRADE ROUTES to reach them. These colonies probably served as places where goods produced in Uruk were traded for those items not available locally.

In the mid-2300s B.C., a king named Lugalzagezi established the first united kingdom in southern Mesopotamia, with Uruk as its capital. However, around 2334 B.C., SARGON I of Akkad defeated Lugalzagezi and destroyed Uruk's walls. The city was revitalized in about 2100 B.C., when the Sumerian king UR-NAMMU founded the Third Dynasty of Ur and undertook an extensive construction program in Uruk. When this dynasty* collapsed

142

100 years later, Uruk went into another decline, and the city's population decreased. It did not grow again until about 1450 B.C., when the Kassites took control of the city. By this time, however, settlement was confined to the Eanna district.

After 1000 B.C., Uruk was controlled first by the Assyrians and later by the Babylonians. Rulers of both empires began new construction in Eanna, and Uruk once again became an important and prosperous city. This may well have been because it lay on one of the main trade routes through the Near East. However, Uruk's prosperity ended when the Parthians conquered Mesopotamia in the 140s B.C. Uruk gradually faded into obscurity, and its final residents probably abandoned the city sometime before A.D. 400. (*See also* **Archaeology and Archaeologists; Cities and City-States; Urbanization.**)

VALLEY OF THE KINGS

* **pharaoh** king of ancient Egypt

The Valley of the Kings is an elaborate cemetery located in the hills on the western side of the Nile River, near the Valley of the Queens. The Valley of the Kings, Valley of the Queens, and temples of Karnak and Luxor were all part of the ancient Egyptian city of Thebes.

The Valley of the Kings is split into two main sections: the West Valley, which contains 4 tombs, and the East Valley, which contains 58 tombs. Although almost all the tombs belong to kings, there are also tombs belonging to two queens, a few important officials, and the many sons of Ramses II.

The valley served as the royal cemetery from around 1539 to around 1075 B.C. The first king to be buried there was the Eighteenth Dynasty pharaoh* Thutmose I. Kings of the Nineteenth and Twentieth Dynasties were also buried there. Ramses XI was the last ruler to be buried at the site.

The tombs at the site were built in a style that had not been used previously. To protect the tombs from robbery, none of them had any aboveground decoration or monuments. They were cut into the secluded hills and their entrances hidden. Also, for the first time since the Early Dynastic period (ca. 3000–2675 B.C.), the tombs in the Valley of the Kings were not built next to mortuary temples. Unfortunately, these attempts at protecting the tombs of the kings were not successful. All the tombs except one were robbed in the centuries that followed.

* **sarcophagus** ornamental coffin, usually made of stone; *pl.* sarcophagi

* **relief** sculpture in which material is cut away to show figures raised from the background

Most of the tombs were of similar structure. They began with a long corridor descending into the hill. This corridor contained deep shafts and, occasionally, rooms of columns that were built to confuse tomb robbers. At the end of the corridor, the burial chamber housed the sarcophagus* of the king. There were also storage rooms that contained furniture and other goods for the king to use in the afterlife. Often, the walls of the tombs were beautifully painted or carved with reliefs* showing the king meeting the gods. Some walls contained magical writings that were meant to help the king as he journeyed through the life after death. The ceilings of the tombs were sometimes painted with stars, astronomical figures, and the sky goddess Nut.

The longest tomb at the site belongs to Queen Hatshepsut. The corridor is almost 700 feet long and drops about 320 feet into the rock. The only tomb that was never robbed belonged to King Tutankhamen. The wealth found in his small tomb gives an indication of the treasure that was robbed from the more ornate tombs. A more recent excavation is that of the enormous tomb meant to house almost all of King Ramses II's 52 sons. This tomb—the largest one found in the Valley of the Kings—was discovered in the early A.D. 1800s but was never fully excavated because it was considered unimportant. In 1988, the tomb was rediscovered, and it is still being excavated. (*See also* **Afterlife; Burials Sites and Tombs; Death and Burial; Egypt and the Egyptians; Kings; Pharaohs; Queens.**)

The Valley of the Queens is an elaborate cemetery located in the hills on the west bank of the Nile River. Along with the temples of Karnak and Luxor and the Valley of the Kings, the Valley of the Queens was part of the ancient city of Thebes.

Around 90 tombs have been uncovered at this site where queens and royal children of the Nineteenth and Twentieth Dynasties (ca. 1292–1075 B.C.) were buried. Some Seventeenth and Eighteenth Dynasty queens were also buried there; however, most queens during those dynasties were buried alongside their husbands.

Most of the tombs at this site are smaller than the tombs at the nearby Valley of the Kings. Each consists of a small room (called an antechamber) that leads into a small passageway. The passageway leads to the burial chamber. Like the tombs in the Valley of the Kings, the tombs in the Valley of the Queens were beautifully painted or carved with reliefs*.

* **relief** sculpture in which material is cut away to show figures raised from the background

The first queen to be buried in the Valley of the Queens was probably Satra, a wife of Ramses I. The most notable person buried there is Nefertari, Ramses II's principal wife. The site also contains the beautiful and well-preserved tombs of the princes Amenherkhopshef and Khaemwaset II, two of Ramses III's sons. (*See also* **Afterlife; Burial Sites and Tombs; Death and Burial; Egypt and the Egyptians; Queens.**)

Vegetables

See *Agriculture; Food and Drink.*

Most of the earth's volcanoes are found in a series of belts located along boundaries between the plates of the earth's crust. Two such boundaries run through portions of the Near East. The more prominent of these, and the one that has produced the most volcanic activity in the region, runs east and west through the Aegean Sea and the northern half of present-day Turkey (ancient Anatolia). Here two plates collide where one slides underneath the other. Another such plate boundary runs along the eastern coast of Africa, through the Red Sea. There the plates are rifting, or pulling apart. The movement of these plates releases molten rock from deep underground, which then rises to the surface. The pressure

קרשתאבגדהוזחטיכדלמסנןסעפףצץזקרשתאבגד

Wall Paintings

forces the surface rock to form a dome- or cone-shaped mountain. When the pressure becomes too great for the overlying rock surface, the top of the mountain explodes, spewing ash and lava.

In ancient times, the most spectacular volcanic eruption occurred on the Aegean island of THERA. Sometime around 1500 B.C. (experts disagree about the exact date), a volcano on Thera erupted with incredibly destructive force. The explosion buried the Late Bronze Age city of Akrotiri under a thick layer of ash and volcanic rock and caused shock waves that were felt for hundreds of miles. The main settlement on the island was apparently evacuated before the eruption, but its burial in ash preserved its remains intact until their excavation in the late A.D. 1960s. At one time, scholars believed that the eruption on Thera was responsible for the destruction of the MINOAN CIVILIZATION on Crete. However, they have since established that Minoan Crete did not fall into decline until around 1450 B.C., disproving their earlier theory. The eruption also may have inspired the legend of the lost continent of Atlantis.

Another well-known volcano in the Near East is Turkey's Mount Ararat, which the Hebrew BIBLE identifies as the resting place of Noah's ark. A few archaeologists* believed that this story was supported by ship-shaped features on the mountain, but these later turned out to be natural formations caused by landslides and lava flows.

Volcanoes exist throughout central Turkey, which is covered with soft volcanic rock that was used in local construction from the A.D. 300s to the 1200s. Lava and volcanic rock are also found in northwestern Arabia, in a region known as Harrat Ash-Shamah. Volcanic eruptions have occurred there as recently as a few hundred years ago. (*See also* **Disasters, Natural; Obsidian.**)

* **archaeologist** scientist who studies past human cultures, usually by excavating material remains of human activity

WALL PAINTINGS

* **deity** god or goddess

Wall paintings represent some of the earliest and most important forms of visual art from the ancient Near East. The earliest wall paintings featured simple geometric designs done in a single color, while later works contained complex images of plants, animals, humans, and deities* in a variety of patterns and colors. Throughout ancient times, such works decorated the walls of palaces, temples, and private homes.

Materials and Techniques. Near Eastern wall paintings were done using paints made from natural pigments, or coloring agents, found in minerals, plants, and animal sources. The earliest and most basic colors used were red (made from iron oxide), white (from the mineral gypsum), and black (from a tarlike substance called bitumen). Other colors, developed later, included blue (from either copper oxide or the semiprecious stone LAPIS LAZULI), green (from the stone malachite), and yellow (from iron oxide mixed with clay or sand).

Ancient painters mixed dry pigments with water and a substance called a binder, which makes paint adhere, or stick, to a surface. Among the binders used were egg whites or a substance in milk called casein. Artists applied paint to a surface with brushes made of reeds, one end of

Wall Paintings

* **fresco** method of painting in which color is applied to moist plaster so that it becomes chemically bonded to the plaster as it dries; also, a painting done in this manner

which had been split and chewed to make the reed fibers soft enough to absorb the pigment.

Two basic techniques were used in wall painting: distemper and fresco*. Distemper, the earliest and easiest technique, involved painting on a wall covered with a layer of plaster, lime, or mud that had been allowed to dry. All wall paintings up to about 1500 B.C. were probably done using this technique. In fresco painting, several layers of plaster or a similar substance were applied to the wall, and the artist painted while the top layer of plaster was still wet. With the distemper technique, the paint formed a film on the surface of the wall. In fresco painting, the particles of pigment were bound to the plaster as it dried. Thus, a fresco actually became a part of the wall itself, which made fresco paintings very durable and allowed them to retain their color longer. However, fresco was a much more difficult technique than distemper because the painter had to work quickly before areas of fresh plaster dried.

Early Wall Paintings. Wall paintings first appeared in the Near East between 8000 and 5000 B.C. in ANATOLIA (present-day Turkey), IRAN, and the coastal areas of the eastern Mediterranean Sea. The earliest works contained simple monochrome (single-color) designs, which remained

This fresco from an Assyrian provincial palace at Til Barsip in Syria shows two officials in profile. Although the palace was decorated with many paintings, stone reliefs were more customary for Assyrian palace art.

* **sixth millennium** B.C. years from 6000 to 5001 B.C.

* **Levant** lands bordering the eastern shores of the Mediterranean Sea (present-day Syria, Lebanon, and Israel), the West Bank, and Jordan

* **third millennium** B.C. years from 3000 to 2001 B.C.

* **archaeologist** scientist who studies past human cultures, usually by excavating material remains of human activity

* **bas-relief** kind of sculpture in which material is cut away to leave figures projecting slightly from the background

* **stylized** referring to art style in which figures are portrayed in simplified ways that exaggerate certain features, not realistically

See color plate 12, vol. 4.

standard for centuries. Multicolored paintings featuring simple geometric patterns appeared around 6000 B.C., and more elaborate patterns and designs began appearing soon afterward. Many such wall paintings have been discovered in Anatolia.

By the early sixth millennium B.C.*, the imagery in wall paintings had expanded to include hunting scenes, birds, and landscapes that attempted to reproduce objects and scenes found in the natural world. Among the earliest examples of such wall paintings are ones found at ÇATAL HÜYÜK in Anatolia and in SYRIA. However, geometric patterns remained the most popular form of wall decoration in Anatolia, Iran, and the Levant* in the fifth and fourth millennia B.C.

The first wall paintings in MESOPOTAMIA were associated with the construction of large temples in the southern region of Sumer between 3500 and 3000 B.C. The walls of Sumerian temples at that time featured primarily geometric designs, although human and animal figures appeared in some wall paintings. The most widely used colors were black, red, and white. Wall paintings in houses of this and later periods continued to feature simple geometric designs done in a single color.

New Images and Colors. Little is known about wall painting during the third millennium B.C.* However, archaeologists* have uncovered many works dating from the 1800s B.C. and later throughout the Near East.

Among the new types of images that appeared during the second millennium B.C. (2000–1001 B.C.) were ceremonial scenes, often depicting acts of worship or processions of people before a ruler. Humans were represented according to the same rules used in bas-relief*. That is, faces appeared in profile, with the fronts of bodies facing outward or turned slightly to the side. Such scenes were intended to support rulers' claims that they were divinely chosen leaders.

Wall paintings from this period often included depictions of rich plant life and plentiful water, suggesting the fertility of the land. Other popular images included hunting scenes and images of sacred trees. Many paintings also incorporated bands of stylized* flowers and palm leaves, as well as groups of the ever popular geometric figures. Some paintings even attempted to imitate the look of materials such as wood or stone. Most wall paintings of this period made use of a variety of colors, including blue, green, yellow, and orange.

Many of the wall paintings that have survived from the second millennium B.C. offer clues to the spread of ideas and influences among the cultures in the Near East. For example, wall paintings from the city of MARI reflect influence from the cultures of Sumer and Babylonia. Elements from the art of the MINOAN CIVILIZATION of CRETE can be seen in wall paintings from northern Syria and Egypt. The artistic styles of the Levant influenced wall paintings in palaces of northern Mesopotamia, while paintings in the Levant featured images of bulls and masks associated with Egypt. Babylonian wall paintings from the 1100s B.C. provided models that were copied widely in Assyrian and Persian art several hundred years later.

Later Developments. One of the major developments in wall painting after 1000 B.C. was the increasing use of glazed BRICKS and tiles, which

* **relief** sculpture in which material is cut away to show figures raised from the background

helped create a more durable form of art. A single ceramic tile might contain an entire scene, with one or several figures or decorative images. More often, however, many individual colored bricks or tiles were arranged together to form larger images and scenes. Artists in Assyria, Babylonia, and Iran created magnificent reliefs* made from colored tiles or molded bricks.

Glazed brick decorations also were used widely by the Persians from the 500s to 300s B.C., but there is little evidence of true wall painting in the PERSIAN EMPIRE. After ALEXANDER THE GREAT conquered the Persian empire in 332 B.C., wall paintings in the westernmost regions of the Near East reflected a strong Greek influence. Later with the expansion of the Roman Empire into the region, Roman artistic influences shaped wall painting styles and techniques. Farther east, artists combined both Western and Asian styles until the decline of Roman influence in the early centuries A.D. (*See also* **Animals in Art; Art, Artisans, and Artists; Bas-Reliefs; Birds in Art; Burial Sites and Tombs; Human Form in Art.**)

WALLED CITIES

* **epic** long poem about a legendary or historical hero, written in a grand style

* **mud brick** brick made from mud, straw, and water mixed together and baked in the sun

* **fortification** structure built to strengthen or protect against attack

* **eighth millennium B.C.** years from 8000 to 7001 B.C.

* **silt** soil or other sediment carried and deposited by moving water

In ancient times, many cities in the Near East were surrounded by walls. Sometimes the walls surrounded an entire city, and as the city grew over time, its walls were extended to enclose new spaces. In other cases, the walls surrounded only the older part of a city or perhaps a central core of special importance, such as a fortress or a district surrounding palaces and temples.

Although historians assume that cities were walled for defense against human attackers, other possibilities exist. For example, in the city of URUK in MESOPOTAMIA, people drove their livestock inside the city's walls each night. In fact, an early version of the epic* of GILGAMESH speaks of the city as a "sheepfold" or "cattle pen." Other early city dwellers may have built walls to protect their animals from wild animals or human raiders, turning their cities into large corrals.

Other city walls originated as flood barriers. Huge walls of mud brick* around the Mesopotamian city of Sippar, for example, were intended as protection from the floodwaters of the Euphrates River. The earliest known city walls are the massive fortifications* built at JERICHO in the eighth millennium B.C.* Scholars have long thought their purpose to be military defense, but a later interpretation suggests that the Jericho walls were built to protect the settlement from silt* carried by a brook.

Walls also served to define areas of settlement and as visible reminders of authority. A wall dating from around 7000 B.C. found at the Mesopotamian village of Maghzalia, for example, probably functioned more as a symbol of the identity of the enclosed community than as a defensive fortification. Another purpose of city walls was to display the wealth and power of their builders. To this end, some walls bore rich decorations intended to win admiration for the city's rulers.

Most city walls were probably military structures built for defensive purposes. In times of war, farmers and people from the countryside sought safety inside walled cities. Between 3500 and 3000 B.C., the Sumerians built a well-planned and fortified colony in northern SYRIA. It was a

קרשתאבגדהוזחטיכדלמסנסעפפצזקרשתאבגד

Wars and Warfare

rectangular city about 44 acres in area, surrounded by a mud-brick wall about ten feet thick. The wall contained nearly 50 square towers from which the people could defend the city during an attack. Uruk, the largest Sumerian city, was surrounded by a defense wall almost six miles long, enclosing nearly 1,360 acres of land. This wall's 900 towers offered vantage points for lookouts or for soldiers.

* **Levant** lands bordering the eastern shores of the Mediterranean Sea (present-day Syria, Lebanon, and Israel), the West Bank, and Jordan

Cities built in the Levant* between 2000 and 1600 B.C. had massive fortifications, such as earthen mounds, steep artificial slopes, and moats, in addition to walls of mud brick or stone. Another impressive walled city was KHATTUSHA, the capital of the Hittites of ANATOLIA. Its fortifications included massive earthen ramps, thick stone walls, and gates with guard chambers and heavy wooden doors. In Egypt, walls were used as fortification as long ago as the Early Dynastic period (ca. 3000–2675 B.C.), although no remains have been found.

* **siege** long and persistent effort to force a surrender by surrounding a fortress or city with armed troops, cutting it off from supplies and aid

Even heavily walled cities, however, could fall to determined attackers and foes. The Assyrians of northern Mesopotamia became expert at conquering walled cities. They laid siege* to the cities surrounding the Assyrian empire and starved out their populations. They also assaulted city walls with battering rams (large logs mounted on wheeled frames), ladders, and axes and undermined them with tunnels. JERUSALEM, with stone walls 23 feet thick and at least as high, was one of the few walled cities in the ancient Near East that was able to hold off the Assyrian army. (*See also* **Cities and City-States; Fortifications; Wars and Warfare.**)

WARS AND WARFARE

* **nomad** person who travels from place to place to find food and pasture
* **city-state** independent state consisting of a city and its surrounding territory
* **imperial** pertaining to an emperor or an empire

Wars and warfare played an important role in the societies of the ancient Near East. The peoples of the region waged war for three main reasons. They fought defensive wars to protect their territories from aggression and offensive wars to conquer new lands. They also fought civil wars, which involved internal rebellions or uprisings.

The earliest wars were disputes between small, loosely organized forces wielding hunting tools such as clubs, spears, and bows and arrows. Nomads* raided the fields and pastures of settled communities, whose inhabitants fought to protect their crops and livestock. City-states* fought for control of land and water resources. Over the course of several thousand years, the states of the Near East grew larger, stronger, and more centrally organized. In some cases, they developed into imperial* powers controlling vast territories. The fighting forces of these states and empires also grew larger and more organized, becoming ARMIES consisting of professional SOLDIERS with an array of WEAPONS AND ARMOR and commanded by ranks of officers.

* **siege** long and persistent effort to force a surrender by surrounding a fortress or city with armed troops, cutting it off from supplies and aid

With the development of large states and empires, wars were fought on a larger scale, and sieges*, fighting at sea, and multiyear campaigns in distant lands became commonplace. The centerpiece of warfare, though, remained the pitched battle, in which land armies maneuvered for position and then clashed on the battlefield.

Reconstructing Ancient Battles. Modern historians have a difficult time reconstructing ancient battles. Surviving information about even the

149

Wars and Warfare

* **Levant** lands bordering the eastern shores of the Mediterranean Sea (present-day Syria, Lebanon, and Israel), the West Bank, and Jordan

* **propaganda** communication deliberately shaped or slanted toward a particular viewpoint

Holy Wars

The ancient Mesopotamians justified warfare on religious grounds, claiming that their enemies had sinned against the gods. Consequently, victory in war was more than military triumph; it was the triumph of divine justice, backed by the gods. Invaders who seized thrones could also be viewed in a religious context. For instance, when Cyrus of Persia defeated Nabonidus of Babylonia, people believed that the Babylonian ruler had sinned against the gods, who had chosen the outsider Cyrus to replace him. So deep were such beliefs that when King Sargon II of Assyria was killed in battle, his son Sennacherib agonized over the sin that his father must have committed to arouse the terrible anger of the gods.

* **fortification** structure built to strengthen or protect against attack

best-documented conflicts is often vague and incomplete. An example is a battle fought at MEGIDDO in the Levant*, which took place around 1456 B.C. This is the earliest Near Eastern battle for which detailed descriptions survive. Yet even the fullest account of the battle, which was recorded on the walls of the great temple of the god AMUN at KARNAK in Egypt, has many missing sections of text. Moreover, scholars realize that it was written in a literary style intended to glorify the achievements of the king. Many ancient accounts of battles were written for a similar purpose—to serve as propaganda*—making the accuracy of their information highly questionable.

The battle at Megiddo pitted THUTMOSE III, the ruler of Egypt, against a coalition of Canaanite forces. The surviving record gives many details of the Egyptian army's long march to the city of Megiddo and its position on the day of battle on the Plain of Jezreel facing the city. However, it includes no details about the size or position of the Canaanite forces or about the actual fight. It says only that when Thutmose appeared on the battlefield, the enemy fled in great disorder.

The battle of Qadesh, in which the Egyptians fought against the HITTITES of ANATOLIA (present-day Turkey) around 1274 B.C., is known in greater detail because pictorial records accompany written accounts in Egypt. However, these pictures and texts fail to reveal that the Egyptians lost the battle. Instead, they focus on the bravery and heroism of the Egyptian king, RAMSES II.

Nearly all accounts of warfare in the ancient Near East contain no reliable information about such things as the location of battlefields, the weather and terrain in which a battle took place, the size and position of troops, the duration of the fighting, and how armies coordinated the movement of people and supplies. In short, information gathered from surviving official accounts of military encounters gives a broad picture of ancient warfare, but it lacks the details that would allow historians to reconstruct those battles.

Siege Warfare. According to ancient texts, the battle of Megiddo was followed by a siege of that city. The ancient armies of the Egyptians, Hittites, Assyrians, Babylonians, and Persians often employed siege warfare, which developed into a highly specialized form of combat with its own tools and weapons.

Siege warfare was a way of capturing cities or fortresses that could not be taken quickly in battle. Fortresses and many ancient Near Eastern cities had strong walls and other fortifications* to help them withstand direct attacks by an enemy. During a siege, however, such protective barriers could become like the walls of a prison, trapping the defenders inside the city or fort.

An attacking army laid siege to a city by surrounding it with troops to make sure that no one could enter or leave. The defenders inside the city could neither send messages to allies asking for help nor obtain fresh supplies or reinforcements. Their ability to endure a siege depended on the quality of their fortifications and the soldiers who operated them, their stockpiles of food, and their access to freshwater from wells or streams.

By the 700s B.C., the Assyrian empire's westward expansion brought the Assyrians into contact with the Arabs, resulting in many battles between them. This relief from Nineveh from the 600s B.C. shows Arab tribesmen fleeing from Assyrian troops. Although some of the Arabs are shown fighting on camelback, most scholars believe that they generally only used camels for transport to battles.

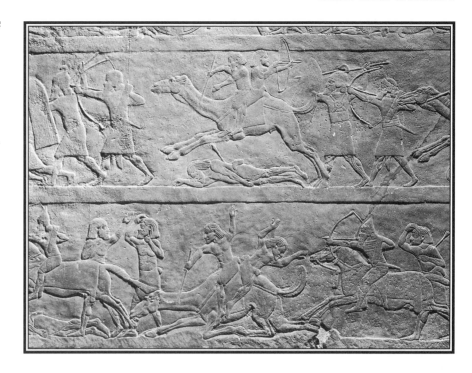

The attackers in a siege had three ways to assault a besieged city or fortress. They could dig tunnels under the walls, climb over them, or smash and burn their way through them. If these methods failed, they could seal off the city and try to starve its inhabitants until they surrendered. Usually, attackers used some or all of these methods at the same time.

Tunneling under city walls required no special equipment other than shovels. Climbing over the walls required the construction of ladders or towers. The attackers might also build huge ramps of earth leading up to the top of the enemy walls. Sometimes these ramps had to cross streams or water-filled ditches that helped protect the approach to the walls.

Attempts to break through walls usually centered on gates, often made of wood, which were the weakest points in the walls. Attackers might try to set the gates on fire or break through them with a battering ram, a huge log or wooden beam mounted in a wheeled frame. Using ropes or chains, the attackers drove the ram as hard as possible against the gates or possibly the walls themselves. If the ram succeeded in making a hole in the defenses, soldiers would charge through to attack the defenders inside. Another tactic involved shooting flaming arrows into a besieged fort or city, hoping to start fires that would cause the inhabitants to panic, flee, and surrender.

It was not easy to carry out siege operations under the watchful eyes of the defenders, who could shoot arrows or hurl stones, hot liquids, or fire from the top of the walls onto the enemy below. Moreover, sieges took time, during which the attacking force also needed food and other supplies. When these ran short, the attackers could suffer from hunger and disease almost as much as the defenders inside the besieged city. The capture of an enemy capital or sacred city had great psychological impact on both the victors and the vanquished. Because siege warfare was so difficult and costly, it tended to be undertaken only as a last resort.

151

Wars and Warfare

* **epic** long poem about a legendary or historical hero, written in a grand style

* **second millennium** B.C. years from 2000 to 1001 B.C.

* **plunder** property stolen by force, usually after a conquest

* **diplomacy** practice of conducting negotiations between kingdoms, states, or nations

Bribery, treachery, or trickery occasionally offered attackers a way into a besieged city. A well-known example of this appears in the *Iliad,* the epic* by the ancient Greek poet Homer, which tells the story of the long siege of Troy in Anatolia by the Greeks. After many years of siege, the Greeks built a giant wooden horse and a small band of soldiers hid inside it. When the Trojans hauled the horse into their city, the Greeks came out of the horse at night and opened the city gates to their armies.

Military Tactics. Warfare involves strategies, which are overall goals, and tactics, which are the means used to reach those goals. The societies of the ancient Near East used different combinations of tactics to achieve their military strategies.

The military history of Assyria illustrates a shift from defensive to offensive strategies and the use of a wide range of tactics, including psychological warfare. At the beginning of the second millennium B.C.*, the city-state of Ashur in northern Mesopotamia slowly built a fighting force to defend itself. The rulers of Ashur, believing that their state had to conquer or be conquered, raided surrounding regions that threatened to attack.

Plunder* proved to be an added advantage to Assyrian raids, and greed became a motive for further campaigns. Another motive for warfare was the growing desire of Assyrian kings to gain prestige through successful military campaigns. By 700 B.C., Assyrian armies had waged offensive wars from the Mediterranean Sea in the west to the Persian Gulf in the south. Campaigns usually began in the spring and lasted through the summer.

The Assyrians made little use of NAVAL POWER in warfare. Because they did not have a navy, they usually used Phoenician ships when they had to go to sea. They made extensive use of pitched battles and siege warfare, but these tactics consumed much time, energy, and labor. The Assyrians came to prefer psychological warfare, which involved breaking down the enemy's will to resist. Once the Assyrians decided to conquer a region, they would try using diplomacy* to get the inhabitants to submit. If diplomacy failed, they surrounded the foreign capital and shouted to its inhabitants, urging them to surrender. The next step was to attack small, weak cities and commit extreme acts of destruction and cruelty as a warning to all who did not submit. Using such methods of psychological warfare, the much-feared Assyrians made some conquests with minimal effort.

During the second millennium B.C., the Hittites of Anatolia had a well-organized and efficient military force that protected their borders and earned them a place among the great powers of the day. The Hittites used sentries, outposts, and spies to gather information about enemy movements. Sometimes Hittite agents disguised as deserters or fugitives deliberately passed false information to the enemy, a tactic that contributed to the victory of the Hittite king Muwattalli II over Ramses II of Egypt at the battle of Qadesh in about 1274 B.C.

The Hittites, just like others in the ancient Near East, believed in seeking guidance from the gods on military matters. The king might ask the gods if they approved of a campaign and if the king would win. He might even ask the gods to approve specific tactics and plans of action. The Hittites favored direct attacks and pitched battles. One favorite tactic was to

152

burn crops and villages in an area until the men of the district were forced to fight the Hittite army. Another was to destroy one town in the hope that neighboring towns would submit without a fight. If a city did not submit and could not be taken by storm, the Hittites mounted a siege. Evidence suggests that, on occasion, a duel between two champions, one representing each side—for example, between David, the Israelite, and the Philistine Goliath; or between Achilles, the Greek, and Hector, the Trojan—might settle an issue. Such contests represented warfare in its most basic form. (*See also* **Assyria and the Assyrians; Cavalry; Chariots; Egypt and the Egyptians; Persian Wars.**)

WATER

Many peoples of the ancient Near East considered water sacred, a symbol of fertility, and the source of life. Access to reliable sources of water was essential for survival, especially in places such as Egypt and Mesopotamia, where rainfall alone did not provide sufficient water to sustain large-scale settlements and AGRICULTURE. The ancient Near Easterners realized the importance of managing their resources so that they could make the most use of the water available to them. How well they were able to do so meant the difference between prosperity and starvation for many farming communities, cities, and even entire empires of the ancient Near East. As a consequence, water became an important resource to safeguard or control.

Climate. About 15,000 years ago, during the most recent Ice Age, the climate of the Near East was cool and dry. There was little precipitation because a large amount of moisture was trapped in large ice sheets. As the earth warmed and the ice melted, the climate became warmer and more humid. Wetter conditions peaked around 7500 B.C. and again in about 4000 B.C., corresponding to times of increased population growth in Egypt and Mesopotamia. By the time the first cities in the Near East were founded, however, somewhat drier conditions had returned. Despite generally less favorable climatic conditions, rapid urbanization* and population growth occurred in the ancient Near East.

* **urbanization** formation and growth of cities

Water Sources and Irrigation. Because most parts of the ancient Near East received little rainfall, the societies there had to rely on other sources of water. Both the Egyptians and the Mesopotamians depended on the annual flooding of local RIVERS to provide the water they needed.

Every year, summer rains steadily increased the water levels of rivers emptying into Egypt's NILE RIVER. These rivers lay far south of Egypt, so the floodwaters traveled a great distance before spilling into low-lying basins adjacent to the Nile, soaking the ground, and depositing silt* rich in nutrients. After the waters receded, farmers plowed and planted the moist soil that was left behind. Consequently, there was little need for man-made IRRIGATION.

* **silt** soil or other sediment carried and deposited by moving water

The main water sources in ancient Mesopotamia, the EUPHRATES RIVER and the TIGRIS RIVER, originated in the mountains of Anatolia (present-day Turkey) and were fed by rapidly melting spring snows. The

153

Water

See
color plate 6,
vol. 4.

floodwaters traveled a shorter distance over steeper terrain, resulting in floods that were difficult to control for purposes of irrigation. Moreover, the timing of the flood was such that it occurred when crops were in the fields. Consequently, unlike those of the Nile, the floodwaters of the Tigris and Euphrates needed not only to be controlled but also to be stored for use prior to the planting. In order to use the floodwaters, the ancient Mesopotamians constructed an elaborate series of CANALS that allowed them to hold the water and channel it to the fields where it was needed.

Another problem in ancient Mesopotamia was that the Tigris and Euphrates carried sediments containing salts that built up in the soil over time, making it unsuitable for farming. The soil in the Tigris and Euphrates Delta became so salty after about 1850 B.C. that the population eventually migrated to more fertile regions where agriculture was still possible.

Outside the main river valleys, people used other sources of water, such as brooks or natural springs into which water flowed by the force of gravity. The earliest permanent settlement in the world was at JERICHO in Canaan, which was located near the Jordan River and a spring.

Protection of Water Resources. In the ancient cities of Canaan, inhabitants constructed public works to tap and protect valuable water sources. They built covered galleries to allow residents access to the streams or pools and to exclude their use by outsiders. In some cities such as MEGIDDO, tunnels were built so that water from a nearby spring flowed into a pool constructed under the city. Bringing the water to the city in this manner was not only more convenient, but it also ensured access to water if the city were attacked or placed under siege*.

Water and Politics. Water had the potential to be used as a tool for destruction. For instance, cities along a river could ruin the economy of neighboring rivals by not maintaining their water-controlling devices or by diverting the water away from other cities, either causing a flood or a drought*. Several early Sumerian texts suggest that this was a cause or result of conflicts between cities. Mesopotamians also fought wars to defend themselves from invaders who wanted to conquer their well-watered land.

Access to water and construction and maintenance of water-controlling devices were important issues in the ancient Near East, because everyone had to share this essential resource. Records of wills and land sales from Mesopotamia and elsewhere in the region show that people carefully defined the water rights associated with their property. Maintenance of canals was crucial, and each city appointed officials who were responsible for this task. Other large-scale projects, such as the construction of regulators* to control the flow of water from the rivers, required the efforts of several villages or even cities working together. These projects were considered so important that several Mesopotamian kings left INSCRIPTIONS celebrating the construction of canals and other steps they took to manage water resources. (*See also* **Drought; Environmental Change; Floods; Geography.**)

* **siege** long and persistent effort to force a surrender by surrounding a fortress or city with armed troops, cutting it off from supplies and aid

* **drought** long period of dry weather during which crop yields are lower than usual

* **regulator** gate or valve to control amount of water passing through a channel

154

Weapons and Armor

WEAPONS AND ARMOR

In the history of the ancient Near East, many battles were fought over territory and resources. The SOLDIERS fighting these battles relied on weapons to attack their foes and on protective armor to escape harm. Over the course of several thousand years, the weapons and armor used by the ARMIES of the region underwent many changes as people developed new materials, new technologies, and new ways of waging war.

Weapons. The first weapons used for war were those used in hunting: spears, bows and arrows, axes, nets, and maces. Most weapons were made of stone or wood, but after about 3000 B.C., advances in metalworking led to the introduction of bronze weapons, with blades that were easier to keep sharp. After about 1200 B.C., bronze was replaced by iron.

The number and variety of weapons increased as people developed implements specifically for combat. Texts, illustrations, and artifacts* of the Egyptians show the array of their weaponry. These weapons fell into two groups: weapons intended to serve as an extension of the arm and used at short range and weapons designed for long-range use. At times, short-range weapons were adapted for long-range use.

Short-range weapons were meant to kill or disable opponents with bone-crushing blows. Maces, clubs, and cudgels* had weighted ends that could strike an opponent with terrific force. Thrusting and stabbing weapons were intended to pierce the body and penetrate vital organs. They included daggers, straight swords, and lances (stabbing spears). Slashing and cutting weapons, such as the battle-ax and single- and double-edged swords combined the qualities of the other two types. That is, they delivered cutting blows over a wide area of the body and, at the same time, struck like clubs and could lop off limbs.

Ancient long-range weapons were missiles (objects that are thrown through the air) launched either by hand or by a launching device. Hand-launched missiles included stones, throwing sticks, throwing axes, and javelins (spears for throwing). The longest-range missiles were those driven by the energy of a launching device. Slingshots could be used to hurl stones with accuracy and force. An example of this is described in the Hebrew BIBLE, when the Israelite David uses a slingshot to kill the Philistine Goliath (1 Kings 17:50). The longest-range weapon, however, was the bow and arrow. Early bows in Egypt consisted of a single long piece of wood bent into a curved shape. The bows that developed later, called composite bows, were shorter and consisted of layers of wood, animal horn, and sinew*. Such bows were more powerful and more accurate than the earlier ones.

Similar weapons came into use across the Near East, but various regions and cultures developed distinctive variations. In MESOPOTAMIA during the third millennium B.C.*, for example, the large number of words for different kinds of axes, such as single-bladed and double-bladed, indicates that axes were widely used not just as weapons but also in ceremonies and as a form of currency. The Scythians and other nomads* of CENTRAL ASIA, who were among the most skilled horsemen and archers of the ancient world, had bows that were small enough to handle on horseback but that could shoot powerfully over a long range. The Scythian arrowheads had thorn-shaped projections that prevented an arrow from being removed from a wound without causing more damage.

* **artifact** ornament, tool, weapon, or other object made by humans

* **cudgel** short, heavy club

* **sinew** tough cord of tissue that attaches muscles to bones

* **third millennium B.C.** period from 3000 to 2001 B.C.

* **nomad** person who travels from place to place in search of food and pasture

155

Weapons and Armor

Armor. Weaponry was only part of a soldier's equipment. Warriors also needed protection from their enemy's attacks. Two main types of protective equipment came into use in the ancient Near East: shields and protective armor. Shields were portable barriers, usually strapped to one forearm, that a soldier could position to block blows aimed at him. Most shields were made of wood or of leather on a wooden frame. Because metal was both heavy and expensive, whole shields were rarely made of metal. However, metal bands, studs, or spikes were used on shields made of other materials.

Egyptian wall paintings illustrating a battle with the HITTITES of ANATOLIA (present-day Turkey) show that they favored a tall shield with indentations on its sides. This shield was probably intended to protect the

The soldier depicted in this Sumerian plaque from the third millennium B.C. wears a helmet to protect him from blows to the head. He also holds two of the earliest types of metal weapons. In his right hand is an ax that was designed for piercing purposes and in his left, he carries a sickle sword.

entire body. By the end of the second millennium B.C. (years from 2000 to 1001 B.C.), smaller, round shields were coming into use.

Ancient armies employed shields in several ways. One widely used tactic was to march infantry, or foot soldiers, forward in a solid block called a phalanx. The soldiers were trained to march in rhythm and close enough together that their shields overlapped, presenting a solid wall to their enemy's arrows or spears. Another important use of shields was to protect the drivers of chariots and the archers who rode in the chariots. The Hittites used three-man chariots, with one soldier who carried the shield to protect both the driver and the fighter.

In addition to shields, soldiers sometimes wore protective clothing, such as helmets or body armor. Helmets were generally made of leather, although metal plates might be attached to them. In Hittite Anatolia, helmets had pointed tops and flaps that protected the wearer's cheeks and neck. The Assyrians made helmets of hammered iron with bronze rivets. Crests and plumes often adorned warrior's helmets. These were sometimes symbols of rank but also may have helped identify members of a particular force during the confusion of battle.

The earliest armor consisted of garments of leather or perhaps heavy felt, a dense woolen cloth. In the later part of the second millennium B.C., as swords and arrows became more powerful and lethal, people began wearing metal plates as armor. Scale armor, which consisted of many small overlapping discs or plates, offered some protection from the enemy's weapons, especially the supreme weapon, long-distance arrows. A soldier portrayed on the King's Gate in the ruins of the ancient Hittite capital of KHATTUSHA wears a sleeveless jacket that may have been made of leather. Underneath it is what looks like a shirt of scale armor. Hittites and other ancient soldiers may also have worn protective garments of chain mail, many small metal rings sewn together in a flexible sheet.

The quest for more powerful weapons was paralleled by a drive to develop lightweight, effective protection from them. For the people of the ancient Near East, improved techniques of weapon and armor making could make the difference between life and death. (*See also* **Cavalry; Chariots; Egypt and the Egyptians; Metals and Metalworking; Wars and Warfare.**)

Uncovering Ancient Armor

The ancient Greeks believed that the Saka people of the Central Asian plains had invented several forms of battle armor, including a large shield. The Greek historian Herodotus wrote that the Saka horses wore armored coats. Modern archaeologists have found evidence that the Saka were skilled armorers. The ruins of the Temple of the Oxus, built in the 300s B.C. in present-day Afghanistan, contain many iron plates from defensive armor. The major part of a complete suit of armor has also survived. Its plates are fastened together in overlapping rows. Those plates may have been the best protection from the hazards of ancient warfare.

Weaving   See *Textiles.*

Wheat   See *Cereal Grains.*

WHEEL

Historians, archaeologists*, and other scholars consider the invention of the wheel one of the most important technological advances that occurred in the ancient Near East. The wheel made the transport of people and goods easier and faster. It also led to developments in many aspects of life, particularly in trade and war.

Wine

* **archaeologist** scientist who studies past human cultures, usually by excavating material remains of human activity

* **artisan** skilled craftsperson

* **fourth millennium B.C.** years from 4000 to 3001 B.C.

* **millennium** period of 1000 years; *pl.* millennia

Archaeologists believe that the wheel used for transport was adapted from the potter's wheel, which was invented around 4000 B.C. The potter's wheel was set on an axle, which in turn was set within a bearing that enabled the wheel to rotate freely. This freely rotating wheel enabled ancient Near Eastern artisans* to mass-produce pottery, which became a necessity with the establishment of cities. The first evidence of wheeled vehicles—depictions in pictographs from URUK—date from the late fourth millennium B.C.* Most archaeological evidence of wheels, however, dates from after 3000 B.C. Before that time, sledges, or sleighs, and pack animals were used to transport people and goods.

The earliest wheels in Mesopotamia were made using three planks of wood that were cut to form a circle and held together by a thin strip of lumber. These disk wheels were then fixed to an axle that was attached to a cart. This type of wheel was soon adopted by the other cultures of the ancient Near East. However, these wheels were heavy and clumsy, making vehicles slow, and people continued to use sledges and animals for transport. When wheeled vehicles were used, they were ox-drawn wagons, two-wheeled or four-wheeled carts, or CHARIOTS, pulled by donkeys or HORSES. These were used for passengers or for carrying goods.

Over the millennia*, ancient Near Easterners improved the wheel in several ways, including the addition of a tire by which the wheel wore down evenly. Eventually, tires of leather, and later, metal were used. The most significant improvement was the creation of openings in the disks. These eventually led to the invention of spokes, which were first portrayed in Hittite and Syrian carvings in the early second millennium B.C. (years between 2000 and 1001 B.C.).

Wheels with spokes were lighter than disk wheels, and they could carry their loads at faster speeds. Because their speed and lightness made them more maneuverable, the spoked wheels were used in chariots to transport soldiers. Around 400 B.C., the Persians turned chariot wheels into weapons by mounting sharp, curved blades on them. When driven into an enemy infantry formation, these blades could cut down troops.

Scholars are unsure of the extent of the impact the invention of the wheel had on ancient Near Eastern society. Some believe that improved TRANSPORTATION enabled people to move into cities even though they were farther away from food sources and supplies because these could now be easily imported. The invention of the wheel also stimulated the economy because it created new professions, such as jobs for people who made wheels and carriages. (*See also* **Science and Technology**.)

WINE

* **commodity** article of trade

The earliest evidence of wine making in the ancient Near East—dating to about 3500 B.C.—was found in sediments inside a large pottery jar at a site in IRAN. However, it is most likely that wine was produced much earlier than that. In addition to grapes, wine was also made from other fruits, including dates, figs, pomegranates, and plums.

Wine was a rare and valuable commodity* in southern MESOPOTAMIA, which contains few regions suitable for the cultivation of grapes. Described as "mountain beer" or "bright wine like the uncountable waters of the river," wine was never plentiful in Babylonia. Wine consumption was limited to the wealthiest classes, and wine was often presented as an OFFERING to the deities. An expensive luxury item of trade, wine reached BABYLON in the form of taxes from northern and western lands or as tribute* from defeated enemies.

Vineyards were more commonly found in northern Mesopotamia, where the terrain was mountainous and the rainfall was sufficient for grape cultivation. For instance, Assyria enjoyed favorable conditions for growing grapes, with the best vineyards in the regions east of the city of NINEVEH. The royal palace at KALKHU contained space for the storage of up to 528 gallons of wine. Several clay tablets found in the palace describe the allocation of wine rations to the members of the royal household, indicating that wine was not as rare a commodity in Assyria as it was in Babylonia.

In Egypt, the cultivation of grapes was easier, and therefore the consumption of wine was greater. However, because the cultivation of grapes required IRRIGATION, wine was still largely a drink of the upper classes. Archaeologists* have found sealed wine jars with labels indicating where and when the wine was made, the name of the vintner (the person in charge of the vineyard), and the quality of the wine inside. The quality listed could vary from simply "wine" to "very good" or "genuine" and, in at least one case, "for merrymaking."

Depictions in tomb paintings as well as INSCRIPTIONS and texts have also yielded considerable information on wine making and consumption in ancient Egypt. As in Mesopotamia, wine was often used to pay taxes and as an offering to the gods. Wine was also well known SYRIA and in the Levant*, as indicated by the many references to it in the Hebrew BIBLE. (*See also* **Food and Drink.**)

* **tribute** payment made by a smaller or weaker party to more powerful one, often under the threat of force

* **archaeologist** scientist who studies past human cultures, usually by excavating material remains of human activity

* **Levant** lands bordering the eastern shores of the Mediterranean Sea (present-day Syria, Lebanon, and Israel), the West Bank, and Jordan

WITCHCRAFT

* **incantation** written or recited formula of words designed to produce a given effect
* **amulet** small object thought to have supernatural or magical powers

The use of MAGIC was widespread in the ancient Near East. Both white magic, or helpful magic, and witchcraft, or black magic, were practiced. Magicians used incantations*, other special words, and objects such as amulets* to control the supernatural world for specific purposes.

White magic, practiced openly in the ancient Near East, was closely related to both religion and medicine. It was generally used to protect people from harm. For example, it might have been used to cure someone by turning away the evil DEMONS who were believed to be causing the person's illness. In contrast, witchcraft was used to deliberately harm others for the benefit of the witch or the witch's client. For instance, it might have been used to cause illness in someone the witch or warlock (male witch) disliked. Because witchcraft was prohibited by law, it was practiced in secret. People believed that witches were frequent and unpredictable causes of harm, and they lived in constant dread of their black magic.

Many written sources from the ancient Near East describe white magic, but little has been found about witchcraft. What is known about witchcraft comes primarily from texts describing the white magic that was used to combat it. Counterspells—spells designed to fight witchcraft—dealing with almost every facet of life have been found, indicating that the practice of witchcraft was common and widespread.

Witchcraft

Methods of Witchcraft. Although their aims were different, witches and people who practiced white magic used the same or similar methods. Of the two techniques most commonly used, one was based on analogy, or similarity, and the other was based on contiguity, or closeness.

In witchcraft based on analogy, an object that bore some resemblance to a person was manipulated by the witch. The assumption was that whatever happened to the object would happen to the person the object represented. For example, a witch might prepare a doll so that it that looked like a particular person. Then the witch would pierce the doll with needles to cause pain or injury to the person the doll resembled.

In witchcraft based on contiguity, an object or objects that had belonged to or been touched by a particular person were manipulated by the witch. The assumption here, as in witchcraft based on analogy, was that whatever happened to the objects would also happen to the people the objects had touched. For instance, a lock of hair or piece of clothing belonging to a person might be damaged or destroyed by a witch to cause harm or death to the person from whom the hair or clothing had been taken.

A special category of witchcraft that was common in the ancient Near East, especially in Mesopotamia, was the "evil eye." This was a curse directed at another person to cause that person harm. In Egypt, ancient texts mention people who were "red of eye," which may be related to the Mesopotamian evil eye. These people were believed to be worshipers of SETH, the god of chaos. The Hebrew Bible describes the evil eye as well, but here it was not a curse. Rather, it was the idea that an envious or jealous person could injure another with a look.

The spirits of dead people were believed to have supernatural powers and knowledge, including that of the future. Necromancy was a method of divination* in which a magician tried to learn about the future by communicating with spirits of the dead. Although necromancy was practiced in many regions in the ancient Near East, it was considered a bad form of magic, practiced only by witches. Consequently, it was punishable by death.

Detecting and Punishing Witchcraft. Witchcraft was illegal throughout the ancient Near East. Several law codes banned it and set procedures to be followed in cases where it was suspected. For example, the law code issued by the Babylonian king HAMMURABI around 1750 B.C. states that both witchcraft and false accusations of witchcraft were punishable by death. The Code of Hammurabi also spelled out how to determine if the person accused of witchcraft was actually a witch. The accused person was to be put through a test called the river ordeal in which he, or more commonly she, plunged into the waters of a river. If the person drowned, he or she was presumed to be guilty of witchcraft. If the person survived, the presumption was of innocence.

Another way of dealing with witchcraft was spelled out in an ancient Mesopotamian ritual called *Maqlu*, meaning "burning." This ritual, which always took place at night, did not require that the witch's identity be known. Instead, an effigy, or model, was used in place of the unknown witch. Much of the ritual and its accompanying incantations

* **divination** art or practice of foretelling the future

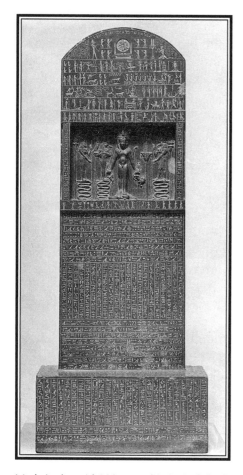

Made in the mid-300s B.C., this 34-inch-high Metternich Stela is an example of a healing stela, or column—one that was believed to have magical properties. It is inscribed with spells, magical representations, and texts directed against dangerous animals. Although some stelae stood in private homes, most were erected in public places.

were aimed at associating the effigy with the real witch. At the end of the ritual, the effigy was burned to punish the witch, whose true identity remained unknown.

Although it is likely that witchcraft was practiced widely in the ancient Near East, it is unlikely that many people were actually accused and put through the river ordeal or some other type of trial. Because witchcraft was always practiced in secret, the identity of a witch usually was not known. Moreover, because a false accusation of witchcraft could mean death for the accuser, people probably avoided accusations of witchcraft whenever possible. (*See also* **Amulets and Charms; Oracles and Prophecy; Rituals and Sacrifice.**)

WOMEN, ROLE OF

In every major civilization of the ancient Near East, men dominated the government, religion, and economy. Women did not enjoy equal status with men although they had more rights in some places and times than in others. Women's legal rights, both within the family and in society as a whole, were generally defined and limited by men.

Although history does not tell of any organized resistance by women to male authority, some individual women achieved considerable status and power. These women usually came from elite, often royal, families. Several were QUEENS who governed their states in their own right. Although most women of the ancient world occupied humbler levels of society, they filled numerous vital roles in addition to those of wives and mothers. Their activities and responsibilities may have been viewed as separate from men's, but they were essential to the functioning of society.

Mesopotamia. Women of the Sumerian, Babylonian, and Assyrian cultures of MESOPOTAMIA could own property in their own names, even when married. As early as the third millennium B.C.*, their names appeared in records as property buyers. In the time of the Old Babylonian empire (ca. 1900–1600 B.C.), women could serve as witnesses to legal transactions, although they later lost this right. Women also served as scribes*, physicians, diviners*, artists, and performers, although in all of these roles they were outnumbered and overshadowed by men.

Information about the status of some Mesopotamian women comes from the ruins of NUZI, a Mitannian town in northeastern Mesopotamia. Free women (as opposed to slaves) in Nuzi were active in the town's economy and in its courts, particularly in connection with the ownership of land, which they acquired by purchase, inheritance, and grants from rulers. They bought and sold goods, lent money, and made investments alone or in partnership with other women and men. Although such activities show that women's legal status was equal to that of men, women participated in economic activities outside the household only when there were no men in their families to do so.

Babylonians developed the custom of sending a rich young woman away to become a *naditum*. She lived apart from the world in an institution called a *gagum*, which was associated with a temple. As a *naditum*, a woman was forbidden to marry and was expected to devote her life to

* **third millennium B.C.** years from 3000 to 2001 B.C.

* **scribe** person of a learned class who served as a writer, editor, or teacher

* **diviner** person who foretells the future

Women, Role of

prayer and religious worship. She controlled some private, portable property from her dowry*, such as money and jewelry, and with these goods she could engage in business activities and investments. Because she was free from the responsibilities of marriage and motherhood, a *naditum* was able to become an important businessperson.

Mesopotamian women of the merchant class sometimes became alewives, or owners and operators of taverns who also lent money to farmers. Lower-class women had fewer opportunities to control their own destinies. Those without men to provide for them sometimes performed forced labor in dire conditions and received smaller rations than their male counterparts. Such women worked in the wool-processing and weaving industries.

Egypt. Ancient Egypt was a male-dominated society that made sharp distinctions between men's and women's roles and occupations. Nevertheless, women enjoyed significant legal rights. They could inherit property, own real estate, and on their deaths, leave it to whomever they pleased. They could own slaves and free them. They could also conduct economic and legal transactions, including lawsuits. Records even tell of one woman who sued her father over ownership of some possessions.

A woman's work in ancient Egypt depended largely on her social status or that of her husband. The titles given to women in Egyptian texts offer clues about their roles. During the Old Kingdom period (ca. 2675–2130 B.C.), elite and noble women bore such titles as "She-who-is-known-to-the-king," the female version of a high-ranking male official's title. Other descriptive titles, such as "inspector of treasure," reveal that women worked in administrative positions as stewards for other powerful women. Some were in charge of state or temple storehouses of food and textiles, while others worked in private households. Female weavers, wigmakers, singers, dancers, and doctors also appear in the records. As in Mesopotamia, however, women formed a minority in most professions.

Women also had roles, although limited ones, in the temple cults* of Egyptian religion. Texts contain accounts of priestesses of the goddess HATHOR and of female singers and dancers in the temples. During the New Kingdom period (ca. 1539–1075 B.C.), a royal wife or daughter headed the priesthood at the temple of AMUN at THEBES.

Married Egyptian women generally ran their households. One Egyptian text even recommended to men that they let their wives run the house without male interference. In addition to overseeing the household, a wife might also have performed textile work for a temple or other state institution or increased family income by selling or trading garden produce, cakes, clothing, or pottery.

Female servants worked in houses and in the tasks of food and textile preparation, but most skilled crafts were limited to men. It is possible that some women worked outdoors as forced laborers as a form of punishment. Generally however, there was a division of labor in Egypt between men's and women's work.

Anatolia. Although the pantheon* of the HITTITES of central ANATOLIA (present-day Turkey) consisted of almost as many goddesses as gods who

Paying for a Man's Mistakes

Although women without male relatives faced many difficulties in the ancient Near East, a husband or father was no guarantee of protection. A man's wife and children were likely to suffer if he had unpaid debts or other legal problems. A letter from the Old Babylonian period describes just such a situation:

Immediately after you left for the trip, Imgur-Sin arrived here and claimed: "He owes me twenty shekels of silver." He took your wife and daughter as pledges. Come back before your wife and daughter die from . . . constantly grinding barley while in detention. Please get your wife and daughter out of this.

Found at Susa and dating from the 800s or 700s B.C., this bitumen-compound relief shows a woman spinning, a process associated with the manufacture of textiles. Many women in the ancient Near East worked in the textile industry, especially as weavers. Many other women worked as oil pressers, nurses for babies, and grain grinders.

received equal space and prominence in shrines and temples, the status of women was less equal in everyday life. An example of this can be found in one Hittite story featuring a husband telling his wife, "You are a woman and of a womanly nature: you know nothing at all."

A Hittite woman's activities were usually limited to her home. Her roles were daughter, wife, mother, and widow. Her power, if she had any, was determined by her husband's status and wealth. A king's daughter or sister, for example, could become queen of a neighboring state. A rich man's wife could command many servants and have time for leisure activities. She supervised the preparation of the family's food and clothing, while ordinary women performed these tasks themselves.

Some women, however, had roles outside the home, although they earned about half as much as men did. Those from the poorer ranks of society performed manual labor for wages. Some women worked in the palace, and temple personnel included priestesses and female singers. Midwives aided in birth, and women skilled in the magic arts were in demand to help people suffering from both physical ills such as headaches and supernatural ones such as attacks by witches.

The most powerful women in Hittite society were queens, some of whom exercised considerable power and conducted official business in their own names. Widowed queens held their power until death, which meant that their influence overlapped with the reigns of their husband's sons or stepsons, resulting in many struggles for power in the palace. Queens were able to strengthen their positions and to influence others by using funds they controlled, their knowledge of state secrets, and even their supposed skills in spells and magic.

163

Wood and Woodworking

See color plate 13, vol. 2.

Iran. Women in the Elamite civilization of western IRAN had higher status than those in neighboring Mesopotamia. This may be reflected in the fact that many cities in Elam had a goddess as their patron* deity. Some scholars also believe that the Elamites had a matrilineal system of inheritance (one that ran from mother to daughter rather than from father to son). Evidence for this comes from a letter from an Elamite king who claimed he should rule Babylon because he was married to the oldest daughter of its king. Other Elamite records show that women could serve as witnesses to the swearing of oaths in legal transactions.

In contrast to the state of Elam, the PERSIAN EMPIRE, which dominated Iran from 550 to 330 B.C., was organized along patrilineal* lines of descent and inheritance. Although women could not inherit their father's goods, they could and sometimes did occupy positions of higher rank than men. Records reveal that women sometimes supervised groups of male workers and received equal or larger shares of rations.

Syria and the Levant. In Syria and the Levant*, as elsewhere in the ancient Near East, women's status and roles depended largely on their male connections. In the third millennium B.C., women of the royal household held a significant place in the society of the Syrian city-state* of EBLA. The king's mother and his primary wife had full access to the palace goods and their management, a privilege they retained in the Canaanite and Israelite cultures that later emerged in the region. The royal harem, or the "women of the king," lived in their own building and were assisted by a group of officials. Sometimes these women were placed in charge of important parts of palace work, especially textile manufacturing.

Among the Israelites, many families raised livestock or engaged in farming. In such households, women and girls shared the work. Although women were raised primarily to be wives and mothers, the Book of Samuel in the Hebrew BIBLE lists jobs that women performed outside the home, including those of performer, cook, and baker. Some women participated actively in trade. Israelite women had few legal rights, however. They could not divorce their husbands, and only rarely could they inherit property. Unlike most Near Eastern societies, Israel barred women from holding religious offices. Although this prohibition set Israelite women apart, the existence of rules that established what roles women could have in society was common in the ancient Near East. (*See also* **Childbirth; Children; Divorce; Egypt and the Egyptians; Family and Social Life; Marriage; Pregnancy.**)

WOOD AND WOODWORKING

The natural abundance of wood, together with its structural qualities and the ease with which it can be worked, has made wood one of the most widely used BUILDING MATERIALS for many millennia*. Throughout history, wood has remained popular not only for building but also for crafts and necessities. Although the Near East is not noted for its extensive timber resources, the inhabitants of the region have made use of wood for a variety of purposes since ancient times.

Wood and Woodworking

* **millennium** period of 1,000 years; *pl.* millennia

* **mud brick** brick made from mud, straw, and water mixed together and baked in the sun

Building the Tabernacle

The Hebrew Bible describes the construction of the tabernacle, a makeshift wooden-framed tent used for worship by the ancient Israelites during their journey to the Promised Land:

He [the craftsman] made upright frames, too, of acacia wood to support the tabernacle. Each board was ten cubits high, and had a width of a cubit and a half; and at the sides of it, two tenon-pieces jutted out, so that each might be mortised to the next; all the frame work of the tabernacle he made in this way.

(Exodus 36:20–23)

* **Levant** lands bordering the eastern shores of the Mediterranean Sea (present-day Syria, Lebanon, and Israel), the West Bank, and Jordan

* **ebony** dark, heavy, and highly prized wood from certain tropical trees

Construction and Building. Circular huts dating to around 8000 B.C. were among the earliest wooden structures built in the ancient Near East. These mud-covered HOUSES consisted of a timber frame with gaps filled with twigs, reeds, and branches. As buildings became larger and more sophisticated, STONE or mud brick* often replaced wood as the primary building material. However, builders did not abandon the use of wood for construction. The remains of early stone houses indicate that wooden posts were used as structural supports on the insides of walls.

Throughout the history of the Near East, certain parts of most structures continued to be made of wood. These included doors, door and window frames, and roof beams. Sometimes roofs also contained twigs and branches that were typically covered with mud or plaster. The roofs on some Greek buildings were made of baked clay tiles set over supporting wooden beams. In larger structures, such as palaces and great halls, tree trunks often served as pillars to support the weight of the roof. Also, the outer walls of many large buildings contained horizontal timber beams laid between layers of stone or masonry. The wooden beams added a measure of flexibility, which was especially important in the many EARTHQUAKE-prone regions of the ancient Near East.

Particularly fine ancient buildings contained wooden floors and walls that were decorated elaborately. Exotic and expensive woods such as cedar were often used for the massive doors of temples and palaces.

The type and amount of wood used for construction depended on the resources available to each region. In ancient times, ANATOLIA (present-day Turkey), IRAN, and the Levant* contained large forests that provided local builders a ready supply of sturdy wood. The cedars of Lebanon were famous for their majestic size and their strength as building materials. Because it was difficult to cut and transport these huge trees across long distances, only empires with substantial financial resources could afford to use them. Pine, oak, and poplar trees provided most of the wood used for building in the Near East.

In contrast to other areas of the region, Egypt and MESOPOTAMIA boasted few timber resources. Those trees that were available, such as sycamore, acacia, and date palms, were often not suited to large-scale construction because they were smaller and their wood was of a lower quality. Societies without access to substantial sources of timber either used the inferior-quality local woods or imported what they needed from other regions. Egypt imported cedar and other conifers (cone-bearing trees such as pine) from Lebanon, as well as ebony* from the Sudan. Mesopotamians also used Lebanese cedar as well as juniper wood from SYRIA and Anatolia. Because of the expense of transporting wood from so far away, imported timber was used primarily in monumental ARCHITECTURE, such as PALACES AND TEMPLES.

Woodworking. Besides its use as a building material, wood was widely employed in the making of FURNISHINGS AND FURNITURE, such as tables, stools, chairs, cabinets, chests, and beds. Woodworkers also created a wide range of items, including screens, coffins, small statues and figurines, utensils, musical instruments, TOOLS, and game boards. One of the more interesting items fashioned from wood in Mesopotamia was an

Wood and Woodworking

* **veneer** thin layer of material bonded to the surface of an object

* **relief** sculpture in which material is cut away to show figures raised from the background

---

Saws, adzes, chisels, and bow drills were some of the typical tools used by Egyptian carpenters around the 1500s B.C. The tools shown here and their uses differ only slightly from the woodworking tools used today. For instance, instead of working a saw in two directions, ancient carpenters used theirs in one direction, pulling it through the wood.

early form of writing tablet consisting of two wooden boards joined with a hinge.

Ancient Egyptian woodworkers achieved a high degree of skill and displayed mastery over many artistic techniques. Some of these skills are evident from remains of furniture found in royal tombs such as that of the pharaoh TUTANKHAMEN. One chest from his tomb contains a veneer* of IVORY and is inlaid with more than 30,000 pieces of ivory and ebony. The Phrygians of Anatolia were known for the beauty and quality of their wooden furniture. Archaeologists have recovered numerous tables, stands, and beds with beautiful inlaid designs. The Greek historian HERODOTUS described a wooden throne donated by the Phrygian king Midas to the temple at Delphi in Greece as "well worth seeing."

Ancient carpenters' tools used for woodworking resembled their modern counterparts. These included saws, axes, chisels, planes, and wooden rulers called cubit sticks. Early carpenters' tools were typically fashioned from copper. After 4000 B.C., bronze became the most widely used material for these tools, and iron tools became common only after 1200 B.C.

Wood in Shipbuilding. In ancient times, many ships were built from wood, and constructing them required skilled woodworkers. Reliefs*

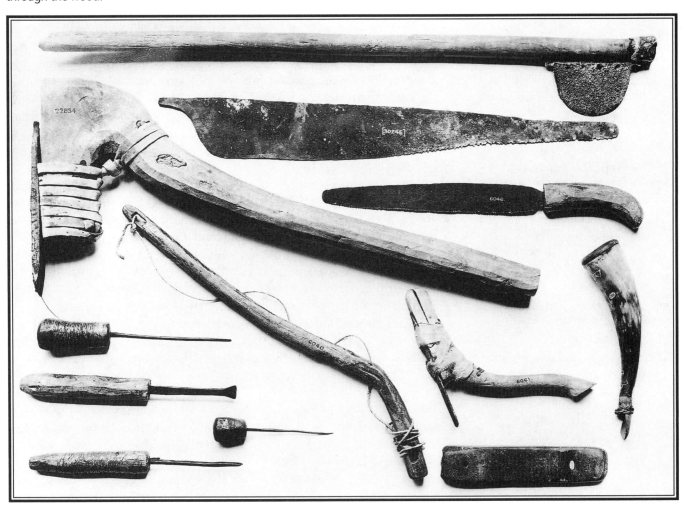

from Egypt depict the process of building a ship, from preparing the trees to be used to putting on the finishing touches. The various reliefs show woodcutters chopping down acacia trees and splitting open the trunks with axes. They also depict artisans* called joiners making planks from the wood from which they constructed the ship's hull. These planks were held together by wooden pegs (called tenons) fitted into holes cut into the edge of each plank (called mortises). This was the basic technique for shipbuilding in the ancient Near East.

* **artisan** skilled craftsperson

Timber was also essential for making other forms of TRANSPORTATION. All wheeled vehicles, from carts and wagons to CHARIOTS, were constructed of wood. Most bridges in the ancient Near East were also wooden structures. (*See also* **Art, Artisans, and Artists; Ships and Boats; Wheel.**)

Wool

See *Clothing; Sheep; Textiles.*

WORK

In the ancient Near East, as in the modern world, most people had to work for their living. As the economy and way of life of the people of the ancient Near East changed over thousands of years, the nature of work also changed. By the end of the ancient period, Near Easterners were engaged in many different types of work and occupations.

Before the development of AGRICULTURE, most people in a given community spent their time performing very similar tasks. The only real differences, perhaps, were between men's and women's responsibilities. However, the role of work in a person's life depended not just on that person's gender but also on his or her social status. The class structure and the economy also shaped the nature of work within each culture.

From Subsistence to Occupation. Before the development of agriculture, nomadic* groups lived by hunting and gathering wild foods. They lived in what economists call a subsistence economy, where individuals or family groups each produce what they need to subsist, or stay alive. Although there may have been some division of duties within bands or communities in ancient subsistence economies, everyone basically had the same "job," which was the daily business of survival—of obtaining food, clothing, and shelter.

* **nomadic** referring to people who travel from place to place in search of food or pasture

The shift from obtaining food by hunting and gathering to agriculture, which began around 9000 B.C., allowed people to occupy permanent settlements and to accumulate, store, and redistribute food. For the first time, not everyone had to obtain each day's or each week's food for himself or his family. Some people could work at other tasks—specializing in craft production, for example—and exchange the products of their labor for food that other people cultivated and harvested. This was the beginning of occupational diversity.

See color plate 12, vol. 2.

Society and Employment. The development of settled communities was closely linked to other trends that affected work. One of these

Work

* **city-state** independent state consisting of a city and its surrounding territory

A Job With Good Benefits

Between 1539 and 1075 B.C., the Egyptian workers who built and decorated the tombs at the Valley of the Kings near Thebes lived at a village called Dayr-al Madina. Because these workers were doing important work for the king, they received many benefits that were not typical for workers of the ancient Near East. Not only were the workers paid generously with different foodstuffs, but they also had people to do their laundry and servants to help them with other daily tasks. Moreover, the workers' children were educated and taught how to read and write, a privilege usually reserved for nobility.

* **bureaucracy** system consisting of officials and clerks who perform government functions

* **scribe** person of a learned class who served as a writer, editor, or teacher

* **diviner** person who foretells the future

* **hierarchical** referring to a society or an institution divided into groups with higher and lower ranks

* **diplomacy** practice of conducting negotiations between kingdoms, states, or nations

* **artisan** skilled craftsperson

* **quarry** to excavate pieces of stone by cutting, splitting, or (in modern times) blasting

* **apprentice** individual who learns skills or a profession from an experienced person in that field

processes was URBANIZATION, the formation of urban centers as some settlements grew into cities and city-states*. The people living in urban centers were able to store large quantities of food for distribution among the population. This allowed some people to work at other occupations or to work at new specialized jobs to meet the needs of large communities.

As these sweeping changes took place in settled states, new social classes emerged. A ruling class developed, and the growth of governments led to the rise of bureaucracies* that employed administrators and later, scribes*. In the same way, the growth of large religious institutions created work not only for priests and priestesses but also for those who served the priesthoods and temples as servants, scribes, stewards, singers, dancers, and diviners*.

A result of these changes was that society became increasingly hierarchical*, and the kind of work people did had much to do with their status. Those in the royal and noble classes perhaps did nothing that a poor, hard-laboring peasant would consider "work," but they had their own obligations, such as administering justice and conducting diplomacy*.

As ruling institutions, the state and the temple influenced other people's work with forced labor. In many ancient Near Eastern societies, people owed the state or the temple a certain number of days of labor each year in exchange for the food and clothing rations they received. Much of that labor was devoted to agricultural production, although it might also be directed toward the construction or repair of roads, bridges, irrigation canals, or public buildings. Some laborers worked on royal or temple estates year-round.

Trade generated much work for people in the ancient world. For instance, MERCHANTS bought and sold goods for long-distance exchange, scribes kept records of their transactions, and handlers and boatmen loaded and moved the goods by ship or animal CARAVAN.

As members of society acquired wealth, they wanted to purchase fine, luxury goods as symbols of their status. Painters, jewelers, sculptors, and crafts workers such as potters and textile weavers worked to supply the demand for such goods. Large numbers of other artisans* were occupied producing everyday textiles, furniture, metalwork, POTTERY, SEALS, TOOLS, and household utensils for the general market.

People in the ancient Near East worked at occupations dealing with many aspects of life. People working on farms might be shepherds, sheep shearers, cattle fatteners, or managers, to name a few possibilities. There were doctors to attend to the sick and people to care for the dead. People were needed to quarry* stones and to mine and process gems and metals. Women worked as grain grinders, weavers, oil pressers, and nurses for babies. Prostitution was also a known occupation, especially for women, some of whom worked for temples.

The Worker's Life. The majority of people in the ancient Near East almost never faced the dilemma of deciding what to do with their lives or what kind of work to pursue. Those lucky enough to be born into a family of artisans, priests, or scribes generally acquired the skills and education to work in these high-status fields. Such opportunities were rarely open to individuals from the lower or peasant classes. Sometimes, however,

This tomb painting, which dates from around 1400 B.C., shows Nakht, an Egyptian official, and his wife watching workers labor on their estate. The workers are seen picking and preparing grapes for wine and netting and preparing birds for the estate kitchen. These workers and others who saw to different tasks were necessary for the running of large estates.

* **creditor** someone to whom a debt is owed

experts took peasant or slave boys into their households as apprentices* to whom they would teach a trade in exchange for a certain number of years of labor.

Highly skilled or talented free laborers received wages for their work, sometimes in the form of silver and sometimes in grain. Such workers probably had some degree of control over their lives. They may have been able to move around freely and choose when and for whom they worked. The same was probably true of those who operated their own businesses. At any given time, however, more people worked as forced or semifree laborers under the control of a public institution or a creditor*. These people did not receive wages but were paid only their rations, the amount of food needed to keep them alive. (*See also* **Art, Artisans, and Artists; Economy and Trade; Labor and Laborers; Slaves and Slavery.**)

Worship

See *Prayer; Religion; Rituals and Sacrifice.*

WRITING

Writing was one of the most important cultural contributions made by the people of the ancient Near East. Before the invention of writing, most information had to be communicated orally and committed to memory. Writing, however, enabled detailed and precise communication between people hundreds of miles away. It also permitted knowledge to be accurately recorded and stored, and then easily retrieved, even after hundreds of years. The ability to record information through writing enabled the development of advanced SOCIAL INSTITUTIONS in the early urban societies of the Near East.

The Development of Writing. The earliest existing evidence of writing consists of inscribed CLAY TABLETS from the Sumerian city of URUK that date to around 3300 B.C. Like most written records from ancient MESOPOTAMIA, these are accounting lists that record inventories of goods. At that

169

Writing

* **urbanization** formation and growth of cities

* **deity** god or goddess

The invention of writing in the ancient Near East was a direct consequence of the demands of developing economies in the region. As early as 3500 B.C., clay tokens and bullae (balls) were used for record keeping and accounting purposes. As cities and city-state emerged, governments became centralized, and trade and administration became more complex, accountants and scribes could no longer depend on this simple method of record keeping. Their needs led to the invention of writing, the aleph-beth, and later the alphabet.

early stage, writing mainly served the administrative function of RECORD KEEPING. However, the need to keep accurate accounting records was not the only inspiration for the invention of writing. Instead, writing was developed as a result of urbanization*. As societies of the ancient Near East became increasingly urbanized, the temples began to take over many of a city's productive activities. In Uruk, the temple of the city's deity* owned not only large tracts of agricultural land but also workshops that produced POTTERY, TEXTILES, SCULPTURE, metalwork, and other goods. The temple was also responsible for coordinating the work of thousands of employees and making sure they were paid by means of food and clothing rations. The needs of administering such a complex enterprise necessitated a system for recording all this information, leading to the invention of writing.

The earliest form of writing is called logographic because it used symbols, or logograms (derived from the Greek words for *word* and *writing*) to communicate words and ideas. For example, the symbol for ox was a picture of an ox's head. The early Sumerian writing system contained more than 1,200 different logograms.

DEVELOPMENT OF WRITING

ca. 4000–3001 B.C.	Tokens and clay balls are used to record and store information. Writing is invented at Uruk. Sumerian scribes develop cuneiform writing. Egyptians develop hieroglyphic script. Proto-Elamite script developed in Iran.
ca. 3000–2001 B.C.	Egyptians develop hieratic, a cursive form of hieroglyphics. Sumerian cuneiform spreads to northern Syria. Elamites develop Elamite cuneiform system. Akkadians adopt the cuneiform script.
ca. 2000–1001 B.C.	Akkadian cuneiform spreads to Anatolia, the Levant and Egypt. Minoans develop hieroglyphic and Linear A scripts. People of Syria and the Levant develop the first examples of the linear aleph-beth. Semitic-speaking northern Syrians create cuneiform-type signs for aleph-beth. Mycenean Greeks develop Linear B script. Hittites develop hieroglyphics.
ca. 1000–1 B.C.	Phoenician traders transmit the aleph-beth to Greeks. Greeks develop vowels for alphabet. South-Semitic aleph-beth is developed in Arabia. Aramaic language and aleph-beth spread throughout ancient Near East. Egyptians develop demotic script. Persians adapt the cuneiform script. Following the Invasions of Alexander the Great, Greek is introduced throughout the ancient Near East.

Shortly after writing was invented in Mesopotamia, a logographic type of writing known as HIEROGLYPHICS appeared in EGYPT. Most scholars believe that the Egyptians borrowed the idea of writing from the Mesopotamians. Others claim that the Egyptians developed it independently. In either case, logographic writing systems were established in both societies by about 3000 B.C., but they were used for quite different purposes. In Mesopotamia, writing served primarily administrative functions, while the Egyptians used it for INSCRIPTIONS and for religious texts.

The earliest Mesopotamian scribes* used a pointed tool called a stylus to scratch signs on their clay tablets. However, they soon began to use a stylus with a triangular-shaped tip to press the shape of the symbol into the clay. The stylus made a wedge-shaped mark; consequently, logograms were transformed into symbols composed of one or more variously oriented wedge-shaped strokes. Over time, these symbols, called CUNEIFORM writing, became more abstract and bore less resemblance to the original logograms.

Meanwhile, scribes also invented symbols that stood for the syllables that formed a word rather than objects representing it. This made it easier to express abstract ideas in writing. For instance, they took the logograms for the noun "water" *(a)*, and the verb "to strike" *(ra)*, and combined them to produce the Sumerian word *ara*, which translates as "to the." Before they began using syllables, such words as *ara* could not be written.

The move away from a purely logographic system was a significant step in the evolution of writing. The early logograms had meaning irrespective of language. Cuneiform symbols that represented syllables could be used to write words in any language that contained similar syllables. Once a word in a particular language was spelled out, it could be sounded out by anyone who could read the script, but it made sense only to a speaker of that language. Compared to fully logographic systems, this method of writing, called a syllabary, was easier to learn and use because it required fewer signs. As Sumerian cuneiform spread across the Near East, local peoples adapted it to write their own languages. They added symbols for syllables in their languages that did not exist in Sumerian. Most of these writing systems, however, continued to use logograms as well as syllables.

In Egypt, hieroglyphics remained in use for more than 3,000 years. Like cuneiform, it consisted of syllabic signs as well as logographic signs. During its long history, two cursive forms of Egyptian hieroglyphics—hieratic and demotic—were adopted for use in writing in everyday practical matters.

The Hittites of ANATOLIA (present-day Turkey) also developed a hieroglyphic writing system of their own during the second millennium B.C. (years from 2000 to 1001 B.C.). This script remained in use in the Neo-Hittite city-states* of northern Syria until about 700 B.C. Hittite hieroglyphs were generally used for royal seals and inscriptions on buildings and sculptures.

Further Developments. The next step in the development of writing was the use of symbols to represent just the individual consonants. This occurred among Canaanite speakers sometime before 1500 B.C. Early Semitic* writing used a system known as the aleph-beth, which had no symbols for vowels. The reader had to supply the proper vowel depending on

* **scribe** person of a learned class who served as a writer, editor, or teacher

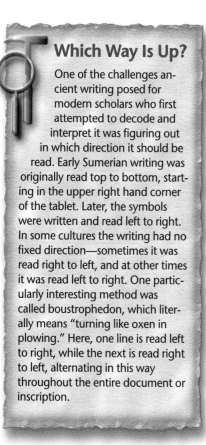

Which Way Is Up?

One of the challenges ancient writing posed for modern scholars who first attempted to decode and interpret it was figuring out in which direction it should be read. Early Sumerian writing was originally read top to bottom, starting in the upper right hand corner of the tablet. Later, the symbols were written and read left to right. In some cultures the writing had no fixed direction—sometimes it was read right to left, and at other times it was read left to right. One particularly interesting method was called boustrophedon, which literally means "turning like oxen in plowing." Here, one line is read left to right, while the next is read right to left, alternating in this way throughout the entire document or inscription.

* **city-state** independent state consisting of a city and its surrounding territory

* **Semitic** of or relating to a language family that includes Akkadian, Aramaic, Arabic, Hebrew, and Phoenician

Xerxes

the context of the writing. For example, it is easy to determine the meaning of the following sentence even without vowels—"Th mn grbs th bttl." The Phoenicians, who traded extensively across the Mediterranean Sea, were probably responsible for the transmission of the aleph-beth writing to the Greeks during the 800s B.C. The Greeks added symbols for their vowels, creating the first true alphabet. Later, the Romans adopted a modified version of the Greek alphabet, which continues to be in use for almost all Western languages.

Literacy. In Mesopotamia and Egypt, only a small segment of the population was literate—able to read and write. Even the majority of kings in the ancient Near East were illiterate. Only three Mesopotamian kings are known to have been trained as scribes—SHULGI of UR, Lipit-Ishtar of Isin, and ASHURBANIPAL of Assyria. In contrast, Egyptian princes were apparently regularly trained as scribes during their youth.

The rate of literacy was low because very few people in the ancient Near East received an EDUCATION. Because schools were controlled by the state or by temples, the political and religious elites effectively controlled a society's knowledge. For instance, it was in the interest of the scribal class to limit the spread of literacy. This enabled them to maintain their high social position, which they gained from their ability to read, write, and keep society functioning smoothly. On the other hand, societies that lacked an established scribal class, such as the ancient Aramaeans, had less reason to restrict literacy and more incentive to adopt new forms of writing that were easier to master.

The development of an alphabetic system made writing and learning more accessible to the people of the ancient Near East. Instead of a confusing system of many hundreds of symbols that took years to master, alphabets had fewer than 30 characters that could be learned in a matter of days or weeks. In Syria, Canaan, Phoenicia, and Israel during the first millennium B.C. (years from 1000 to 1 B.C.), many people learned to read and write well enough to conduct their daily business. Some scholars estimate the literacy rate in classical Greece (ca. 500 B.C.) at about 30 percent, which was dramatically higher than in Mesopotamia or Egypt. (*See also* **Books and Manuscripts; Communication; Epic Literature; Languages; Literature; Schools; Scribes; Semitic Languages; Sumer and the Sumerians; Sumerian Language.**)

XERXES

ruled 486–465 B.C.
Persian king

Best known for his campaigns against Greece, Xerxes (ZUHRK•seez) was one of the most famous kings of the PERSIAN EMPIRE. He was the son of the Persian ruler DARIUS I and Atossa, the daughter of CYRUS THE GREAT. Named heir to the throne instead of his elder brother, Artabazanes, Xerxes became ruler of Persia after the death of his father in 486 B.C. By that time, Xerxes had had a great deal of administrative experience, having governed the province of Babylonia for more than a decade.

When Xerxes ascended the throne, one of his first concerns was to regain control of Egypt, where a local ruler had usurped* power. In 484 B.C.,

* **usurp** to wrongfully occupy a position
* **delta** fan-shaped, lowland plain formed of soil deposited by a river

* **fortification** structure built to strengthen or protect against attack
* **plunder** to steal property by force, usually after a conquest

* **strait** narrow channel that connects two bodies of water

Xerxes and his armies invaded the delta* region of Egypt and put down the revolt, regaining control of the country.

When Xerxes learned of a rebellion in BABYLON, he sent his son-in-law to reconquer the city in 482 B.C. This reconquest was followed by violent repression during which temples and fortifications* were plundered* and destroyed. Xerxes also canceled the special status that Babylon had enjoyed since its incorporation into the Persian empire.

After Xerxes had resolved the difficulties in Egypt and Babylon, he planned an invasion of Greece. Responding to pressure from his advisers, he became determined to avenge the defeat that his father, Darius, had suffered at the hands of the Greeks nearly a decade before. After three years of preparation, Xerxes was ready to invade Greece.

In 480 B.C., Xerxes led a force of at least 300,000 soldiers and hundreds of ships across the Hellespont (present-day Dardanelles), the narrow strait* separating Europe and Asia, and entered Greece. The Persians enjoyed a few early successes, including victory over a small band of Greeks at a mountain pass called Thermopylae and the capture and plunder of the city of Athens. However, the tide of war changed when the Greeks destroyed the Persian fleet at the battle of Salamis. Without a fleet to bring supplies, Xerxes and his armies were forced to retreat into ANATOLIA (present-day Turkey). The following year, a Greek victory at a battle near Plataea in central Greece forced the Persian troops to withdraw from the region.

Little is known of Xerxes' last 14 years except that he launched a vast building program at PERSEPOLIS. Xerxes and the crown prince were assassinated by a member of his bodyguard in 497 B.C. He was succeeded by his son ARTAXERXES I. (*See also* **Babylonia and the Babylonians; Persian Wars; Susa and Susiana.**)

YAHWEH

* **monotheistic** referring to the belief in only one god
* **Semitic** of or relating to a language family that includes Akkadian, Aramaic, Arabic, Hebrew, and Phoenician
* **patriarch** male leader of a family or tribe

* **exodus** migration by a large group of people, usually to escape something unpleasant

Yahweh is the God of the Hebrews (or Israelites) whose worship led to the development of Judaism, the first monotheistic* religion. The early Israelites often referred to Yahweh as EL, a Semitic* term meaning "god," and also as Elohim, a Semitic term for "gods" that was understood to apply to the one God. The name *Yahweh,* which comes from the Hebrew root word *hayah,* "to be," is often interpreted to mean "I am that I am"; "He was, He is, He ever will be"; or "He causes [things] to be."

According to the Hebrew BIBLE, the sacred book of Judaism, Yahweh is the creator of the universe and everything in it. Jews trace the foundation of their religion to the time when Yahweh made a covenant, or solemn agreement, with the patriarch* Abraham (also called Abram). Yahweh promised Abraham that he would have an heir and many descendants and that the land of CANAAN (known as the Promised Land) would belong to them.

Yahweh first revealed his true name to the Israelite leader MOSES during the exodus* of the Israelites from Egypt. At that time, Yahweh made a new covenant with the Israelites and gave them the TEN COMMANDMENTS, a set of laws to observe.

Ziggurats

Some scholars believe that worship of Yahweh developed from worship of the Canaanite god El, who was the king of the gods and the creator of the earth. Eventually, the Israelites began to identify El with Yahweh, a storm god. Although Yahweh could be portrayed as a warlike god, he eventually came to be seen as a benevolent father who had chosen the Jews to fulfill a special destiny.

While it is possible that the early Israelites believed that Yahweh had a human form, they certainly later believed that he did not have a specific form and therefore could not be represented. As a result, Yahweh is not depicted in art or sculpture. (*See also* **Hebrews and Israelites; Judaism and Jews; Mosaic Law; Sinai, Mount.**)

ZIGGURATS

* **archaeologist** scientist who studies past human cultures, usually by excavating material remains of human activity

Found mainly in ancient Mesopotamia, ziggurats were large, multistory structures with steps leading to a temple at the top. Although their general shape resembled that of the Egyptian pyramids, there were many differences between the two structures. While most later pyramids had smooth, sloping walls, ziggurats, like the earlier stepped pyramids, resembled a series of rectangular boxes, set one atop the next. Also, the pyramids were built as tombs and funeral shrines for deceased kings, whereas ziggurats served as temples for the local gods of the cities in which they were located. Although no intact ziggurat exists today, archaeologists* have been able to reconstruct them by studying their ruins and ancient descriptions that have survived.

HISTORY OF ZIGGURAT CONSTRUCTION

The first ziggurats, built in SUMER sometime before 3000 B.C., were simply a single, large platform on top of which sat a temple. The temple was reached by climbing a stairway or ramp. Over time, the ziggurat changed to include additional platforms stacked on top of one another. The earliest "true" ziggurat, consisting of more than one level, was probably constructed by King UR-NAMMU, founder of the Third Dynasty of UR, around 2100 B.C. Its base is believed to have measured 210 by 160 feet, and the completed building might have been nearly 50 feet high. A reconstructed version of this early ziggurat, which was dedicated to the moon god Nanna, remains at the site of the ancient city. Like many early ziggurats, it consisted of three platforms, topped by a temple. The basic design soon evolved to consist of four stories, and later ziggurats were built with as many as seven levels. Moreover, some earlier ziggurats were expanded to include additional stories.

See color plate 14, vol. 3.

The most famous ziggurat was a seven-story structure built in the city of BABYLON in the early 500s B.C. by King Nebuchadnezzar II, on a foundation that possibly dates back to King HAMMURABI, who ruled in the early 1700s B.C. According to some ancient sources, the ziggurat rose some 300 feet above the ground and might have been the inspiration for the story of the Tower of Babel in the Hebrew BIBLE. The largest surviving ziggurat, built in the 1200s B.C., is at Chogha Zambil in Elam. Rising more than 78 feet from the ground, the ziggurat still stands at half its original height.

STRUCTURE AND FUNCTION OF ZIGGURATS

Although they all originated from the same basic plan, ziggurats were constructed in different forms in different regions of Mesopotamia. Despite the differences in architecture, all ziggurats were designed to serve as a platform for the temple of the city's god.

Southern Ziggurats. The civilizations of southern Mesopotamia—Sumer and Babylonia—built ziggurats in what is considered the classic form. The ziggurat was situated in a walled courtyard that was entered by means of gateways. A large platform covering an area of about an acre formed the base of the structure. The corners of the platform were aligned with the four major points of the compass. This lower platform, like the ones above it, was a solid structure made of clay and sun-dried mud brick*. Unlike the pyramids, ziggurats had no interior passageways or chambers.

Most ziggurats had three staircases that led from the ground to the lower level. All the staircases were on one side of the building. Two of them ran along the outside wall, and the third was perpendicular to the wall face and extended some distance away from the base of the ziggurat. Remains of a ziggurat at Ur indicate that only one staircase led to the top of the building. At the top of the ziggurat was a "high temple" to the local god. A "lower temple" for other gods was usually located at the base of the ziggurat.

Although impressively designed and built, ziggurats were not very durable. During heavy rain, water penetrated the mud brick interiors and caused them to soften. Over time, the weight of the upper levels would

* **mud brick** brick made from mud, straw, and water mixed together and baked in the sun

Construction of the ziggurat at Ur, the remains of which are shown here, was begun by King Ur-Nammu in the 2100s B.C. and completed by King Shulgi shortly thereafter. It was restored around 1,500 years later by the Babylonian king Nabonidus. The ziggurat and the complex surrounding it dominated the skyline of Ur.

Zimri-Lim

The Tower of Babel

The ancient Mesopotamians believed that the temple on top of a ziggurat was a place where their god might come down to earth. However, according to the Hebrew Bible, its purpose was quite different. According to the story of the *Tower of Babel* in the Book of Genesis 11:1-9, Noah's descendants attempted to build a tower that they hoped would reach heaven. However, to prevent them from completing construction, their god made them speak different languages so they could not understand one another. The tower was never completed, and Noah's descendants scattered over the face of the earth. This story is said to account for the origin of the world's different languages.

* **deity** god or goddess

cause the lower walls to bulge and eventually collapse. Several texts from ancient Mesopotamia indicate that the rulers expected this to happen. To try to preserve the structure as long as possible, all ziggurats incorporated features such as internal drainpipes to drain water away from the building. Some ziggurats also contained layers of reeds and bitumen (tarlike substance used for waterproofing) between each level to absorb extra moisture. Notwithstanding these precautions, many ziggurats had to be rebuilt every 100 years or less.

Northern Ziggurats. The ziggurats in northern Mesopotamia were similar in design and construction to southern ones, but with a few differences. Assyrian ziggurats were typically square, not rectangular like the ones in the south. The four corners were not always aligned to the points of the compass, nor were the external stairways the only means of reaching the temple at the top. However, the most important difference between the two types of ziggurats was their physical surroundings. Sumerian and Babylonian ziggurats stood alone on a site, while the Assyrians incorporated their ziggurats into larger temple complexes that contained other buildings. These temple complexes were constructed on three platforms. The first, or lowest, platform was simply a courtyard surrounding the buildings on the site. The second platform contained the main temple of the god. The ziggurat was the third, and highest, platform in the group.

Function of Ziggurats. The ancient Mesopotamians believed that the ziggurats served as a link between humans and the gods. Every important city contained a ziggurat dedicated to its local god. The structure rose to the sky, enabling the deities* to descend from heaven to visit their subjects. The high temple on top of the ziggurat received the god when he or she first descended from the sky. The lower temple at the base received the deity upon reaching the earth. The names given to many ziggurats express the idea that ziggurats were the stairways of the gods. The name of the ziggurat in the city of Sippar meant "the staircase to holy heaven," while the great ziggurat in Babylon was called "the temple which is the foundation of heaven and earth." In some ziggurats, the high temple had a bedchamber in which sacred marriage ceremonies took place. In these ceremonies, the king would enact a ritual with a priestess of the temple to ensure the fertility and prosperity of the kingdom. (*See also* **Architecture; Assyria and the Assyrians; Palaces and Temples.**)

ZIMRI-LIM

ruled ca. 1776–1761 B.C.
King of Mari

Zimri-Lim was the king of MARI, a city-state* located on the upper EUPHRATES RIVER in present-day Syria. Historians know more about second millennium B.C.* Mari than about any other Near Eastern culture of this period because official records and many of the king's personal letters have survived. These sources have enabled historians to reconstruct a detailed picture of Mari society during Zimri-Lim's reign.

Zimri-Lim was the son of a former king of Mari who had been defeated and removed from power by the Assyrian king SHAMSHI-ADAD I.

* **city-state** independent state consisting of a city and its surrounding territory
* **second millennium** B.C. years from 2000 to 1001 B.C.

Around 1776 B.C., shortly after Shamshi-Adad's death, Zimri-Lim reclaimed his father's throne. When the city-state of ESHNUNNA allied itself with his enemies and attacked Mari, Zimri-Lim joined forces with the neighboring Syrian city-state of Aleppo. He successfully defeated his rivals and increased his power by forcing the rulers of several cities near Mari to swear loyalty to him.

Zimri-Lim had a friendly political relationship with the great Babylonian king HAMMURABI. He sent troops to aid Hammurabi's attack on the city-state of LARSA. Still, Zimri-Lim did not trust his more powerful neighbor, and his suspicions were soon justified. After the siege of Larsa, the Babylonians entered Mari. Over the next two years, they recorded the city's valuables, seized them, and then burned Mari to the ground. Zimri-Lim's fate is unknown, and scholars are still unsure why Hammurabi decided to destroy his ally's capital. (*See also* **Assyria and the Assyrians; Babylonia and the Babylonians.**)

ZODIAC

* **constellation** group of stars that is thought to resemble, and is named after, an object, animal, or mythological character

* **Hellenistic** referring to the Greek-influenced culture of the Mediterranean world and western Asia during the three centuries after the death of Alexander the Great in 323 B.C.

Babylonian astronomers were the first to observe that the SUN, moon, and PLANETS move across the sky within a narrow, imaginary band. This band, called the zodiac, extends about nine degrees on either side of the ecliptic—the path in which the sun appears to travel during the course of a year. The astronomers also identified constellations* on the ecliptic. By about 1100 B.C. they had named 17 such constellations and used them to mark the locations of the moon and planets.

Around 500 B.C., Babylonian astronomers divided the band of the zodiac into 12 equal sections, each named for a prominent constellation contained within the section. The name of each constellation became the name of that segment, or sign, of the zodiac. The 12 signs of the zodiac in modern astrology are direct descendants of the signs of the Babylonian zodiac. Their modern names—Aries, Taurus, Gemini, Cancer, Leo, Virgo, Libra, Scorpio, Sagittarius, Capricorn, Aquarius, and Pisces—are nearly direct translations of the original names given to the constellations by the Greeks when they borrowed the zodiac from the Babylonians during the late Hellenistic* period.

Over a period of many hundreds of years, Babylonian astronomers, using the zodiac, compiled enormous amounts of data about the positions of planets and STARS. They were eventually able to use MATHEMATICS to determine the location of planets. Using these data, they could predict where the heavenly bodies would be on any given date, even if the sky was too overcast for direct observation. The Babylonians were able to use this information in their practice of astrology—the interpretation of the movement and relationships of the sun, moon, visible planets, and stars in order to predict eclipses as well as human affairs and events. Because astrologers could refer to the zodiac to determine exactly where each planet was when a person was born, they could draw a horoscope—a map of the heavens at the moment of birth. Astrologers then interpreted that map, determining what the positions of the planets at birth meant for a given person's life. At first, horoscopes related only to the king or to the state as a whole. However, by the 300s B.C., astrologers had begun to draw

177

Zoroaster and Zoroastrianism

Dating from the third millennium B.C., this clay tablet from Uruk is inscribed with the drawings of several constellations, or groups of stars. On the left, Corvus, a raven, pecks at the tail of a serpent, Hydra. The star (center) represents the planet Mercury, and the figure holding a spike (right) symbolizes Virgo.

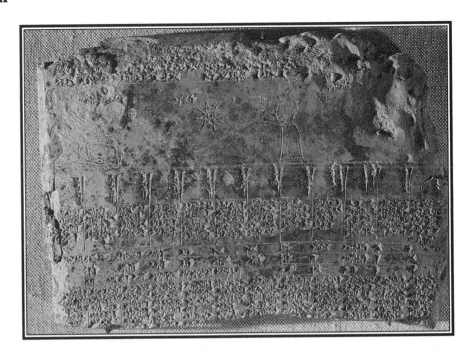

horoscopes for individuals as well. Beginning in the 200s B.C., Babylonians, especially at Uruk, began to use images of the signs of the zodiac, either individually or in groups of twos or threes, as decorations on finger rings that could be used as seals. (*See also* **Astrology and Astrologers; Astronomy and Astronomers; Lunar Theory; Oracles and Prophecy.**)

ZOROASTER AND ZOROASTRIANISM

* **prophet** one who claims to have received divine messages or insights

* **monotheism** belief in only one god

founded by a Persian prophet* and religious reformer named Zoroaster (ZOH•ruh•as•tuhr) in the late 600s B.C., Zoroastrianism (zoh•ruh•AS•tree•uh•ni•zuhm) is a Persian religion that still survives in some parts of IRAN and India. One of its notable features is a belief in monotheism*, and some scholars believe that this aspect of Zoroastrianism may have influenced other monotheistic faiths, including Judaism, Christianity, and Islam.

Little is known about Zoroaster, who was also known as Zarathustra. According to tradition, he was born in eastern Iran in about 628 B.C. Perhaps a member of a family of knights, he was credited with having knowledge of magical practices. When Zoroaster became a priest, however, local religious and civil authorities opposed his teachings. This was largely because Zoroaster focused his teachings on one god, AHURA MAZDA, or "Wise Lord", whom he considered the highest god and the only one worthy of worship. Zoroaster believed that he had received a vision from Ahura Mazda in which the god told him to teach the truth. At that time, however, most religions were polytheistic, or based on a belief in many gods.

According to Zoroaster, Ahura Mazda was the creator of heaven and earth, the supreme lawgiver, the center of nature, and the originator of order in the universe. Although supreme, Ahura Mazda was not the only

Zoroaster and Zoroastrianism

Fire is a sacred symbol to the Zoroastrians, who keep their altars, shown here, perpetually lit. The importance that ancient Persians accorded fire is evident from a relief in the tomb of Darius I, which shows the king praying before a blazing fire altar.

The Magi

Before the establishment of Zoroastrianism, the priests of Persia were known as Magi or Magians. Famed for their skills in astrology, they adopted the religion of Zoroaster as their own. In fact, it is possible that Zoroaster himself was a Magi. The Magi acquired great power because of their knowledge of sacred rituals, and at times, they exerted great influence on the Persian government. Many ancient writers revered them as wise men, and their supposed power over demons gave rise to the word *magic*. The Magi also appear in the Christian religion as the three wise men who followed a star and brought gifts to the infant Jesus at Bethlehem.

spirit, however. He was surrounded by several immortal beings called *amesha spentas,* whom he had also created. These beings represented such qualities as truth, justice, righteousness, devotion, and salvation. Because Zoroaster maintained that the world was divided into good and evil, he also believed that there were evil spirits—*daevas*—ruled by a being named Angra Mainyu, or AHRIMAN, the source of darkness and lies. According to Zoroaster, there was a great war in progress, both on earth and in the heavens, between the forces of good and evil. He believed that Ahura Mazda allowed humans to choose between good and evil and to decide which side to serve.

Because humans were free to determine their own fate, those who chose good and proved their worth through good words, thoughts, and deeds would be rewarded. Those who chose evil would be punished. Zoroaster taught that after death, the soul of every human received judgment from Ahura Mazda. The good entered the kingdom of everlasting joy and light, while the evil fell into the kingdom of misery and darkness. Zoroaster also taught that, in the end, good would triumph over evil, Ahriman would be destroyed, and the world would be renewed and inhabited by the good.

Zoroaster's teachings are compiled in the *Gathas,* which form part of the Zoroastrians' holy book, the *Avesta.* The *Gathas* include early HYMNS believed to have been written by Zoroaster. These hymns contain many

179

Zoroaster and Zoroastrianism

12,000 Years of Existence

According to Zoroastrianism, the history of the universe is divided into four periods of 3,000 years each. During the first three periods, totaling 9,000 years, a great battle rages between Ahura Mazda and Ahriman—the forces of good and evil—for dominance. In the fourth 3,000-year period, however, a savior, known as Saoshyant, is expected to appear and help forces of good triumph over evil. The dead will then rise for a final judgment, and good will reign forever after.

references to the basic beliefs of Zoroaster and are the only evidence of what the prophet actually taught. In addition to hymns, the *Avesta* also contains sections dealing with ritual and sacrifice that were to be followed by Zoroastrian priests during worship.

According to tradition, Zoroaster lived for 77 years and died in about 551 B.C. Many legends about him arose after his death, including stories that credited him with being a skilled healer, artisan, astrologer, and magician. He also was said to have founded sacred fires. This idea may have been associated with the ancient Persian respect for fire, which was later incorporated into Zoroastrianism. The Zoroastrians believed that fire was a symbol of Ahura Mazda, and a fire was always kept burning in Zoroastrian temples.

The early Persian kings were among the first followers of Zoroaster, although other Persians soon adopted Zoroastrianism as well. By the early 500s B.C., Zoroastrianism had become the major religion of the PERSIAN EMPIRE, and it was made the official state religion of Persia in the A.D. 200s. When the Muslims took over Persia in the 600s, many Zoroastrians sought refuge in India, where they became known as Parsis. (*See also* **Gods and Goddesses; Magic; Monotheism; Mythology; Religion.**)

קרשתאבגדהוזחטיכדלמסנןסעפףצץקרשתאבגד

SUGGESTED READINGS

ATLASES AND ENCYCLOPEDIAS

Aharoni, Yohanan, and Michael Avi-Yonah. *The Macmillan Bible Atlas.* Rev. ed. New York: Macmillan, 1977.

Baines, John, and Jaromír Malék. *Atlas of Ancient Egypt.* New York: Facts on File, 1980.

Bienkowski, Piotr, and A. R. Millard. *Dictionary of the Ancient Near East.* Philadelphia: University of Pennsylvania Press, 2000.

Branigan, K., ed. *The Atlas of Archaeology.* New York: St. Martin's Press, 1982.

Freedman, David Noel, ed. *Anchor Bible Dictionary.* New York: Doubleday, 1992.

Grant, Michael. *Ancient History Atlas.* New York: Macmillan, 1971.

———. *From Alexander to Cleopatra: The Hellenistic World.* New York: Charles Scribner's Sons, 1982.

*Haywood, John. *The Encyclopedia of Ancient Civilizations of the Near East and Mediterranean.* Library Reference ed. Armonk, N.Y.: Sharpe Reference, 1997.

Kuhrt, Amélie, and Susan Sherwin-White, eds. *Hellenism in the East: Interaction of Greek and Non-Greek Civilizations from Syria to Central Asia After Alexander.* London: Duckworth, 1987.

Leick, Gwendolyn. *Who's Who in the Ancient Near East.* London and New York: Routledge, 1999.

Manley, Bill. *The Penguin Historical Atlas of Ancient Egypt.* New York and London: Penguin Books, 1996.

McEvedy, Colin. *The Penguin Atlas of Ancient History.* London: Penguin Books, 1967.

Pritchard, James B., ed. *The Ancient Near East; Supplementary Texts and Pictures Relating to the Old Testament.* Princeton, N.J.: Princeton University Press, 1969.

Radice, Betty. *The Penguin Who's Who in the Ancient World.* New York: Penguin Books, 1973.

Roaf, Michael. *Cultural Atlas of Mesopotamia and the Ancient Near East.* Oxfordshire, England: Andromeda Oxford Ltd., 1996.

Sasson, Jack M., ed. *Civilizations of the Ancient Near East.* 4 vols. New York: Charles Scribner's Sons, 1995.

Speake, Graham, ed. *The Penguin Dictionary of Ancient History.* New York: Penguin Books, 1995.

Whitehouse, Ruth D., ed. *The Facts on File Dictionary of Archaeology.* New York: Facts on File, 1983.

HISTORY

Bright, John. *A History of Israel.* 3rd ed. Philadelphia: Westminster Press, 1981.

The Cambridge Ancient History. 3rd ed. 12 vols. New York: Cambridge University Press, 1970–1998.

The Cambridge History of Iran. 7 vols. Cambridge, England: Cambridge University Press, 1968–1991.

Clayton, Peter A. *Chronicle of the Pharaohs: The Reign-by-Reign Record of the Rulers and Dynasties of Ancient Egypt.* New York: Thames and Hudson, 1994.

*Corbishley, M. J. *The Near East.* The Legacy of the Ancient World Series. Hemel Hempstead, England: Macdonald Young Books, 1995.

*Currah, Ann. *From Cities to Empires.* This Is Our World Series. Glasgow, Scotland: Collins, 1975.

Dunstan, William E. *The Ancient Near East.* Fort Worth, Tex.: Harcourt Brace College Publishers, 1998.

Herodotus of Halicarnassus. *The Histories.* Edited by Carolyn Dewald. Translated by Robin Waterfield. New York: Oxford University Press, 1998.

Kuhrt, Amélie. *The Ancient Near East.* 2 vols. London and New York: Routledge, 1995.

Nissen, Hans J. *The Early History of the Ancient Near East, 9000–2000 B.C.* Translated by Elizabeth Lutzeier and Kenneth J. Northcott. Chicago: University of Chicago Press, 1988.

Oates, Joan. *Babylon.* London: Thames and Hudson, 1986.

Potts, Timothy. *Mesopotamia and the East: An Archaeological Study of Foreign Relations ca. 3400–2000 B.C.* Oxford, England: Oxford University Committee for Archaeology, 1994.

Pritchard, James B., ed. *Ancient Near Eastern Texts Relating to the Old Testament.* 3rd ed. Princeton, N.J.: Princeton University Press, 1969.

Reade, Julian. *Mesopotamia.* Cambridge, Mass.: Harvard University Press, 1991.

Saggs, H. W. F. *Civilization Before Greece and Rome.* New Haven, Conn.: Yale University Press, 1989.

Starr, Chester G. *A History of the Ancient World.* New York: Oxford University Press, 1991.

*Asterisk denotes book for young readers

Suggested Readings

CULTURE AND SOCIETY

*Anatolia: Cauldron of Cultures. Lost Civilizations Collection. Alexandria, Va.: Time-Life Books, 1995.

*Bianchi, Robert Steven. The Nubians: People of the Ancient Nile. Brookfield, Conn.: Millbrook Press, 1994.

*Church, Alfred J., and Arthur Gilman. The Story of Carthage. Austin, Tex.: BookLab, 1996.

Crawford, Harriet E. W. Dilmun and Its Gulf Neighbors. New York: Cambridge University Press, 1998.

Curtis, John. Ancient Persia. Cambridge, Mass.: Harvard University Press, 1990.

David, A. Rosalie. Handbook to Life in Ancient Egypt. New York: Facts on File, 1998.

Dicks, Brian. The Ancient Persians. How They Lived and Worked Series. North Pomfret, Vt.: David and Charles, 1975.

Dothan, Trude Krakauer, and M. Dothan. People of the Sea: The Search for the Philistines. New York: Macmillan, 1992.

Dumbrill, Richard J. The Music of the Ancient Near East. London: Athlone, 1999.

*Egypt: Land of the Pharaohs. Lost Civilizations Collection. Alexandria, Va.: Time-Life Books, 1992.

Frankel, David. The Ancient Kingdom of Urartu. London: British Museum Publications, 1979.

*The Holy Land. Lost Civilizations Collection. Alexandria, Va.: Time-Life Books, 1992.

Hoerth, Alfred J., Gerald L. Mattingly, and Edwin M. Yamauchi, eds. Peoples of the Old Testament World. Grand Rapids, Mich.: Baker Books, 1994.

Kramer, Samuel Noah. History Begins at Sumer: Thirty-Nine Firsts in Man's Recorded History. 3rd ed., rev. Philadelphia: University of Pennsylvania Press, 1981.

Macqueen, J. G. The Hittites and Their Contemporaries in Asia Minor. Rev. ed. New York: Thames and Hudson, 1986.

Maisels, Charles Keith. The Emergence of Civilization: From Hunting and Gathering to Agriculture, Cities, and the State in the Near East. London and New York: Routledge, 1993.

*Mesopotamia: The Mighty Kings. Lost Civilizations Collection. Alexandria, Va.: Time-Life Books, 1995.

Moscati, Sabatino, ed. The Phoenicians. New York: Rizzoli Bookstore, 1991.

Murnane, William J. The Penguin Guide to Ancient Egypt. London: Penguin Books, 1983.

*Odijk, Pamela. The Phoenicians. The Ancient World Series. Englewood Cliffs, N.J.: Silver Burdett Press, 1989.

*———. The Sumerians. Ancient World Series. Englewood Cliffs, N.J.: Silver Burdett Press, 1990.

*Perl, Lila, and Erica Weihs. Mummies, Tombs, and Treasure: Secrets of Ancient Egypt. New York: Clarion Books, 1987.

*Persians: Masters of Empire. Lost Civilizations Collection. Alexandria, Va.: Time-Life Books, 1995.

Postgate, J. Nicholas. Early Mesopotamia: Society and Economy at the Dawn of History. London: Routledge, 1994.

Potts, D. T. The Archaeology of Elam: Formation and Transformation of an Ancient Iranian State. Cambridge, England: Cambridge University Press, 1999.

———. Mesopotamian Civilization: The Material Foundations. Ithaca, N.Y.: Cornell University Press, 1997.

Roux, Georges. Ancient Iraq. New York: Penguin, 1992.

Schulz, Regine, and Matthais Seidel, eds. Egypt: The World of the Pharoahs. Cologne, Germany: Könemann, 1998.

*Sumer: Cities of Eden. Lost Civilizations Collection. Alexandria, Va.: Time-Life Books, 1994.

Welsby, Derek. The Kingdom of Kush: The Napatan and Meroitic Empire. London: British Museum Press, 1996.

*Wondrous Realms of the Aegean. Lost Civilizations Collection. Alexandria, Va.: Time-Life Books, 1993.

MYTHS AND LEGENDS

Curtis, Vesta Sarkosh. The Legendary Past: Persian Myths. Austin: University of Texas Press, 1993.

*Epics of Early Civilization: Middle Eastern Myth. Myth and Mankind Collection. Alexandria, Va.: Time-Life Books, 2000.

Gray, John. Near Eastern Mythology. London: Hamlyn Publishing Group, 1969.

Hamilton, Virginia. In the Beginning: Creation Stories from Around the World. San Diego: Harcourt Brace Jovanovich, 1988.

Harris, Geraldine, David O'Connor, and John Sibbick. Gods and Pharaohs from Egyptian Mythology. New York: Peter Bedrick Books, 1982.

Leick, Gwendolyn. A Dictionary of Ancient Near Eastern Mythology. London and New York: Routledge, 1991.

McCall, Henrietta. The Legendary Past: Mesopotamian Myths. Legendary Past Series. Austin: University of Texas Press, 1990.

Skinner, Fred Gladstone. Myths and Legends of the Ancient Near East. New York: Barnes & Noble Books, 1993.

*The Way to Eternity: Egyptian Myth. Myth and Mankind Collection. Alexandria, Va.: Time-Life Books, 1998.

RELIGION

Black, Jeremy, and Anthony Green. *Gods, Demons and Symbols of Ancient Mesopotamia.* Austin: University of Texas Press, 1992.

Clark, Peter. *Zoroastrianism: An Introduction to Ancient Faith.* Sussex Library of Religious Beliefs and Practices Series. Porland, Oreg.: Sussex Academic Press, 1998.

Graf, Fritz. *Magic in the Ancient World.* Revealing Antiquity Series. London and Cambridge, Mass.: Harvard University Press, 1998.

Jakobsen, Thorkild. *The Treasures of Darkness: A History of Mesopotamian Religion.* New Haven, Conn.: Yale University Press, 1976.

Pinch, Geraldine. *Magic in Ancient Egypt.* Austin: University of Texas Press, 1994.

Quirke, Stephen. *Ancient Egyptian Religion.* New York: Dover Publications, 1997.

Ringgren, Helmer. *Religions of the Ancient Near East.* Translated by John Sturdy. Philadelphia: Westminster Press, 1973.

ART AND ARCHITECTURE

Amiet, Pierre. *Art of the Ancient Near East.* Translated by John Shepley and Claude Choquet. New York: Harry N. Abrams, 1980.

Aruz, Joan, Prudence Oliver Harper, and Françoise Tallon, eds. *The Royal City of Susa: Ancient Near Eastern Treasures in the Louvre.* New York: Metropolitan Museum of Art, 1992.

Cadogan, Gerald. *Palaces of Minoan Crete.* University Paperbacks Series. London and New York: Routledge, 1991.

Caubet, Annie, and Patrick Pouyssegur. *The Ancient Near East: The Origins of Civilization.* Translated by Peter Snowdon. Paris: Terrail, 1998.

Collon, Dominique. *Ancient Near Eastern Art.* Berkeley: University of California Press, 1995.

Doumas, Christos. *The Wall-Paintings of Thera.* Translated by Alex Doumas. Athens: Thera Foundation, 1992.

Downey, Susan B. *Mesopotamian Religious Architecture: Alexander Through the Parthians.* Princeton, N.J.: Princeton University Press, 1988.

Frankfort, Henri. *The Art and Architecture of the Ancient Orient.* 4th ed., rev. impression. Harmondsworth, England: Penguin Books, 1970.

Klengel, Horst. *The Art of Ancient Syria.* Translated by Joan Becker. Cranbury, N.J.: A. S. Barnes, 1971.

*Leacock, Helen, and Richard Leacock. *The Buildings of Ancient Mesopotamia.* Reading, Mass.: Addison-Wesley, 1974.

Leick, Gwendolyn. *A Dictionary of Ancient Near Eastern Architecture.* London: Routledge, 1988.

Lloyd, Seton. *The Art of the Ancient Near East.* New York: Frederick A. Praeger Publisher, 1961.

Lundquist, John M. *The Temple: Meeting Place of Heaven and Earth.* New York: Thames and Hudson, 1993.

Perrot, Georges. *History of Art in Phrygia, Lydia, Caria, and Lycia.* Boston: Longwood Press, 1977.

Polin, Claire C. J. *Music of the Ancient Near East.* New York: Vintage Press, 1954.

Robins, Gay. *The Art of Ancient Egypt.* Cambridge, Mass.: Harvard University Press, 1997.

————. *Proportion and Style in Ancient Egyptian Art.* Austin: University of Texas Press, 1994.

Weiss, Harvey, ed. *Ebla to Damascus: Art and Archaeology of Ancient Syria: And Exhibition from the Directorate-General of Antiquities and Museums, Syrian Arab Republic.* Washington, D.C.: Smithsonian Institution Traveling Exhibition Service, 1985.

Woolley, Leonard. *The Art of the Middle East Including Persia, Mesopotamia and Palestine.* New York, Crown Publishers, 1961.

THE JEWISH WORLD

Barclay, John M. G. *Jews in the Mediterranean Diaspora: From Alexander to Trajan (323 BCE–117 CE).* Berkeley: University of California Press, 1996.

Crenshaw, James L. *Education in Ancient Israel: Across the Deadening Silence.* New York: Doubleday, 1998.

Galil, Gershon. *The Chronology of the Kings of Israel and Judah.* Vol. 9 of *Studies in the History and Culture of the Ancient Near East.* New York: E. J. Brill, 1998.

Gordon, Cyrus H., and Gary A. Rendsburg. *The Bible and the Ancient Near East.* 4th ed. New York: W. W. Norton, 1998.

Jaffee, Martin S. *Early Judaism.* Upper Saddle River, N.J.: Prentice Hall, 1996.

Josephus, Flavius. *The Jewish War.* Edited by Mary E. Smalley. Translated by G. A. Williamson. New York: Penguin Books, 1984.

Modrzejewski, Joseph. *The Jews of Egypt: From Ramses II to Emperor Hadrian.* Princeton, N.J.: Princeton University Press, 1997.

Niditch, Susan. *Ancient Israelite Religion.* New York: Oxford University Press, 1998.

Pixley, Jorge V. *Biblical Israel: A People's History.* Minneapolis, Minn.: Fortress Press, 1992.

Shanks, Hershel. *Ancient Israel: From Abraham to the Destruction of the Temple.* Washington, D.C.: Biblical Archaeology Society, 1999.

Tcherikover, Victor. *Hellenistic Civilization and the Jews.* Peabody, Mass.: Hendrickson Publishers, 1959.

Uffenheimer, Benjamin. *Early Prophecy in Israel.* Translated by David Louvish. Jerusalem: Magnes Press, 1999.

Weber, Max. *Ancient Judaism.* New York: Free Press, 1967.

Suggested Readings

DAILY LIFE

Countenau, George. *Everyday Life in Babylonia and Assyria.* New York: W. W. Norton, 1966.

Nemet-Nejat, Karen Rhea. *Daily Life in Ancient Mesopotamia.* Daily Life Through History Series. Westport, Conn.: Greenwood Press, 1998.

Oppenheim, Adolf Leo, trans. *Letters from Mesopotamia: Official Business and Private Letters on Clay Tablets from Two Millennia.* Chicago: University of Chicago Press, 1987.

Poliakoff, Michael. *Contact Sports in the Ancient World.* New Haven, Conn.: Yale University Press, 1987.

Saggs, H. W. F., *Everyday Life in Babylonia and Assyria.* New York: G. P. Putnam's Sons, 1965.

Snell, Daniel C. *Life in the Ancient Near East.* New Haven, Conn.: Yale University Press, 1997.

Time Frame 3000–1500 B.C.: The Age of God Kings. Time Frame Series. Alexandria, Va.: Time-Life Books, 1987.

What Life Was Like on the Banks of the Nile: Egypt 3050–30 B.C. What Life Was Like Series. Alexandria, Va.: Time-Life Books, 1997.

SCIENCE AND TECHNOLOGY

Bobula, Ida Miriam. *Sumerian Technology: A Survey of Early Material Achievements in Mesopotamia.* Washington, D.C.: Smithsonian Institution, 1960.

*Gonen, Rivka. *Fired Up! Making Pottery in Ancient Times.* Minneapolis, Minn.: Runestone Press, 1993.

Hodges, Henry. *Technology in the Ancient World.* New York: Barnes & Noble Books, 1992.

James, Peter, and Nick Thorpe. *Ancient Inventions.* New York: Ballantine Books, 1995.

Moss, Carol. *Science in Ancient Mesopotamia.* New York: Franklin Watts, 1989.

Nemet-Nejat, Karen Rhea. *Cuneiform Mathematical Texts as a Reflection of Everyday Life in Mesopotamia.* American Oriental Series, Vol. 75. New Haven, Conn.: American Oriental Society, 1993.

Neugebauer, Otto. *The Exact Sciences in Antiquity.* 2nd ed. Copenhagen: Munksgaard, 1957.

WRITING AND RECORD KEEPING

Ben-Tor, Daphna. *The Scarab: A Reflection of Ancient Egypt.* Jerusalem: Israel Museum, 1989.

Cohen, Mark E. *The Cultic Calendars of the Ancient Near East.* Bethesda, Md.: CDL Press, 1993.

Collon, Dominique. *First Impressions: Cylinder Seals in the Ancient Near East.* Chicago: University of Chicago Press, 1987.

———. *Near Eastern Seals.* Interpreting the Past Series. Berkeley: University of California Press, 1990.

Damerow, Peter, R. K. Englund, and Hans J. Nissen. *Archaic Bookkeeping: Early Writing and Techniques of Economic Administration in the Ancient Near East.* Translated by Paul Larsen. Chicago: University of Chicago Press, 1993.

Daniels, Peter T, and William Bright, eds. *The World's Writing Systems.* New York: Oxford University Press, 1996.

Gelb, Ignace J. *A Study of Writing.* 2nd ed. Chicago: University of Chicago Press, 1963.

Pedersén, Olof. *Archives and Libraries in the Ancient Near East 1500–300 B.C.* Bethesda, Md.: CDL Press, 1998.

Reading the Past: Ancient Writing from Cuneiform to the Alphabet. Berkeley: University of California Press, 1990.

Robinson, Andrew. *The Story of Writing.* London: Thames and Hudson, 1995.

Schmandt-Besserat, Denise. *Before Writing.* Vol. 1 of *From Counting to Cuneiform.* Austin: University of Texas Press, 1992.

*Woods, Geraldine. *Science in Ancient Egypt.* New York: Franklin Watts, 1998.

LITERATURE

Andrews, Carol, ed. *The Ancient Egyptian Book of the Dead.* Translated by R. O. Faulkner. New York: Macmillan, 1985.

Foster, Benjamin R. *Before the Muses: An Anthology of Akkadian Literature.* 2nd ed. 2 vols. Bethesda, Md.: CDL Press, 1996.

Kovacs, Maureen Gallery, trans. *The Epic of Gilgamesh.* Stanford, Calif.: Stanford University Press, 1989.

Lichtheim, Miriam. *Ancient Egyptian Literature: A Book of Readings.* 3 vols. Berkeley: University of California Press, 1973–1980.

Pritchard, James B., ed. *Ancient Near Eastern Texts Relating to the Old Testament.* 2nd ed. Princeton, N.J.: Princeton University Press, 1955.

Reiner, Erica. *Your Thwarts in Pieces, Your Mooring Rope Cut: Poetry from Babylonia and Assyria.* Ann Arbor: Horace H. Rackham School of Graduate Studies at the University of Michigan, 1985.

Roth, Martha. *Law Collections from Mesopotamia and Asia Minor.* Vol. 6 of *Writings from the Ancient World.* Atlanta: Scholars Press, 1995.

Schiffman, Lawrence H., and James C. VanderKam, eds. *Encyclopedia of the Dead Sea Scrolls.* New York: Oxford University Press, 2000.

קרשתאבגדהוזחטיכךלמסןננסעפּפֿצץקרשתאבגד

Suggested Readings

ARCHAEOLOGY

Ben-Tor, Amnon, ed. *The Archaeology of Ancient Israel.* Translated by R. Greenberg. New Haven, Conn.: Yale University Press, 1994.

Bibby, Geoffrey. *Looking for Dilmun.* London: Stacey International, 1996.

Clapp, Nicholas. *The Road to Ubar: Finding the Atlantis of the Sands.* Boston: Houghton Mifflin. 1998.

Dineen, Jacquelin, and Philip Wilkinson. *The Lands of the Bible.* New York: Chelsea House, 1994.

Duchêne, Hervé. *Golden Treasures of Troy: The Dream of Heinrich Schliemann.* Translated by Jeremy Legatt. New York: Harry N. Abrams, 1996.

Farnoux, Alexandre. *Knossos: Searching for the Legendary Palace of King Minos.* Translated by David J. Baker. New York: Harry N. Abrams, 1996.

Foreman, Laura. *Cleopatra's Palace: In Search of a Legend.* Del Mar, Calif.: Discovery Books, 1999.

Maisels, Charles Keith. *The Near East: Archaeology in the Cradle of Civilization.* Experiences of Archaeology Series. London and New York, Routledge, 1993.

McIntosh, Jane. *The Practical Archaeologist: How We Know What We Know About the Past.* London: Facts on File, Paul Press, 1986.

Meyers, Eric M. *The Oxford Encyclopedia of Archaeology in the Near East.* 5 vols. New York: Oxford University Press, 1997.

Wood, Michael. *In Search of the Trojan War.* Berkeley: University of California Press, 1985.

WOMEN

Bach, Alice, ed. *Women in the Hebrew Bible: A Reader.* New York: Routledge, 1999.

Barber, Elizabeth Wayland. *Women's Work: The First 20,000 Years.* New York: W. W. Norton, 1994.

Ide, Arthur Frederick. *Women in the Ancient Near East.* 2nd ed. Mesquite, Tex.: Ide House, 1982.

Lesko, Barbara S. *The Remarkable Women of Ancient Egypt.* 3rd ed., rev. and enl. Providence, R.I.: B. C. Scribe Publications, 1996.

*Nardo, Don. *Cleopatra.* San Diego: Lucent Books, 1994.

Robins, Gay. *Women in Ancient Egypt.* Cambridge, Mass.: Harvard University Press, 1993.

Tyldesley, Joyce. *Hatchepsut: The Female Pharaoh.* London: Penguin Books, 1998.

———. *Nefertiti: Egypt's Sun Queen.* New York: Viking Press, 1999.

Vivante, Bella, ed. *Women's Roles in Ancient Civilizations.* Westport, Conn.: Greenwood Press, 1999.

ECONOMY

Aberbach, M. *Labor, Crafts, and Commerce in Ancient Israel.* Jerusalem: Magnes, 1984.

Aubet, Maria Eugenia. *The Phoenicians and the West: Politics, Colonies and Trade.* New York: Cambridge University Press, 1997.

Finley, M. I. *The Ancient Economy.* Sather Classical Lectures Series. Updated ed. Berkeley: University of California Press, 1999.

Groom, Nigel. *Frankincense and Myrrh: A Study of the Arabian Incense Trade.* New York: Longman, 1981.

Parkins, Helen, and Christopher John Smith, eds. *Trade, Traders, and the Ancient City.* London and New York: Routledge, 1998.

Pastor, Jack. *Land and Economy in Ancient Palestine.* London and New York: Routledge, 1997.

Powell, Marvin A. *Labor in the Ancient Near East.* New Haven, Conn.: American Oriental Society, 1987.

Price, B. B. *Ancient Economic Thought.* Routledge Studies in the History of Economics, Vol. 1. London: Routledge, 1997.

Wright, Christopher J. H. *God's People in God's Land: Family, Land, and Property in the Old Testament.* Grand Rapids, Mich.: W. B. Eerdmans, 1990.

WARS AND WARFARE

*Brewer, Paul. *Warfare in the Ancient World.* Austin, Tex.: Raintree Steck-Vaughn Publishers, 1998.

Briant, Pierre. *Alexander the Great: Man of Action, Man of Spirit.* Translated by Jeremy Leggatt. New York: Harry N. Abrams, 1996.

*Gonen, Rivka. *Charge! Weapons and Warfare in Ancient Times.* Minneapolis, Minn.: Runestone Press, 1993.

Herodotus of Halicarnassus. *The Persian Wars.* Translated by George Rawlinson. New York: Modern Library, 1942.

*Nardo, Don. *The Battle of Marathon.* San Diego: Lucent Books, 1996.

Stillman, Nigel, and Nigel Tallis. *Armies of the Ancient Near East, 3000 B.C. to 539 B.C.: Organisation, Tactics, Dress, and Equipment.* Devizes, England: Wargames Research Group Publications, 1984.

Time Frame: Barbarian Tides, 1500–600 B.C. Alexandria, Va.: Time-Life Books, 1987.

*Woods, Michael, and Mary B. Woods. *Ancient Warfare.* Minneapolis, Minn.: Runestone Press, 2000.

Yadin, Yigael. *Art of Warfare in Biblical Lands.* 2 vols. New York: McGraw-Hill, 1963.

185

קרשתאבגדהוזחטיכדלמסנןסעפּףצץקרשתאבגד

ON-LINE RESOURCES

Abzu: Guide to Resources for the Study of the Ancient Near East. *Contains information about the study of the ancient Near East. Provides links to other sites about the ancient Near East.*
http://www-oi.uchicago.edu/OI/default.html

Ancient Persia. *Contains a historical overview and a gallery of art and artifacts from ancient Persia.*
http://dolphin.upenn.edu/~pps/

Architecture in the Ancient Near East. *Discusses building techniques used in ancient structures, with images and descriptions.*
http://www-lib.haifa.ac.il/www/art/archimedia.html

Canaan and Ancient Israel. *Contains information about the University of Pennsylvania's Museum of Archeology and Anthropology's permanent exhibit on Canaan and ancient Israel. Provides links to its galleries on Mesopotamia, Egypt, and the Mediterranean world.*
http://www.upenn.edu/museum/Collections/canaanframedoc1.html

The Hermitage Museum. *Provides information about and examples of art from ancient Mesopotamia, Egypt, Central Asia, and the Caucasus.*
http://www.hermitagemuseum.org/html_En/03/hm3_5.html

Hittite Home Page. *Provides information about resources for Hittite and ancient Anatolian studies and information about other regions of the ancient Near East.*
http://www.asor.org/HITTITE/HittiteHP.html

The Iraklion Archaeological Museum. *Contains information about exhibits on ancient Minoan art and artifacts from Crete. Also provides information about the history of Crete and archaeological sites.*
http://www.interkriti.org/museums/hermus.htm

The Israel Museum, Jerusalem. *Provides information about archaeological and historical discoveries in Israel and presents visual images of artifacts.*
http://www.imj.org.il/archaeology/index.html

Learning Sites, Inc. *Contains information on archaeological sites in Greece and the ancient Near East, including Anatolian, Assyrian, and Egyptian sites.*
http://www.learningsites.com

Lost City of Arabia. *Contains information about the discovery and excavation of the site of ancient Ubar, a "lost city" in Arabia.*
http://www3.pbs.org/wgbh/nova/ubar

The Louvre Museum. *Contains information about the Louvre's ancient Near Eastern collections, with photographs of art and artifacts from ancient Mesopotamia, Iran, Anatolia, the Levant, and Arabia.*
http://www.louvre.fr/anglais/collec/coll_f.htm

Metropolitan Museum of Art. *Contains information and photographs of the museum's ancient Near Eastern art collection. Also provides an introduction to ancient Near Eastern art.*
http://www.metmuseum.org/collections/department.asp?dep=3

National Archaeological Museum of Athens. *Provides images and information on the museum's collections of ancient Greek and Egyptian art.*
http://www.culture.gr

Near East—Cradle of Civilization. *Contains information about the peoples and contributions of ancient Near Eastern civilizations.*
http://www.emory.edu/CARLOS/ODYSSEY/NEAREAST/homepg.html

Oriental Institute. *Provides information on the ancient Near East. Also contains a video tour of the University of Chicago's collection of Near Eastern art.*
http://www-oi.uchicago.edu
http://www.oi.uchicago.edu/OI/MUS/OI_Museum.html

Science Museum of Minnesota: Mysteries of Çatalhöyük. *Contains information about archaeological excavations and artifacts from Çatal Hüyük.*
http://www.sci.mus.mn.us/catal

The Seven Wonders of the Ancient World. *Provides information about the Seven Wonders of the Ancient World, including the Hanging Gardens of Babylon and the Great Pyramid of Giza.*
http://ce.eng.usf.edu/pharos/wonders/list.html

Smith College History of Science: Museum of Ancient Inventions. *Provides an on-line exhibit of ancient inventions, with photographs and accompanying text.*
http://www.smith.edu/hsc/museum/ancient_inventions/hsclist.htm

PHOTO CREDITS

VOLUME 1

Color Plates for Religion

1: Erich Lessing/Art Resource, New York; **2:** Corbis/Gianni Dagli Orti; **3:** Metropolitan Museum of Art, New York/Gift of Norbert Schimmel Trust/Schecter Lee; **4:** Erich Lessing/Art Resource, New York; **5:** British Museum, London/Bridgeman Art Library; **6:** British Museum, London/Bridgeman Art Library; **7:** Erich Lessing/Art Resource, New York; **8:** Courtesy Oriental Institute, University of Chicago; **9:** Israel Museum; **10:** Louvre Museum, Paris/Explorer/SuperStock; **11:** Erich Lessing/Art Resource, New York; **12:** Corbis/Gianni Dagli Orti; **13:** SEF/Art Resource, New York; **14:** Archaeological Museum, Iraklion, Crete/Bridgeman Art Library; **15:** Erich Lessing/Art Resource, New York

Black-and-White Photographs

1: SuperStock; **4:** Corbis/Werner Forman; **7:** Egyptian National Museum, Cairo/ET Archive, London/SuperStock; **15:** Egyptian National Museum, Cairo/Index, Barcelona/Bridgeman Art Library; **17:** Louvre Museum, Paris; **21:** Iraq Museum, Baghdad; **25:** Alinari/Art Resource, New York; **32:** Bildarchiv Preussischer Kulturbesitz, Berlin; **34:** The Granger Collection, New York; **36:** Ekrem Akurgal, *Die Kunst der Hethiter;* **42:** Werner Forman/Art Resource, New York; **46:** Museum of Archaeology and Anthropology, University of Pennsylvania, Philadelphia; **55:** Oriental Division, New York Public Library, Astor, Lenox and Tilden Foundations; **58:** French Archaeological Expedition in Abu Dhabi Emirate; **67:** The Granger Collection, New York; **72:** Corbis/Bettmann; **77:** The Granger Collection, New York; **85:** British Museum, London; **86:** British Museum, London; **101:** Corbis/Michael Nicholson; **105:** Louvre Museum, Paris; **106:** Pierpont Morgan Library, New York; **114:** Brooklyn Museum, New York; **116:** Kelsey Museum of Archaeology, University of Michigan, Ann Arbor; **120:** Corbis/Archivo Iconografico, S.A.; **120:** Louvre Museum, Paris/SuperStock; **129:** Courtesy Oriental Institute, University of Chicago; **139:** Louvre Museum, Paris; **149:** Louvre Museum, Paris/Bridgeman Art Library; **152:** Alinari/Art Resource, New York; **154:** Courtesy B.A. Litvinsky; **156:** Metropolitan Museum of Art, New York; **161:** Louvre Museum, Paris/Bridgeman Art Library; **171:** Friedrich Schiller University, Jena; **172:** Erich Lessing/Art Resource, New York

VOLUME 2

Color Plates for Daily Life

1: Egyptian National Museum, Cairo/Bridgeman Art Library; **2:** Werner Forman/Art Resource, New York; **3:** Christie's Images/SuperStock; **4:** Erich Lessing/Art Resource, New York; **5:** Corbis/Gianni Dagli Orti; **6:** Corbis/Chris Hellier; **7:** Erich Lessing/Art Resource, New York; **8:** Scala/Art Resource, New York; **9:** Louvre Museum, Paris/Bridgeman Art Library; **10:** Corbis/Gianni Dalgi Orti; **11:** Corbis/Gianni Dagli Orti; **12:** World Photo Service Ltd./SuperStock; **13:** Erich Lessing/Art Resource, New York; **14:** Corbis/Adam Woolfitt; **15:** Scala/Art Resource, New York

Black-and-White Photographs

2: Corbis; **4:** Corbis; **8:** British Museum, London; **10:** Archaeological Museum, Teheran; **12:** Egyptian Museum, Cairo; **14:** Bridgeman Art Library; **17:** J.D.S. Pendlebury, *A Handbook to the Palace of Minos at Knossos;* **25:** After M. Matousova-Rajmova, Archiv Orientalni; **27:** Kelsey Museum of Archaeology, University of Michigan, Ann Arbor; **31:** Minneapolis Institute of Arts; **37:** Louvre Museum, Paris; **51:** Louvre Museum, Paris; **55:** British Museum, London; **60:** Hirmer Archives, Munich; **62:** SuperStock; **68:** Louvre Museum, Paris; **71:** Louvre Museum, Paris; **82:** H. Von Minutoli, *Reise zum Tempel des Jupiter Ammon in der Libyschen Wuste;* **85:** Louvre Museum, Paris; **86:** Courtesy Oriental Institute, University of Chicago; **93:** Corbis; **102:** SuperStock; **106:** Adapted from Peter R. S. Moore and P. E. Newberry, Beni Hasan; **108:** Hermitage Museum, St. Petersburg; **111:** Art Resource; **122:** British Museum, London; **125:** Art Resource; **127:** National Museum of the Syrian Arab Republic, Aleppo; **128:** Art Resource; **135:** Art Resource; **145:** Art Resource; **147:** Louvre Museum, Paris; **152:** Metropolitan Museum of Art, New York; **161:** Hieroglyphic text from Alan Gardiner, *Egyptian Grammar;* **163:** British Museum, London; **167:** Museum of Anatolian Civilizations, Ankara; **172:** Corbis; **173:** French Archaeological Expedition in Abu Dhabi Emirate; **176:** British Museum, London; **179:** British Museum, London; **180:** The Granger Collection, New York; **181:** Metropolitan Museum of Art, New York; **185:** J. Black and A. Green, *Gods, Demons and Symbols of Ancient Mesopotamia*

Photo Credits

VOLUME 3

Color Plates for Architecture and Tombs

1: Scala/Art Resource, New York; 2: Erich Lessing/Art Resource, New York; 3: Erich Lessing/Art Resource, New York; 4: Corbis/Michael Nicholson; 5: Israel Museum/Nachum Slapak; 6: Corbis/Michael Nicholson; 7: Scala/Art Resource, New York; 8: Erich Lessing/Art Resource, New York; 9: Art Resource, New York; 10: Erich Lessing/Art Resource, New York; 11: SuperStock; 12: Vanni/Art Resource, New York; 13: Erich Lessing/Art Resource, New York; 14: Corbis/Charles & Josette Lenars; 15: SuperStock

Black-and-White Photographs

3: Louvre Museum, Paris; 7: Museum of Archaeology and Anthropology, University of Pennsylvania, Philadelphia; 16: Louvre Museum, Paris; 22: Museum of Archaeology and Anthropology, University of Pennsylvania, Philadelphia; 25: Biblical Archaeology Review; 34: Ashmolean Museum, Oxford/Bridgeman Art Library; 36: British Museum, London; 40: Fritz Hintze and Ursula Hintze, *Alte Kulturen Im Sudan;* 43: Louvre Museum, Paris; 52: Erich Lessing/Art Resource, New York; 55: Erich Lessing/Art Resource, New York; 60: Metropolitan Museum of Art, New York; 64: Courtesy Trevor R. Bryce; 66: Courtesy Crawford M. Greenwalt, Jr.; 69: Courtesy Oriental Institute, University of Chicago; 70: British Museum, London/Bridgeman Art Library; 74: Museum of Anatolian Civilizations, Ankara; 76: British Museum, London; 81: Corbis/Adam Woolfitt; 84: Corbis/Bettmann; 89: Courtesy Oriental Institute, University of Chicago; 92: Courtesy Klaas R. Veenhof; 97: British Museum, London; 102: Hirmer Archives, Munich; 110: Christos G. Doumas, *The Wall-Paintings of Thera;* 112: N. Angell, *The Story of Money;* 118: The Granger Collection, New York; 120: British Museum, London; 122: National Museum of Athens; 124: Courtesy Oriental Institute, University of Chicago; 131: British Museum, London/Bridgeman Art Library; 134: Bildarchiv Preussischer Kulturbesitz, Berlin; 139: Courtesy Elizabeth C. Stone; 142: Courtesy Frank Hole; 145: Courtesy Frank Hole; 146: Fritz Hintze and Ursula Hintze, *Alte Kulturen Im Sudan;* 150: Richard F. S. Starr, *Nuzi,* Vol. 2; 152: Phoebe Hearst Museum of Anthropology, University of California at Berkeley; 154: British Museum, London; 160: Helen Leacroft and Richard Leacroft, *The Buildings of Ancient Mesopotamia;* 165: Giraudon/Art Resource, New York; 170: Ernst Herzfeld, *Iran in the Ancient Near East;* 175: Courtesy Oriental Institute, University of Chicago; 182: Israel Department of Antiquities, Jerusalem; 187: Private Collection

VOLUME 4

Color Plates for Arts and Culture

1: Scala/Art Resource, New York; 2: Courtesy Oriental Institute, University of Chicago; 3: Erich Lessing/Art Resource, New York; 4: Scala/Art Resource, New York; 5: British Museum, London/Bridgeman Art Library; 6: Erich Lessing/Art Resource, New York; 7: Museum of Baghdad/Silvio Fiore/SuperStock; 8: Ashmolean Museum, Oxford/Bridgeman Art Library; 9: Erich Lessing/Art Lessing, New York; 10: Scala/Art Resource, New York; 11: Erich Lessing/Art Resource, New York; 12: Scala/Art Resource, New York; 13: Erich Lessing/Art Resource, New York; 14: Erich Lessing/Art Resource, New York; 15: Scala/Art Resource, New York

Black-and-White Photographs

2: Museum of Archaeology and Anthropology, University of Pennsylvania, Philadelphia; 8: Arnaldo Mondador, Ed., *Anatolia: Immagini di Civilita;* 15: Erich Lessing/Art Resource, New York; 22: Courtesy John Ruffle; 25: NY Carlsberg Glyptothek, Copenhagen; 28: Louvre Museum, Paris.; 33: Museum of Anatolian Civilizations, Ankara; 37: Erich Lessing/Art Resource, New York; 42: British Museum, London; 47: Giovanni Lilliu, *La Civilta Nuragica;* 53: British Museum, London; 57: Ekrem Akurgal, Ed., *The Art and Architecture of Turkey;* 64: British Museum, London; 67: Courtesy Oriental Institute, University of Chicago; 75: Erich Lessing/Art Resource, New York; 81: Carnegie Museum of Natural History, Pittsburgh; 95: SEF/Art Resource, New York; 98: *Archaeology in the United Arab Emirates,* Vol. 4; 104: State Museum, Berlin; 109: Courtesy Francois Vallat; 113: National Museum of the Syrian Arab Republic, Damascus; 119: Sergei I. Rudenko, *The World's Most Ancient Artistic Carpets and Textiles;* 126: Hermitage Museum, St. Petersburg; 131: Ashmolean Museum, Oxford/Bridgeman Art Library; 133: Courtesy Hans G. Jansen; 136: Louvre Museum, Paris; 138: Museum of Archaeology and Anthropology, University of Pennsylvania, Philadelphia; 142: Hirmer Archives, Munich; 146: Erich Lessing/Art Resource, New York; 151: British Museum, London; 156: Giraudon/Art Resource, New York; 160: Metropolitan Museum of Art, New York; 163: Metropolitan Museum of Art, New York; 166: British Museum, London; 169: Metropolitan Museum of Art, New York; 175: Museum of Archaeology and Anthropology, University of Pennsylvania, Philadelphia; 178: Giraudon/Art Resource, New York; 179: Corbis/Roger Wood

INDEX

Page numbers of articles in these volumes appear in boldface type.

Index

Index

Index

Index

Index

Index

Index

Index

Index

Index

Index

קרשתאבגדהוזחטיכדלמסמןנסעפפצץקרשתאבגד

Index

Index

Index

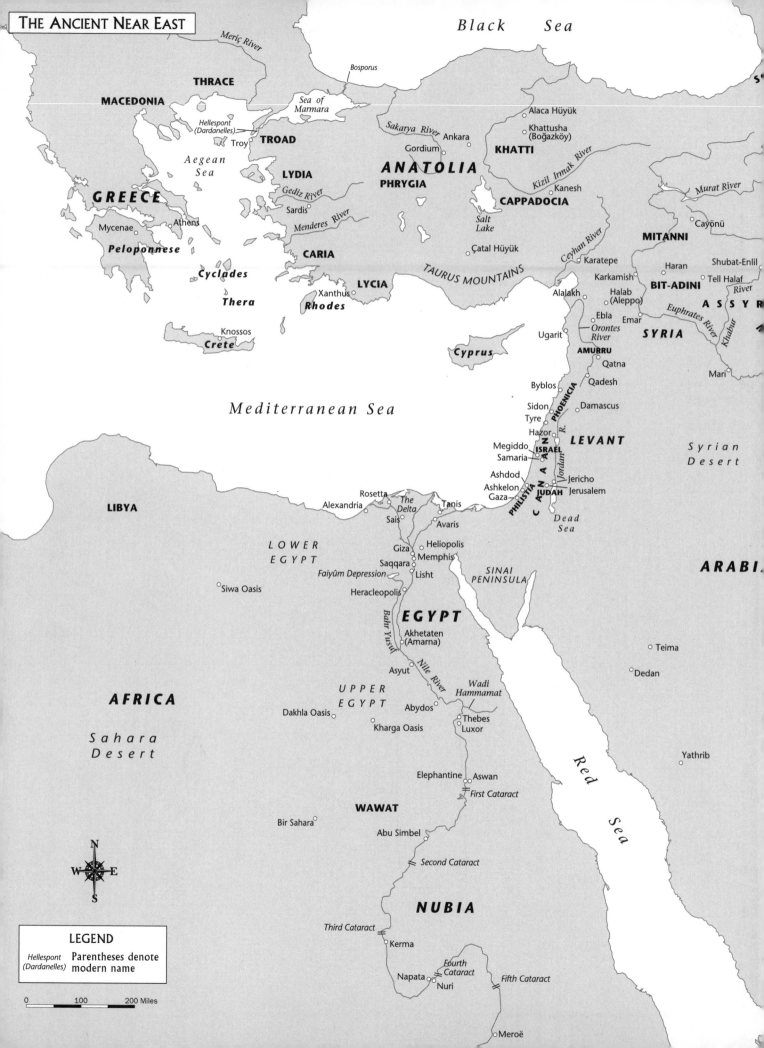

THE ANCIENT NEAR EAST

Black Sea

Meriç River

THRACE

Bosporus

MACEDONIA

Sea of Marmara

Hellespont (Dardanelles)

TROAD

Aegean Sea

Troy

Sakarya River

Ankara

Gordium

ANATOLIA

Alaca Hüyük

Khattusha (Boğazköy)

KHATTI

GREECE

LYDIA

PHRYGIA

Kizil Irmak River

CAPPADOCIA

Kanesh

Murat River

Çayönü

Sardis

Gediz River

Menderes River

Mycenae

Athens

Peloponnese

Salt Lake

MITANNI

Çatal Hüyük

Karatepe

Ceyhan River

Haran

Shubat-Enlil

Karkamish

Tell Halaf

Cyclades

CARIA

Thera

Rhodes

LYCIA

Xanthus

Knossos

Crete

Alalakh

Halab (Aleppo)

BIT-ADINI

A S S Y R

SYRIA

Ebla

Emar

Euphrates River

Khabur River

Ugarit

Orontes River

Cyprus

AMURRU

Qatna

Mari

Byblos

PHOENICIA

Qadesh

Sidon

Damascus

Tyre

Mediterranean Sea

Hazor

Jordan R.

LEVANT

Syrian Desert

Megiddo

Z

ISRAEL

Samaria

C

A

N

A

Ashdod

Jericho

Ashkelon

JUDAH

Jerusalem

Gaza

PHILISTIA

Rosetta

Alexandria

The Delta

Tanis

Dead Sea

LIBYA

Sais

Avaris

Giza

Heliopolis

ARABIA

Saqqara

Memphis

Faiyûm Depression

Lisht

SINAI PENINSULA

LOWER EGYPT

Siwa Oasis

Heracleopolis

Bahr Yusuf

EGYPT

Akhetaten (Amarna)

Teima

Asyut

Nile River

Dedan

AFRICA

UPPER EGYPT

Wadi Hammamat

Dakhla Oasis

Abydos

Sahara Desert

Kharga Oasis

Thebes

Luxor

Elephantine

Aswan

First Cataract

Red Sea

Yathrib

WAWAT

Bir Sahara

Abu Simbel

Second Cataract

NUBIA

Third Cataract

Kerma

LEGEND

Hellespont (Dardanelles) Parentheses denote modern name

0   100   200 Miles

Fourth Cataract

Napata

Nuri

Fifth Cataract

Meroë